CW01512831

THE RETURN OF RUSSIA

THE RETURN OF RUSSIA

FROM YELTSIN TO PUTIN, THE STORY OF A VENGEFUL KREMLIN

James Rodgers

YALE UNIVERSITY PRESS
NEW HAVEN AND LONDON

For information about this and other Yale University Press publications, please contact:
U.S. Office: sales.press@yale.edu yalebooks.com
Europe Office: sales@yaleup.co.uk yalebooks.co.uk

Set in Adobe Garamond Pro by IDSUK (DataConnection) Ltd

Printed and bound in the UK using 100% renewable electricity at CPI Group (UK) Ltd

Library of Congress Control Number: 2025947243
A catalogue record for this book is available from the British Library.
Authorized Representative in the EU: Easy Access System Europe, Mustamäe tee 50, 10621 Tallinn, Estonia, gpsr.requests@easproject.com

ISBN 978-0-300-27081-5

10 9 8 7 6 5 4 3 2 1

Dedicated to the memory of Margaret Rodgers, 1941–2024

Contents

CONTENTS

Plates and Maps

Maps

Preface

In early September 1991, I stood on the square in front of the building of the Supreme Soviet of the Ukrainian Soviet Socialist Republic. I was a TV news producer, three years out of university, where I had studied Russian and French. That summer was my first international assignment. I had gone to Moscow in June to cover the first elections for the presidency of Russia. I ended up staying much longer than expected, witnessing the collapse of the USSR, a superpower that had been a major part of global politics for all of my life, and most of the twentieth century. That day in Kyiv – or Kiev, as we at Reuters news agency and other Western media invariably spelt it then – I was surrounded by a crowd, whose singing, sunburnt faces were turned upwards to the sky of late summer. Their eyes were focused on the flag-pole atop the Verkhovna Rada, as the Supreme Soviet was called in Ukrainian. Eventually, they saw what they had been waiting for: the hauling down of the flag of Soviet Ukraine, and its replacement with the yellow and blue flag familiar today.

Two months earlier, I had been in the Ukrainian capital for the first time, when President George H.W. Bush visited on his way back from attending a summit meeting in Moscow with the Soviet leader, Mikhail Gorbachev. It was to be the last-ever Soviet–US summit. By the end of the year, the USSR had ceased to exist. The Cold War was finally over, and Moscow and the West were seeking to be friends and partners, perhaps even allies. At the same time, the USSR – 'an indestructible union' – was breaking up. In the process, Moscow was losing control of territory over which it had had sovereignty for centuries – even if there had been brief periods of independence for some peoples between the collapse of the Russian Empire after 1917 and the consolidation of Soviet power in 1922. Russia was about to enter a whole new era in its relations with the West and with its near neighbours, and in its own politics.

Three weeks after I first proposed my idea for this book to Yale University Press, in January 2022, Russia took its war on Ukraine to a completely new level, sending a massive invasion force in an attempt to capture much more territory than it already held and to take Kyiv. The main reason for writing the book became all the more pressing. It seemed to me important to try to set down what had happened in between. There may be many motives for writing a book: literary, academic, commercial. Whichever is true, there is often a personal motive, too – an initial curiosity about the subject that is driven by an enthusiasm that provides the energy for the research and writing. That is true in this case. I was inspired to write this book to tell for as wide an audience as possible the story of Russia at a unique period in its history: one in which its attempts to adapt to Western ideas of democracy and capitalism failed and instead led it into renewed confrontation with the West. It is a story that fascinates me as an author and historian – and one that is also personal for my generation, who grew up in the last stages of the Cold War and now see Europe at war again.

I was born in the 1960s and came of age at the end of the Cold War. I remember my grandparents' tales of the Second World War. As a teenager, as the US and the USSR sped up their arms race in the 1980s, I was terrified of the possibility of nuclear war – especially as I lived in the suburbs of Manchester, a major British city that must certainly have been a major Soviet target if the nuclear missiles ever were launched. For my generation, the end of the Cold War was a liberation from threats such as these. It was also an opportunity to travel with far greater ease to places – like the USSR – that had previously been much more difficult to visit. From the start of my career as a journalist in the early 1990s to the end of my final correspondent posting for the BBC in Moscow from 2006 to 2009, I was able to see Russia as few Westerners had before.

It was a period when Russia was open to the West in a way it may not be again for a long time. It is now harder to go to Russia than at any time during my life – and perhaps even more risky. The recent arrests and imprisonment of Westerners such as the American journalist Evan Gershkovich show what can happen if things go wrong. Such a fate was impossible to imagine for young Western journalists of my generation working in Russia, though not without historical precedent. In writing this book, I seek to explain how Russia's view of the West moved from hope, to humiliation, to hatred in such a short time.

So, having explained *why* I have tried to tell the story of this period in Russian history, and of Russia's relations with the West during that period, I will move on to *how*. Because this is a work of contemporary history, open archive resources are limited, but I have been able to draw on valuable sources both in the UK and the US. I have also been fortunate enough to have had the opportunity to interview a number of key figures from both sides of the Atlantic. Beyond that, I have drawn extensively on the many secondary sources – news reports, diplomatic memoirs, official statements – available for the period.

To that I must add that, to my regret, I was not able to travel to Russia to conduct interviews and other research. Instead, I have drawn on official Russian online resources – such as the Kremlin and foreign ministry websites – to trace the evolution of Russian foreign policy throughout the period. News reports – some of them remarkably revelatory, considering the kind of reporting that is allowed in Russia today – have also been useful. The ever-more-burdensome restrictions placed on journalism in Russia during the Putin era mean that such resources will not be available to future writers as they have been to me.

That in itself is part of the history of this period, and it is one of the subjects I discuss. As Maureen Perrie noted in the introduction to *The Cambridge History of Russia*, 'Striking the appropriate balance between thematic and chronological organisation is a perennial problem for historians'.[1] My approach has been to organise this book chronologically, and also to address themes over a more extended period at a point where such an assessment seems most relevant. So the book contains sections on subjects such as energy supplies, espionage, the Russian Orthodox Church, arms treaties, the media and protest against Putin. Russia's internal political development, together with the country's vast changes in economic fortune, is covered throughout the period. So too are its relations with the West: primarily here the US and the UK, but also the EU, Germany and France. NATO enlargement, and Russia's responses, are considered throughout. Whatever your views of the alliance's policies since the end of the Cold War, there is no question that Russian leaders, especially Vladimir Putin, have been troubled and angered by the way NATO has evolved.

Inevitably, there are periods and issues I could have considered in greater detail, and I ask the reader's understanding for omissions made necessary by the need to keep this as a single volume offering an overview of the events and themes of an age that started with so much hope, and ended in hatred.

As a Western European who lived and worked in Russia for many years, I offer this book in the hope that it can go some way to explaining what went wrong. The costs of the failure to build a better relationship between Russia and the West have already been heartbreakingly high.

James Rodgers
London, June 2025

A Note on Transliteration

For transliteration from Russian to English, I have tried generally to follow Library of Congress transliteration rules. There are exceptions. Where there is a recognised form in standard use in English, I have tended to use that: for example, the Russian forename Александр is rendered not as Aleksandr, but as Alexander, and the name of the last leader of the USSR as Gorbachev, not Gorbachëv.

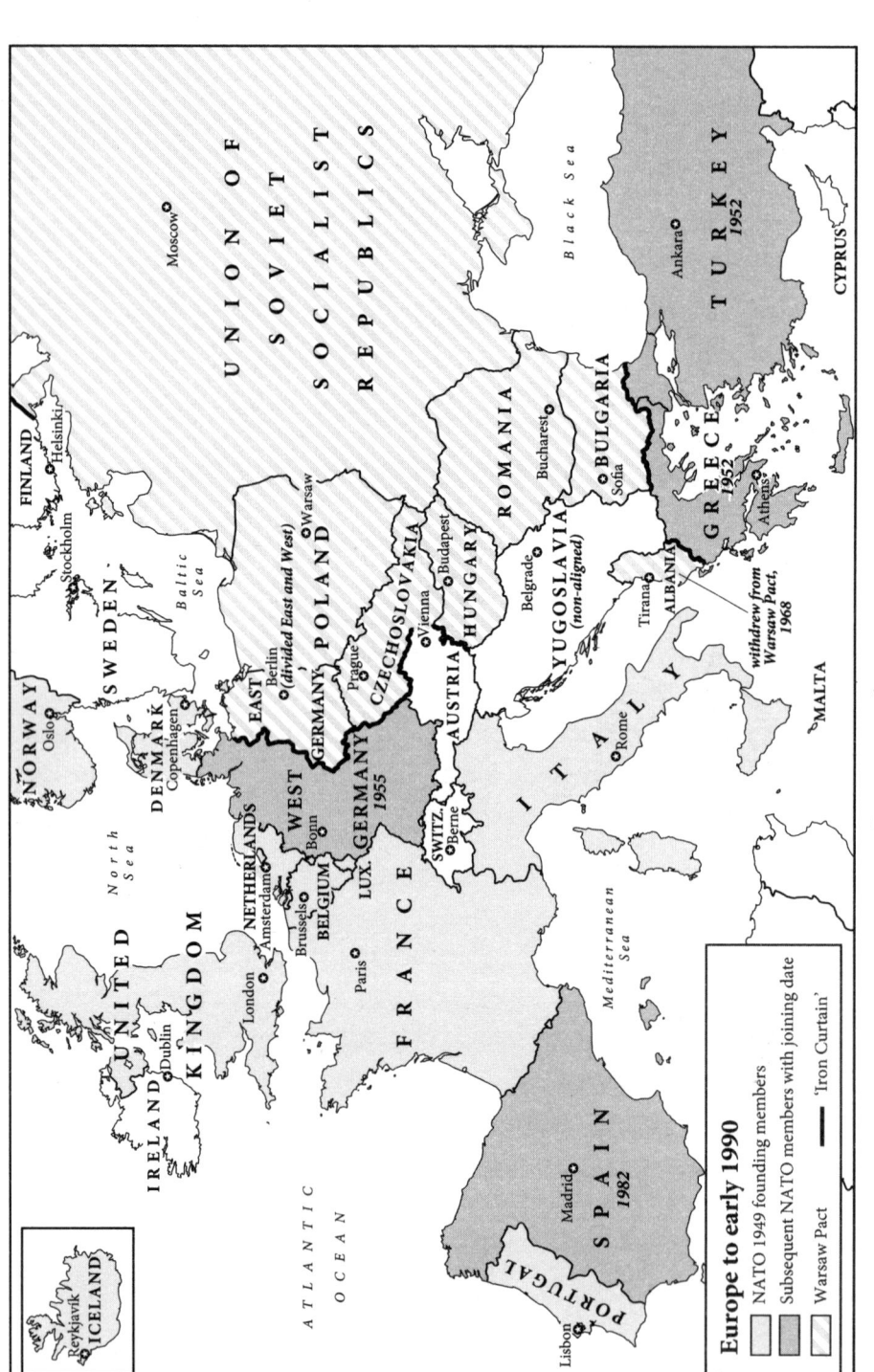

1. Europe to early 1990.

2. *Europe to 2025.*

1

Making Up the Rules as He Goes Along

By the side of the road that leads from Sheremetyevo airport to central Moscow, three huge 'Czech hedgehogs' – monumental versions of the barricades made to stop approaching enemy tanks – form a memorial to those who defended the city against Hitler's armies in 1941. For many new arrivals in Moscow during the decades when Russia welcomed visitors from the West, this, in Khimki on the edge of the city, was one of the first things they saw. The monument marked the limit of the invaders' advance on the Soviet capital. Hitler's drive to capture Moscow was halted here. His failure to conquer Russia joined the retreat of Napoleon in the chronicles of Russian martial glory. The war memorial was raised to record the gratitude of the city's inhabitants. Generations of newlywed couples dutifully came here on their wedding days to offer their respects.

In the 1990s Russia experienced a different kind of encounter with the West. New ideas, beliefs, people and products flooded in, filling the space left by the collapse of communism. The area around the monument began slowly to change. Trucks bearing goods from beyond Russia's borders made the traffic heavier, as did the cars that more people could now buy. The seedier side of Russia's new capitalism was represented here, too, with sex workers sometimes soliciting at the roadside of a highway that went not only to the airport but also, eventually, to Saint Petersburg. As Leningrad, Saint Petersburg too had been a Soviet hero city of the Second World War – or the Great Patriotic War as it is more usually known in Russia – but the name went in 1991, as the Soviet system struggled through its final summer. The result of a referendum renamed the city as its founder, Tsar Peter the Great, had intended. Before that change, while bearing the name of the leader of the revolution that led to the creation of the Soviet system, it was also the birthplace of the man who dominated the country after its collapse: Vladimir Putin.

During Putin's leadership, Khimki has changed yet again: tower blocks of apartments were built behind the war memorial, lessening the effect of the striking silhouette of the 'hedgehogs' but satisfying just some of the soaring demand for housing in and around Moscow as its economy took off. As if in anticipation of such a boom, and the changing tastes that might come with it, IKEA opened its first Russian store here in 2000, the year Putin was first elected president. Its store sign, within sight of the war memorial, spoke of a new harmonious and mutually profitable era of cooperation between Russia and the countries which lay to the west. Later still, Sheremetyevo, memorable to many travellers in the 1990s for the way the smell of boiled cabbage carried from distant kitchens along the airport's shabby corridors to mingle with the smell of smoke from poor-quality Soviet cigarettes, received its own major makeover: splendidly and shiningly renovated, and smoke-free, in preparation for the football World Cup held in Russia in 2018. By then, the threat of renewed conflict and confrontation cast a shadow over Russia's commercial ties with the West. The annexation of Crimea from Ukraine in 2014, and the intervention in the Syrian civil war on the side of President Assad, loathed by the West for his murderous treatment of those who opposed his regime, were the first parts of a renewed enmity that would only grow, until in 2022 Western airlines landed at Sheremetyevo no more. Instead, Russia's embattled neighbour, Ukraine, begged the West for warplanes.

2

The Russian system that Putin built after he first came to power in 2000 was a response to what had gone before. In the space of just a few years, Russia had fallen from being the largest, and leading, part of the superpower that was the Union of Soviet Socialist Republics, to a state where it was forced to seek food aid from the West. With that aid came a new ideology: the market economy (the phrase preferred in official discourse to 'capitalism', which carried such negative associations after seven decades and more of communism). The transition was not easy. The Soviet system, as it neared its end, had increasingly failed to provide for its people's basic needs. Yet its collapse led not to improvement but to continuing decline. If 11 per cent of the population were designated poor in 1989, by 1992–93 that had surpassed 30 per cent, and, by the middle of the decade, in 1995, the figure stood at around 40 per cent.[1]

Boris Yeltsin, elected president of the Russian Soviet Federative Socialist Republic, as it still then was, in 1991, found himself by the end of that year in the Kremlin. Mikhail Gorbachev's post as president of the USSR had disappeared with the union itself. But if Yeltsin had made sure that communism came to an end in Russia – including by opposing those who in August 1991 sought to return the country to a more severe Soviet system – then he proved incapable of delivering the stability and prosperity that many hoped would follow. Inevitably, there were serious political consequences. The hope remained in the West that Yeltsin, if given time, and the right kind of support, could deliver a democratic and prosperous Russia at peace with its neighbours. Yet the 1990s actually saw the start of trends that would eventually be integral parts of the Russia that came to see the West as an enemy once more: the use of violence to settle political and territorial disputes, and corrupt elections.

Instead of enjoying prosperity, many Russians found that the end of communism meant poverty. A British government briefing document on Russia prepared in September 1993 noted that 'inflation has risen to 29 per cent per month, the highest since February'.[2] Such hardship naturally led to widespread discontent among an electorate who, in

1991, had voted for Boris Yeltsin in such large numbers that he was elected Russia's first president without the need for a run-off.

The euphoria and excitement, the joy of seeing and saying those things that had for long been forbidden or frowned upon, carried the Russian people through their revolutionary year of 1991 but soon evaporated against the reality of soaring inflation and collapsing infrastructure. There were bold policy attempts to try to get ordinary people to buy in to the new changes: literally, in one case. A year after he had faced down the attempted coup of August 1991, Yeltsin announced that every Russian citizen would receive a voucher for 10,000 roubles (then worth about $25) that would permit them to buy shares in newly privatised industries. This was presented at the time as a bold move giving people literal ownership over what was theirs. The people were soon largely disillusioned. The vouchers did not create a nation of small shareholders. Not all vouchers went the way the state intended. Some ended up being sold for hard currency, or even traded for vodka,[3] in an early example of the more cynical and short-term ways a population brought up under communism exercised the consumer choice that capitalism now permitted them. Still, stability eluded society, and prosperity belonged to the few who had been canny or ruthless enough to position themselves to take advantage of the instability and uncertainty. Of course, the vouchers sold for vodka and other short-term luxuries or necessities did not disappear. They ended up, along with the industries in which they represented shares, in the hands of a small stratum of post-Soviet society. By 1999, 10 per cent of the population owned half of Russia's wealth.[4] Communist warnings about capitalism meaning wealth for the few and misery for the many seemed to be coming true. Poverty and inequality bred discontent that spread through the political system.

The revolution that had ended communism had been incomplete. Along with Gorbachev's office in the Kremlin, Yeltsin had also inherited a parliament that had been elected in 1990 for a five-year term. While Yeltsin, and the team of young reformers he had put in charge of economic policy, believed that the country's interests were best served by pursuing a rapid and radical transition to capitalism, many members of the parliament were fundamentally opposed. The winter of 1992–93 saw a series of confrontations between Yeltsin and the Congress of People's Deputies, particularly over the choice of prime minister. The Congress refused to confirm Yegor Gaidar, author of the economic 'shock therapy', as the reforms were known, as prime minister – a position he held in an acting capacity from June to December 1992. Instead, they agreed to the appointment of Viktor Chernomyrdin, who had been a minister in the Soviet government and then head of the giant state gas company, Gazprom. Yeltsin's entire political career had been built on a series of bold populist gestures, some of them, like his defiant appearance on the tank in the August 1991 coup, risky to the point of recklessness. Yeltsin was not a politician to play the long game, calculating several moves ahead like many of the fine chess players Russia has produced. He could still thrive in a crisis, though. In March 1993, the Congress launched impeachment proceedings against him, but they failed to pass. The following month, Yeltsin gambled on a referendum in which the electorate was asked, among other things, whether they trusted the president. Yeltsin prevailed, giving him a new boost of political capital just as his reserves threatened to run low. His rivals were undaunted, and now included those he had once counted on as staunch allies. That summer, I interviewed the vice president of Russia, Alexander Rutskoi, in his office in the Kremlin, for what was then the main morning news programme on British commercial television, GMTV. In the interview, Rutskoi warned of 'civil disobedience' if the constitutional crisis were not resolved. What he did not say then was that he would be among its leaders.

On 21 September, Yeltsin issued a decree dissolving the legislature in preparation for early elections and a new constitution – one which would limit the power of the Congress, and of the smaller standing body drawn from it, the Supreme Soviet. Rutskoi was joined by the speaker of the Supreme Soviet, Ruslan Khasbulatov, in his defiance of

Yeltsin. Together with many of the deputies, they barricaded themselves in the building that housed the Supreme Soviet, the 'White House', on an embankment of the Moskva River, close to the main road leading from the west into the centre of the Russian capital, towards the Kremlin. Yeltsin, apparently satisfied that the referendum gave him a mandate to defy the constitution, had the building surrounded. The standoff put a complete stop to any attempts to solve Russia's economic crisis. Demonstrations descended into street fighting, just as Rutskoi had predicted. Then street fighting briefly threatened to become civil war. On the afternoon of Sunday 3 October, armed supporters of the parliament broke the siege and, having gathered enough vehicles, men and weapons, headed to the north of the capital to try to take over the television station at Ostankino. They failed, but only after a gun battle that stopped them taking to the airwaves not only of the entire Russian Federation, but of the whole former USSR. Getting their message out across the whole of the world's largest country might have helped their uprising against the president to succeed. As it was, by the next morning, the parliament building, where the leaders still had their headquarters, was under attack. Troops advanced towards the White House, cover provided by tanks that blocked the Kiev bridge across the Moskva River, a bridge that should normally early on a Monday morning have been choked instead with commuter traffic. Some people had made it to the city centre, though. On a golden afternoon in autumn, Muscovites abandoned their workplaces to watch the war. By the end of the day, the White House was ablaze, having been blasted by tank shells. Rutskoi and Khasbulatov were in the same jail, 'Sailor's Rest', where those whom Yeltsin had defied in 1991 had been locked up.

Writing of the failed 1991 coup, Vladislav Zubok has persuasively argued that one of the plotters, Vladimir Kryuchkov, the then head of the KGB – the Soviet security force responsible for everything from the suppression of internal dissent to international espionage – 'was well aware of the requirements for a successful coup, but he simply lacked the guts to implement them'.[5] In the case of the would-be putschists, a successful coup would have meant using force against those thousands of civilians who had sided with Yeltsin and had surrounded the White House to protect it, and him. While Yeltsin was not faced with a decision as to whether to give an order to open fire on unarmed civilians, he did not flinch from using violence to secure his political survival. By the end of two days of bloodshed, 147 people had been killed.[6] When calm returned to the streets, the White House stood as a reminder of the rebellion and its aftermath, its upper floors blackened like a decaying tooth by the fires started during the fighting.

This was not the kind of transition to democracy that Western policy-makers had foreseen, much less hoped for. The president of the US, Bill Clinton, in his first year in office was, according to his Russia advisor, 'shaken by the turn of events in Russia'. Clinton, his advisor Strobe Talbott later wrote, 'could see that even though Yeltsin had, for the moment, prevailed over his most extreme and conspicuous enemies, the shelling of the White House was a political setback of considerable proportions and potentially lasting consequences for a leader who had claimed, with good reason, to have introduced "civilized" politics to Russia'.[7]

Clinton himself later recalled that it was his view 'that Yeltsin had "bent over backwards" to avoid using excessive force, and that the United States would support him and his efforts to hold free and fair elections to parliament'.[8] Clinton spoke to Yeltsin by phone on 5 October, telling him, 'You did everything exactly as you had to and I congratulate you for the way you handled it.'[9] That message was reinforced even more warmly on Clinton's behalf by the US secretary of state, Warren Christopher, when he met Yeltsin in Moscow later that month. Christopher told Yeltsin that Clinton 'was extremely interested in President Yeltsin's superb handling of the crisis'.[10] In public, Christopher was more measured. In a speech at the Academy of the National Economy, he explained 'that while the United States doesn't easily support dissolving – or shelling – democratic institutions, President Yeltsin had taken these steps under "exceptional circumstances" '.[11]

Roderic Lyne had completed postings to the British embassy in Moscow in both the 1970s and 1980s, and he would return in 2000 as ambassador. At the time of the October rebellion, he was working for the British prime minister, John Major, as foreign affairs adviser. The British government's response was affected by the fact that Major was at the time on a trip to Malaysia, a trip on which Lyne was accompanying him. Lyne recalled the evening for a speech made by the host, the Malaysian prime minister, Mahathir Mohamad, in which he criticised British policy on the war in Bosnia. Later that evening, Lyne remembered, 'News starts coming through of events in Moscow – but at this point we are incredibly jetlagged, incredibly tired.'[12] Perhaps the fact that policymakers are only human is not always sufficiently taken into account when judging decisions with hindsight. Still, Lyne recalled, 'The spectacle of Yeltsin shelling his parliament was pretty alarming. On the other hand, one had seen a clear buildup of people who were trying to oust Yeltsin. And these were not good people.' Washington and London stood by Yeltsin because they had invested a lot of political capital in supporting him and could see no alternative other than the kind of government that would be much more hostile to the West. Having ended half a century of ideological confrontation backed by nuclear arsenals, there was a strong desire not to return there.

Now Yeltsin moved to consolidate his power by enshrining it in law. The constitution in force at the time that his parliamentary enemies had challenged him was replaced – within weeks – by a new one. As Russia had only had constitutions during its decades of communism, Western experts were involved in the drafting, including some paid for by the United States Agency for International Development (USAID)[13]. The constitution was approved in a referendum on 12 December. Elections for a new parliament were held the same day. The results of that vote also caused some alarm in the West. The largest single bloc that emerged, although it won only 64 seats out of 450, was the Liberal Democratic Party, led by Vladimir Zhirinovsky. Despite its name, the party had a far-right, Russian nationalist agenda. Zhirinovsky was given to making populist gestures such as offering free vodka to the electorate should he win (this during his unsuccessful bid for the presidency which Yeltsin won in 1991) but never seriously emerged as a challenger to the Kremlin's authority.

The new constitution came into force on 25 December. It was designed to prevent a repetition of the rebellion against Yeltsin, whether it was he who occupied the Kremlin or another. It provided for a strong presidential republic, in which the president had the right to dissolve the parliament.[14] Yeltsin had crushed his rivals by sending troops against them at the very spot where his former enemies had once lacked the resolve to do the same to him. The British ambassador to Moscow, Brian Fall, was clear on the significance of what had unfolded. 'It is only now beginning to be understood how radically the events of the past few weeks have changed the political landscape in Russia. There is plenty of good news, but also a fair amount for us and thoughtful Russians to worry about,' he wrote in a despatch to the Foreign Office in London on 22 October. Among the causes for concern, 'Yeltsin, issuing floods of decrees unconstrained by parliament or Constitutional Court, sometimes seems to be making up the rules as he goes along.'[15]

Yeltsin's victory in the conflict of October 1993 is important for three main reasons. Firstly, the constitution that resulted could be a fearsome tool in the hands of a future strongman president who would find few legal restraints on his power. Secondly, the West had been prepared to give Yeltsin the benefit of the doubt, despite his resort to armed force to win a political battle, if only because policymakers were convinced that the alternative was worse. Thirdly, a precedent had been established in which military force and other acts of violence were used to solve political disputes in post-Soviet Russia.

A year after the new constitution came into effect, the Russian army was again sent into action on the territory of the Russian Federation. The first of two wars in Chechnya, a region in southern Russia, broke out in December 1994. Chechnya's shared history with its rulers in Moscow had been scarred by violence since the region was first conquered and incorporated into the Russian Empire in the nineteenth century. Chechnya's capital, Grozny, began life as a fort, part of 'a chain built to intimidate the highlanders'[16] who were resisting the Russian state's attempts to bring them under its control. Grozny means 'formidable' or even 'threatening' in Russian. The name's endurance tells much about the relationship the Kremlin has had with this far corner of its territory. On 31 December 1994, the Russian army launched a major assault on Grozny with the aim of ending the de facto independent regime. Armed separatists, led by Dzhokar Dudayev, a decorated Soviet air force veteran, had declared they would no longer accept the authority of the government in Moscow. The Russian defence minister, Pavel Grachev, had boasted before the operation that 'Grozny could be taken by a single parachute regiment in the space of two hours'.[17]

In fact, it was a military catastrophe that lasted until the summer of 1996 and cost as many as 100,000 civilian lives.[18] Many of the Russian soldiers killed were conscripts, scared teenage boys there often because their parents lacked the connections or the cash to prevent their being sent to the front. In their book *Chechnya: A Small Victorious War*, the correspondents Carlotta Gall and Thomas de Waal wrote that the figure circulating among the troops was 2,000 dead on the first day of the attack.[19] Gall and De Waal quoted the French photographer Patrick Chauvel, who was in Grozny on 1 and 2 January, when Chechen fighters took him 'for a long and dangerous tour of the battlefield'.[20] Chauvel estimated he saw 800 Russian dead.[21] I was in Grozny as a BBC producer in January 1995 and remember scared and slightly built Russian captives being shown to us correspondents by their Chechen captors. The boys – for they were no more than boys – were produced from a nearby cellar where, the Chechen fighters told us, they were cooking and washing for them. It was a piece of impromptu public relations for the Western media, which also had the effect of making me wonder what on earth the Kremlin was thinking by sending soldiers such as these into combat against a guerilla force that knew Grozny well and was also ready to fight for it in a way these unwilling conscripts never could be.

The first Chechen war showed Yeltsin's willingness to use overwhelming force against an insurgent movement with no care for civilian casualties. His actions troubled the West but did not lead to any change of policy. On assignment in April 1995, my BBC colleagues and I encountered a Russian soldier who was enraged to learn that we were from the UK. 'Go and film in Ulster!' he yelled, waving his rifle. 'Quick march!' In a sense, the comparison was more apt than he can have known. In the first Chechen war, the Kremlin's approach to defeating the uprising against its rule was the equivalent of the British government deciding to carpet-bomb Belfast because a small section of the population had taken up arms against the British crown. The first Chechen war was significant too for what it said at that time about Russia's attitude to empire, and its willingness and ability to enforce it. The Russian army's failure to take Grozny for weeks – let alone in two hours – with a force that amounted to a great deal more than a single parachute regiment showed how far the military superpower had fallen, and how quickly.

This was not lost on senior Western military personnel, who had themselves recently been allowed a look at what once had been beyond the iron curtain. In the summer of 1992, Lieutenant General Sir Jeremy Mackenzie, then commanding NATO's Allied Command Europe Rapid Reaction Corps, had the opportunity to visit Russia and the newly independent Kyrgyzstan. It was, he wrote to Sir Charles Guthrie, then commander of the British Army of the Rhine, 'a mystery we believed the USSR to be a superpower'.[22] The USSR had ceased to exist, and so had the status its army had enjoyed. Mackenzie's host was Dmitry Volkogonov. Volkogonov was a colonel general and the author – thanks to his access to archives that had been closed for decades – of a critical biography of Lenin. Mackenzie wrote that Volkogonov had told him that the Russian army, in its post-Soviet state, having withdrawn from parts of the former Eastern bloc, had 198,000 officers with nowhere to live.[23] Even for those fortunate enough to have accommodation, it could be less than impressive, by NATO standards, at least. Another British officer who visited Russia in the 1990s was invited to a Russian major's apartment. The Russian major and his family had to share a bathroom, toilet and kitchen (the last only 10' x 10', or a little over 9 square metres). The apartment, the British officer added, unkindly in regard to one of the UK's major cities, was 'on the 16th and top floor of a high-rise building which would not look out of place in one of the less attractive areas of Liverpool'.[24]

The first Chechen war was not simply about restoring the Russian state's control over the region. It was also about reversing – to however small and symbolic an extent – the colossal loss of prestige that had come with the collapse of a superpower. By 1996, Moscow had more or less accomplished the first objective, regaining control, although that grip would loosen again as the 1990s neared their end. The war was a disaster from the point of view of restoring martial pride. Instead, the Russian armed forces were embarrassed. Only a short time before, they had believed they were in the world's greatest army defending the world's greatest country. In reality, the end of the USSR had shown them that if that had ever been so, it certainly no longer was. Instead, former Cold War foes, now allowed to survey that which they had so long feared from a distance, expressed their surprise that they had ever believed in their enemy's might. The superpower's soldiers, returning from the Soviet bloc to poverty and uncertainty, were humiliated: both in their modest accommodation, and by their insurgent enemies on the country's southern edge.

In May 1995, the Russian army's humiliation on the battlefield was briefly set aside. The celebration of the fiftieth anniversary of the allied victory over Nazi Germany allowed the Kremlin to remind its partners in Western Europe and the US of the role it had played in their common struggle to defeat Hitler. It was an opportunity for post-Soviet Russia to draw on Soviet glory to stand tall on the international stage – for a few days, not a supplicant for bailouts, but an equal. Veterans from all parts of the USSR were invited to Moscow, many of them lodged in the

Rossiya, a giant of a hotel built during the 1960s. Its great size spoke of the confidence of a Soviet regime that could hardly have believed then that it would not survive until the end of the century. The hotel did not long outlive the USSR. After it closed in 2006, it was demolished. That morning in May 1995, though, in bright spring weather, Soviet military prowess and Soviet-era architecture shone together. The fine weather had been all but guaranteed by the Soviet-era habit of dispersing any rain clouds that threatened to approach the capital on days of major celebration. The technique, known as cloud-seeding, involves firing silver iodide into potential rainclouds, causing either the clouds to disperse or the rain to fall soon afterwards, away from the city centre. The corridors of the Rossiya filled with the sound of countless Soviet military medals of thin metal tinkling against each other as war veterans made their way around. Victory was their greatest, but not their only, achievement. This was a time when life expectancy in Russia, especially male life expectancy, was falling rapidly (in the first half of the 1990s, it was below sixty[25]). Given that the war had finished fifty years before, and that to have fought in it they must at the very least have been in their mid-teens, even having lived this long in Russia in the second half of the century was a significant achievement. With quiet dignity, and no doubt many memories they perhaps had never shared with any but the comrades-in-arms they met that May, the veterans paraded across Red Square that cool, bright morning. History, and their role in it, would also come to be an important part of Russia's political future. Later the same day, there was a second parade, this one including military hardware. That took place at Poklonnaya Gora, the site of a war memorial on raised ground to the west of the city centre. The name in Russian comes from the words for 'to bow' and 'hill'. There was also a rare outing on Victory Day for warplanes. They tore across the clear skies above the Russian capital in tribute to the fallen, and the victorious.

Speaking at the opening ceremony of the memorial complex, the British prime minister, John Major, drew a comparison between the changing generation, and the changing times: 'Political leadership has passed to a generation too young to have fought in that war. We face instead the responsibility of peace. Having banished the divisions of the past, we must let not even the shadow of a new division fall across Europe. We need to forge a chain of new relationships binding us together in a durable peace.'[26]

In a sign of post-Cold War unity, more than fifty national leaders were in Moscow to mark the anniversary. There were still tensions, though. The two parades were held separately for diplomatic as much as logistical reasons. Western leaders such as Major and Clinton were content to watch the veterans march across Red Square in the morning. They did not show similar enthusiasm for observing military aircraft and other materiel that might have seen recent action in Chechnya. The *New York Times* correspondent Steven Erlanger described Clinton waiting in his hotel until the last jet had flown over, as 'this was the parade that President Clinton and most other Western leaders refused to see, in a quiet protest over Russian military behaviour in secessionist Chechnya'.[27] Other correspondents covering the ceremonies pointed out the contradiction that the Kremlin was hosting a celebration of the end of Europe's mid-century, continent-wide war while its forces continued to attack Chechnya. Defence ministry denials that operations were ongoing were rapidly undermined by video footage of Russian helicopter gunships attacking Chechen villages.

This note of discord aside, Clinton, like Major and other Western leaders, had come to Moscow with a clear message that the Cold War really was over, and that a new era of relations between Russia and the West was beginning. Clinton articulated this most clearly the day after the main ceremonies in a speech he gave at Moscow State University. There, he addressed an audience of faculty and, more importantly, given his theme, students. This was before the children of Russia's business and political elites had the funds or the access to universities abroad. An audience then studying at Moscow State could reasonably be considered to be Russia's future leaders. Clinton addressed directly one of Moscow's perennial complaints about the history of the Second

World War: that Western accounts tended to underplay, or even over-look, the Soviet role. The president's opening remarks referred to the 'almost unimaginable price the peoples of the Soviet Union paid for survival and for victory'.[28] He continued, 'Because our alliance with you was shattered at the war's end by the onset of the cold war, Americans never fully appreciated, until yesterday, the true extent of your sacrifice and its contribution to our common victory.' At a time when the Russian military and political establishments were stung by their humil-iating fall from superpower status, Clinton sought to be as generous as possible in recognising past glories.

The rest of his speech was clearly written with the students in the audience most in mind. Clinton extolled the importance of democracy, and especially of elections and a free press as indispensable constituent parts thereof. Under the latter category, Clinton noted two recently murdered journalists: 'Dmitriy Kholodov and Vladislav Listyev were murdered in pursuit of the truth.' Kholodov, investigating corruption in the military, had been killed when he opened a briefcase he had been led to believe contained documents for his story (his death and its significance is discussed in more detail in Chapter 4). Listyev was believed to have fallen foul of criminals who stood to lose from planned changes to advertising on Russia's biggest TV channel, of which he – aged just thirty-eight – had recently been appointed head. Tens of thousands of people came to the television studio at Ostankino, north of the centre of Moscow, to file past his open coffin. Newspapers published front pages bordered in black in a sign of mourning and respect that had traditionally been used when reporting the death of a Soviet leader.[29]

With parliamentary elections due later that year, and presidential elections – the first since the fall of communism – due the following year, 1996, Clinton praised Yeltsin's commitment to keeping to the schedule (as often in politically unstable societies, there had been spec-ulation that Yeltsin might postpone the elections on the grounds of national security or some similar pretext). Clinton said that Yeltsin had 'shown that he understands what has often been said about a new democracy: The second elections are even more important than the first, for the second elections establish a pattern of peaceful transition of power.'

But the second elections presented a problem for Yeltsin, his supporters in Russia and his allies in the West. This was not the euphoric, optimistic Russia of 1991 when Yeltsin easily won a Russian presidential election without the need for a run-off. This was a Russia in which millions of people now struggled to put food on the table, while a small number became fantastically wealthy: a Russia in which, in effect, Marxist-Leninist warnings about life under capitalism (plenty for the few, not much for the many) had largely come true. At the top end, business disputes were often resolved with violence. Scores were settled with shootings in the centre of Moscow and Russia's other big cities. On the edges of markets, and even on main streets at night, impoverished Muscovites, many of them seemingly of pension age, would stand, even in the depths of the Russian winter, selling personal possessions in the hope of raising cash. It was an echo of what the British journalist Malcolm Muggeridge had seen in the early Soviet period, when what he termed 'the relics of the old Russian bourgeoisie brought their family treasures'[30] to shops to sell.

Wages were often unpaid. By the time the election year, 1996, came around, 'According to official statistics, government arrears of wage payments, settling of state orders, and pension payments amounted to about 2 per cent of GDP.'[31] The restructuring of the economy according to market principles had meant a loss of the certainties that went with working for a state enterprise. The greater opening of the Russian economy to imports had demonstrated the poor quality, in many cases, of Soviet goods that then struggled to compete with new products. This inevitably had political consequences. The first elections Clinton had in mind when he spoke in Moscow in May 1995 were for the Russian parliament, by now known again by its pre-Soviet name, the Duma, in December that year. Their vote no doubt swelled by dissatisfaction at the failure of the market economy and democracy to improve life as so many had hoped when they had voted for Yeltsin in the summer of 1991, the Communist Party took the largest share of the vote. They won 157 seats in the 450-seat assembly.[32] It was a warning of what might come in the race for the Kremlin that was to follow half a year later. In January 1996, the month after the Duma elections, Yeltsin was polling at only 6 per cent. The leader of the Communist Party and their presidential candidate, Gennady Zyuganov, enjoyed more than twice as much support.[33]

In addition to the problems with wages, the Chechen war still raged. Unthinkable though a return to communism might have seemed less than three years earlier, when Yeltsin crushed his opponents' armed insurgency and quickly won a referendum on the new constitution, it was now plausible. Clinton had said in his speech at Moscow State that 'the United States supports the forces of democracy and reform here in Russia because it is in our national interest to do so'. The US and its allies knew that the return of a reheated version of Soviet communism would be very likely to signal the end for democracy and reform in Russia, very possibly for good. Having let power be grabbed from their grasp once in the name of democracy, newly empowered communists would be unlikely to risk repeating the error. The election would decide Russia's future direction, and whether the first five years after communism would come to be seen as the foundation of something new, or simply a brief detour before returning to the normality that had prevailed for most of the century that was now almost at an end.

Having given Yeltsin the benefit of the doubt over his shelling of the parliament in 1993, and having confined expressions of concern over the slaughter in Chechnya to polite protest, Western governments and institutions would not stop their support just when Yeltsin seemed to need it most. In the spring of 1996, as Yeltsin and his team began their attempt to build the president's woeful poll ratings into a launchpad for victory, help was forthcoming from a number of quarters. The International Monetary Fund (IMF) agreed to provide $10 billion to

Russia in the coming three years, with $4 billion of that to be provided in the next twelve months.[34] Clinton made another visit to Russia in April that year, boosting Yeltsin's credentials on the international stage. There was assistance from the US in other forms, too – political consultants 'paid $250,000 plus all expenses and have an unlimited budget for polling, focus groups and other research',[35] as *Time* magazine reported in July. The report suggested that the funds came from Russia. The techniques were all American.

Yeltsin's Western supporters willing him to win was not sufficient on its own. Daniel Treisman's conclusion that 'Yeltsin won the election in large part through state largess'[36] is convincing, especially for those of us who remember a re-energised Russian president taking to the campaign trail in the far-flung regions of the world's largest country, and getting off his plane to speak, joke, dance and, most importantly, dispense cash to regions that really needed it. This followed government initiatives in the spring to reduce wage arrears as polling day approached. In the end, Yeltsin won – defeating Zyuganov in a second-round run-off on 3 July. It would be a last political triumph for the man who played such a decisive role in changing Russia forever. He had had help from a loyal network of regional officials, and of course from Western governments, institutions and spin doctors – but his own irrepressible and sometimes unpredictable personality showed its positive side here too, as he rose to meet and overcome a challenge that had seemed set to defeat him only months earlier. Yeltsin's victory was also notable for the fact – only revealed later – that he had suffered a heart attack in the run-up to polling day. It was one of five he had while in office, as he admitted in an interview in 2004.[37] He had survived, and so had his presidency. Neither enjoyed the healthy strength of earlier years.

His support from the West had not weakened. During this period, there was close cooperation especially with the US in the form of the Gore–Chernomyrdin Commission, named for the US vice president, Al Gore, and the Russian prime minister, Viktor Chernomyrdin, who led its activities. In Talbott's view, the committee had the benefit that 'foreign economic assistance would be politically more palatable in Russia – less like "patronizing charity" – if it were put in the framework of US–Russia cooperation'.[38] This commitment to Yeltsin and his team even extended to Gore's deciding publicly to criticise Zhirinovsky's populist-nationalist agenda after his party's strong showing in the 1993 Duma elections. Zhirinovsky's views were, Gore said on a visit to Moscow, 'reprehensible and anathema to all freedom-loving people in Russia, the United States and everywhere in the world'. Such opinions might often be expressed in private, but offering views on the domestic politics of a host country during a visit was a departure from diplomatic convention. Gore's words were an expression of how strongly Washington was taking sides as post-Soviet politics took shape.

Yet there was also a recognition that things were not going well in Russia. Gore also took issue with the IMF. It had, he argued, been 'slow to recognize some of the hardships that are caused by some of the conditions that have been overly insisted upon in the past'.[39] Christopher admitted in his later memoir, 'We did overestimate the popularity and strength of reform in Russia.'[40] Members of Yeltsin's team would agree, especially his first foreign minister, Andrei Kozyrev, in office during the initial post-Soviet period. In a 2020 memoir, Kozyrev was sharply critical of the abilities and attitudes of Clinton and those of his administration who were dealing with Russia. Noting that Clinton 'inaugurated the era of Bill and Boris' (as the two leaders were sometimes referred to on the basis of the warm personal relationship they seemed to have in public), Kozyrev wrote: 'Untested in foreign affairs, Clinton depended on the audiences he was playing to, with Congress and the public expecting him to deliver first of all on his campaign assurances to boost the domestic economy.'[41] Kozyrev, who had moved to the US by the time he published his memoir, argued further that 'nor did the grandly promised aid materialize in amounts large enough to move the reform efforts forward. The Americans seemed not to understand the dire social situation of the Russian population and the effect on its fledgling democracy.'[42]

Kozyrev's verdict on Clinton was understandable from the point of view of a Russian who desperately wanted his country to be a close ally of the West, yet it also showed a certain lack of understanding of the pressures politicians in democracies faced. For the pro-Western Russian political elite in this period, the US was the potential source of all that they sought: funding for their reforms, giving them a greater chance of success, thereby hopefully limiting the appeal to voters of Vladimir Zhirinovsky or similar firebrand nationalists. US support would also show that Russia, while no longer feared as the foe it had been in the Cold War, was still seen as important, and therefore respected. For the US and its Western allies, Russia was a major policy issue – but it was just one issue. For the collapse of the USSR had not only meant new policies towards the countries that had made up the USSR: it had created other issues that had consequences around the world, as Lyne's memory of Mahathir Mohamad's criticism of British policy in Yugoslavia demonstrated. It was also an age in which the media was changing. CNN, established in the 1980s, was increasingly available and would soon inspire the launch of other twenty-four-hour television news channels. These technological developments would drive new editorial approaches and also change the way that policymakers looked at the media – because historical events could now be watched live around the world.

Some of the assault on the White House in Moscow in October 1993 was broadcast live. Talbott later wrote that during the fighting he was on the phone to Georgi Mamedov, Kozyrev's deputy with special responsibility for US–Russia relations. Talbott and Mamedov realised they were watching the same pictures. The battle for Russia's future, with all its bloody consequences, was thus a moment not only in world history but also in the history of diplomatic communication – and one in which the White House in Washington, DC and the Moscow Kremlin were seeking the same outcome. As the centre of Moscow became a war zone during the course of Sunday 3 October, Talbott talked to Clinton. The president sounded 'weary and grim – but not because of what has happening in Russia'. Two American Blackhawk helicopters had been shot down in Mogadishu in Somalia. Five Americans were dead. In his memoir, Talbott remembers that the 'pitched battle in the heart of Moscow dominated the news'.[43] In his, Clinton remembered that 'the news in America led with a different story' – that from Mogadishu.[44] Russia was important, but the deaths of American soldiers on active service overseas was more politically pressing. Clinton and Christopher's firm support, both in public and in private, for Yeltsin after he used military force against his armed opponents showed how strongly the US was prepared to back him. But the fall of the USSR had created a new world, and a new Europe. That meant new policies for Washington and the wider West. Even the bonhomie of 'Bill and Boris' would not be enough to overcome the differences in outlook that remained between the capitals that had led opposing sides in the Cold War.

2

Our Hopes Have Not Come True

If Western allies supported Yeltsin throughout the 1990s, in other ways they caused him problems. During the Cold War, Moscow had led The Warsaw Pact, a military alliance with satellite socialist states in the Eastern bloc. The Warsaw Pact did not survive even as long as the USSR itself. After the revolutions against communist governments in Eastern Europe in 1989, the alliance began to crumble. It was formally dissolved on 1 July 1991. The North Atlantic Treaty Organization (NATO) had been established by treaty on 4 April 1949, with the aim of 'deterring Soviet expansionism, forbidding the revival of nationalist militarism in Europe through a strong North American presence on the continent, and encouraging European political integration'.[1] With the USSR gone, and its officers and soldiers returning in their thousands to Russia, 'Soviet expansionism' was no longer a threat that needed to be deterred. NATO did not consider that it might follow the example of its Cold War foe and – albeit for different reasons, the political systems in Western Europe and the US not being in transition – disband. In the early 1990s, Jamie Shea was speechwriter to the then secretary general, Manfred Wörner – just one role that Shea held in a NATO career that spanned almost four decades. 'At the time of great instability in Europe, you hang on to the stable factors. You can't afford to have everything in flux all at once,' he explained in a 2023 interview. 'So if the Warsaw Pact is collapsing, you keep NATO.'[2] Echoing the official reasons for NATO's creation, Shea also maintained that NATO was 'more than simply a deterrent against the Soviet Union. It was a kind of organizing principle for European integration.'

Yeltsin did not see it in those terms. Even with the goodwill and warm personal relations of the 'Bill and Boris' era, NATO's future and ambitions soon became grounds for disagreement. On 15 September 1992, less than a year after the USSR had formally ceased to exist, Yeltsin wrote to Major to express concerns at the direction in which he felt new plans for European security were heading. Among the points he raised was a long-held Russian belief that Moscow had been given guarantees that, Germany reunited and the Cold War over, NATO would not enlarge eastwards: 'I would also like to draw the [sic] attention to the fact that the Treaty on final settlement with respect to Germany signed in September of 1990, and especially its provisions which ban stationing of foreign troops in the eastern lands of the FRG do rule out by their own sense the possibility of the expansion of the NATO zone to the east.'[3]

Yeltsin's letter touched on the issue that, more than any other, has led to confrontation between Russia and the West since the end of the Cold War: the acceptance into NATO of countries that were once in the Warsaw Pact, and therefore under Moscow's military authority. In the years since, even the terminology has become a matter of controversy, with NATO itself, and its members, preferring to talk of 'enlargement'. Its critics often prefer 'expansion'. In his memoir, published in 2004, Clinton used the terms interchangeably.[4] Christopher, in 1998, wrote of expansion: 'In moving forward on expansion, we had to weigh the risks of aggravating Russian anxieties and undermining President Yeltsin. Particularly with the Duma elections scheduled for December 1993, we needed to allay any Russian impression that expanding NATO was anti-Russian.'[5] The distinction has become more sharply drawn as time has passed. Those who support NATO's growth since the end of the Cold War use 'enlargement', arguing that the alliance has grown by accepting applications from willing new members. 'Expansion', they would argue, suggests that NATO has itself initiated the increase in its number of members.

For Christopher was right to worry about an impression that expanding NATO was anti-Russian. In Russia, it was not simply an impression but an opinion unshakeably held. It was a concern that preoccupied Yeltsin, facing nationalist and communist domestic opposition. Major's reply was suitably diplomatic, only becoming more direct towards its conclusion, when he addressed the point about the treaty on Germany. 'Neither the letter nor the spirit of that treaty affects the sovereign rights of other countries to belong to Alliances, with all the rights and responsibilities which follow.' Major concluded, 'I understand the sensitivities in Russia about any enlargement of NATO. I have no wish to cause you political difficulties.'[6] Towards the end of his letter, Yeltsin wrote, 'One cannot rule out also our entry into NATO. This is a theoretical issue, however.' And theoretical it remained, although it was an idea that did not disappear for some time to come – enduring into the Putin era, as will be seen later, though never of course becoming reality. NATO enlargement, however, did not remain theoretical. In early 1994, Clinton's secretary of state, Madeleine Albright, travelled to Central and Eastern Europe on a diplomatic mission ahead of that year's NATO summit. She was accompanied by General John Shalikashvili, Chairman of the US Joint Chiefs of Staff. She later wrote, 'The leaders we met wanted the protection of the NATO security guarantees because they worried that the Russian bear might not remain gentle for long.'[7] Albright was aware of the way that NATO's incorporation of new members would be seen by Russia. 'An open and deliberate process would help reassure Moscow that NATO's enlargement east would be a step toward Russia, not against it.'[8] The nuance of the choice of preposition was not enough to reassure the Kremlin.

By the end of the decade, Poland, Hungary and Czechia (then known as the Czech Republic), all three of them former Warsaw Pact countries, had become members of the alliance. Seen from Moscow, this was a breach of agreements reached at the end of the Cold War, at least as successive occupants of the Kremlin said they understood it. Western policymakers have generally insisted – as Major did in his letter to Yeltsin in the autumn of 1992 – that no such agreement, written or unwritten, existed. Others closer to events at the time have different recollections. At a discussion at the Chatham House research institute in London in 2011, held to mark the twentieth anniversary of the end of the USSR, Rodric Braithwaite, last British ambassador to the USSR, said: 'I think that the inclusion of the East European countries into NATO and the EU was inevitable and a good thing. I think we handled it badly, because, among other things, despite what you read, we did, the British, at least, did officially assure the Russians we would not expand NATO to the east, so they feel double-crossed.'[9]

In his memoir, Talbott (also using the word 'expand') argued that 'NATO had already expanded since the end of the cold war [. . .] East Germany had pulled out of the Warsaw Pact, abandoned communism, ceased to exist as a separate country, and merged with West Germany. The Bush administration gave the Soviet leadership assurances that NATO would stop there.'[10] This famously included the phrase, used by the US secretary of state James Baker, that NATO would 'not shift one inch eastward' from the border of a united Germany. As M.E. Sarotte has written, 'A controversy erupted over this phrase almost immediately, at first behind closed doors, and then publicly.'[11]

For Russia, especially later, under Putin, the feeling would endure that NATO enlargement was carried out when Russia was weak, and with the intention of preventing its becoming strong again. The belief that Russia somehow had a right to influence over countries on or near its borders was deep rooted, and it did not vanish with the end of the Cold War. John Lough was NATO representative in Moscow from 1995 to 1998. He was in the room when, in 1996, the visiting NATO secretary general, Javier Solana, met the Russian defence minister, Pavel Grachev. Grachev, Lough remembered in a 2024 interview, 'said that

Russia wanted to keep Central Europe as a grey zone, and sort of drew a map to show it as such'.[12]

This impression of weakness hampered Russian attempts to project both hard and soft power in the 1990s. If Soviet officers were returning from foreign postings to poverty at home, its diplomatic service was struggling to keep up appearances abroad. In January 1992, a British diplomat in Berlin described a meeting with a Russian colleague, who 'proudly showed me the menu for our lunch printed on cards bearing the Russian flag'. The new flag was apparently the only thing the Russian embassy could show for its new status. 'The Embassy Office was currently receiving nothing from Moscow. They were living off their resources.' In a gesture of sympathy, or some form of diplomatic solidarity, the British diplomat had brought 'some whisky and chocolates to keep the wolf from the door'.[13] Another British diplomat, at the UK's delegation to NATO in 1993, reported a lunch he and a colleague had with two Russian diplomats. 'The alacrity with which they accepted our invitation, and indeed their comment at the end that they could not reciprocate such hospitality for the moment, confirmed that they are being kept on a short rope financially.'[14] Two years earlier they had been a superpower, in name at least. Now the Russian diplomatic service could not even afford lunch. One of those invited that day was Andrei Kelin. He later became, in November 2019, Russian ambassador to London – a post he still held at the time of Russia's full-scale invasion of Ukraine in February 2022.

Yeltsin's victory in the 1996 presidential election was a relief for Western governments, and for those parts of the Russian political system that still supported him after five hard years of economic instability, falling living standards and war in Chechnya. The relief would be relatively short lived. In some respects, the early years of Yeltsin's second term saw things getting better. The Russian stock market 'quadrupled in value in 1996 and 1997'.[15] At the same time, the problem of unpaid wages and all that went with it continued to plague the lives of everyday Russians. In July 1998, my BBC colleagues Allan Little and Andrew

Kilrain and I reported from Rostov-on-Don, where the once-mighty Rostselmash agricultural machinery factory was working at a fraction of its normal capacity. The factory had recently sold some combine harvesters to Bulgaria, but the buyers were themselves so short of cash that they had paid in jars of pickled gherkins – a commodity that was already plentiful in southern Russia. As the factory had no roubles for wages, the workers received some of their pay in gherkins. One employee we interviewed lived mainly on what he grew at his tiny dacha outside the city. His family's only cash income was his mother-in-law's pension. This was not an isolated example. It was common on the roads approaching a town to see workers from that town's main enterprises trying to sell products – glassware, biscuits, whatever it might be – that they had been given in lieu of wages.

By August that year, the month after our trip to Rostov, a staggering 54 per cent of Russia's industrial sales were in the form of barter.[16] August was the month that crisis hit. The booming stock market notwithstanding, as Anders Aslund has written, 'investor sentiment to emerging markets suddenly reversed in the wake of the Asian financial crisis in late 1997. Contagion effects from the East Asian crisis hit Russia hard.'[17] This coincided with a crisis in Russian politics. Chernomyrdin had been sacked as prime minster in March. It took a month's wrangling with the Duma before his successor, Sergei Kiriyenko, was confirmed in his post. Poor tax collection rates worsened the paucity of the public finances.

A storm was gathering. Rising oil prices have sometimes come to Russia's rescue. But demand had fallen as a result of the Asian financial crisis. Prices were in the doldrums at $10 a barrel. The Russian government's solution was to issue treasury bills at increasingly implausible rates. By August 1998, it was over 120 per cent.[18] In the end, the repayments could not be met. On 17 August, the Russian government defaulted on its debt and let the rouble exchange rate float downwards, from 6 to 24 roubles to the dollar. The immediate consequences for ordinary people were devastating. Imported goods, paid for in dollars, soon became all but unaffordable and rapidly disappeared from shelves, recalling the bad not-so-old days of the dying USSR. For the second time in less than a decade, savings were wiped out, and desperate customers hammered on the firmly locked doors of banks to try to get back some – any – of their money. The inflation rate for 1998 was 85 per cent.[19]

To this sense of financial insecurity was added a fear for physical safety. In November 1998, the democratic politician and opponent of the Chechen war, Galina Starovoitova, was shot dead in the entrance to her apartment block in Saint Petersburg.[20] Her murder presaged later assassinations of Kremlin critics. For capitalism had come to Russia on the crest of a crime wave. Gunshots were sometimes even heard resounding across the nighttime streets of the Russian capital. The aftermath of heavy-handed police raids, or the settling of scores among rival gangs, could sometimes be seen in the shape of corpses covered in sheets on city-centre pavements. While much of the bloodshed was a consequence of warring business and crime elites (the distinction often blurred), ordinary people could hardly feel safe when the battles sometimes even erupted by day in busy city streets. As William Burns, later US ambassador to Moscow and later still director of the Central Intelligence Agency (CIA), recalled of his time as minister-counsellor for political affairs at the US embassy in the 1990s, 'Moscow had its own unique charms'. Burns remembered a visit to the Moscow mayor's office during that wild decade. Arriving, he 'noticed a number of Russians in suits lying spread-eagled in the snow with a group of armed, uniformed men wearing black ski masks standing over them'.[21] The men in black were part of the Kremlin's presidential guard, whose powerful boss, Alexander Korzhakov, had a dispute with one of Russia's wealthiest men, Vladimir Gusinsky. This was Korzhakov's way of teaching Gusinsky's company executives a lesson.

While such episodes had the capacity to shock, one firearms incident in March 1999 had greater significance, because it was an attack on the US embassy. Earlier that week, NATO had bombed targets in Belgrade in an attempt to stop the Serbian authorities' military action against the separatist ethnic Albanian population in Kosovo. Enraged by airstrikes on a fellow Slavic nation and traditional Russian ally, demonstrators – including, as the *New York Times* reported, 'beer-drinking toughs' – had gathered to protest.[22] Days later, the embassy was the target of a failed attack by assailants who attempted to launch a rocket-propelled grenade. That misfired, but when officers policing the demonstration and guarding the embassy fired back, one of the attackers opened fire from an assault rifle, before escaping in the car in which they had arrived. As the *New York Times*'s correspondent also wrote, the car 'reportedly had been stolen from the police'.

While Russia struggled at home to cope with the economic hardship and political uncertainty that came with the collapse of communism, it faced yet more challenges finding its place in the new world that followed the end of the Cold War. By the end of the 1990s, any enthusiasm for Yeltsin had long vanished: crushed as the reality of post-Soviet life turned out to be very unlike the change for the better for which so many had hoped. A poll published by the All Russian Center for Public Opinion (VTsIOM) in April 1999 gave the ailing Russian president an approval rating of just 6 per cent.[23] His time in office had seen the Russian people hit with two devastating financial blows: the sky-high inflation and unpaid wages at the dawn of the post-Soviet era, and the additional shock of the default in the later summer of 1998. To this domestic struggle for survival was added a sense of being pushed around, or simply ignored, in the international arena.

A transatlantic flight just days before the attack on the embassy summarised neatly this sense of helplessness and humiliation. The flight did not reach its destination. Its principal passenger, the Russian prime minister, Yevgeny Primakov, used his authority to order the pilot to turn around and return to Moscow. Primakov had been flying to the US to try to negotiate a loan for the Russian government. He ended his mission without even seeking to accomplish it. Already in the air, he learnt that NATO airstrikes on Serbia had started. Primakov had led

Russia's foreign intelligence service from 1991 to 1996, and may also have been a KGB agent himself while ostensibly working as a Soviet foreign correspondent in the 1960s.[24] Sitting politely asking for financial assistance from a former Cold War foe – while a military alliance of which that foe was the most powerful member bombed a Russian ally – was clearly too much. Yet this was the stage that Russia's strength and standing relative to the West had reached. The Russian government's opinion disregarded, they still had to seek help. Russia's poverty and impotence were plain for the world to see.

This sense of humiliation only worsened as NATO's operation in Kosovo continued. In the summer of 1999, the Serbian president, Slobodan Milosevic, ended attacks on Kosovo, persuaded to do so by a combination of NATO's military action and Russian diplomacy. When NATO forces prepared to move into Kosovo to take up a peacekeeping role, however, they discovered that Russian troops, which had been stationed in Bosnia, were already on the move and seeking to seize Pristina airport. The US general, Wesley Clark, NATO's supreme allied commander, ordered 500 British and French paratroopers to be moved to the airport to block the Russian advance. The force's British commander, General Sir Mike Jackson, refused – reportedly telling Clark, 'General, I am not going to start the Third World War for you.'[25]

Jackson did not order the troops under his command to block the Russian advance; instead, he allowed the Russians to take up positions at the airport, and then, when he realised that the Russian forces were short of supplies – especially water – in the oppressive heat of a Balkan summer, came to their aid. In the words of the then NATO spokesman, Jamie Shea, Jackson decided to 'absorb the problem rather than confront the problem'. Speaking many years later, Shea saw the Russian advance in the following terms: 'The Russian move into Kosovo was obviously a face-saving move. It all worked out very well in the end because the Russians took the airport. And NATO moved up to the Film City[26] and had put its headquarters up there, right near the airport.' What followed was much more amicable, in Shea's view, than the looming confrontation in the summer of 1999 had threatened to be. 'It all worked very well for a number of years. They eventually departed quite quietly, I think, for economic reasons.'[27] Given the state of the Russian economy, that is perfectly plausible. The Russian contingent seems, after all, not to have had sufficient food or water – perhaps not surprising given the British diplomats' accounts from the 1990s suggesting that their Russian counterparts were similarly financially embarrassed.

The fact that the Russian and NATO forces seem to have cooperated during the time they were both there, though, speaks of a broader diplomatic relationship that would have been unthinkable before the end of the USSR. This was an age in which – despite the fury that led Primakov to return to Russia without reaching Washington – there was a desire to work together on international issues, including conflict in the Balkans. The standoff at Pristina airport was important mostly for what it showed about the gap between Russia's ambitions to be a power able to project its might beyond its borders, and its inability to realise those ambitions. For the Russian armed forces themselves, there was a much bigger challenge in 1999: renewed war in Chechnya.

August has often been a time of crisis in modern Russian history: the coup against Gorbachev; the financial crisis of 1998; the sinking of the Kursk submarine, in 2000; the war with Georgia in 2008. The year 1999 also fitted this pattern, although it began with an incident the significance of which was not fully appreciated, taking place as it did in a region far from Moscow, and not initially attracting a great deal of attention. On 11 August, Islamist separatists in Dagestan, a southern Russian region between the Caspian Sea and Chechnya, declared that they had appointed Shamil Basayev, a Chechen rebel commander, as their leader. In statements published on the Kavkaz-Tsentr (Caucasus Centre) website, the Dagestani separatists called on Basayev 'to lead the holy jihad in Dagestan until the infidels have been driven completely from the Muslim land of Dagestan'.[28] Basayev, then aged just thirty-four, was already notorious in Russia. Four years earlier, in the summer of 1995, he had led a murderous raid on the southern Russian town of

Budennovsk. Fighters under Barayev's command took over a hospital: their attack, and the resulting attempt by the Russian security forces to regain control of the site, ended with the killing of more than 100 people, some of them patients. The fact that Basayev was able to negotiate safe passage for his fighters back to Chechnya was widely seen as a sign of weakness on the part of the Russian state under Yeltsin. Now Basayev and his followers had returned to threaten again the Kremlin's authority. They were seeking to establish their form of Islamic rule in part of the north Caucasus. 'If Russia goes away from the Caucasus by itself, we will leave it alone,' Basayev was quoted as saying at the time. 'If it does not, we will force it to go.'[29]

Worse still was to come – and much closer to the centre of power than the restive regions at the Russian Federation's southern edge. In the early hours of Thursday 9 September 1999, an explosion destroyed an apartment block in Guryanova Street, in the Pechatniki district of south Moscow. More than 90 people were killed and some 250 injured. The time of the blast, shortly after midnight, meant many residents were at home in bed, and so probably increased the large number of casualties.[30] The city authorities' first version of events was that it had been a gas explosion. By the following afternoon, it was being blamed on a bomb, a deliberate act of terrorism. Days earlier, a car bomb had gone off outside a block of flats in the town of Buinaksk, in Dagestan, killing twenty-two people. The block was home to Russian service personnel and their families.[31] On 13 September, four days after the Pechatniki explosion, another blast destroyed an apartment block on Kashirskoye Shosse in Moscow. One hundred and nineteen people were killed. On 16 September, there was a bomb in the city of Volgodonsk. Seventeen people were killed in that explosion. This series of bombings shocked Russia for their random cruelty. While the target in Buinaksk might have been chosen because it was home to military personnel, the same was not true of the apartment buildings in Moscow, ordinary residential blocks in an unremarkable suburb. There was great fear among Muscovites that their home might be the next target.

The bombings themselves, and the contradictory accounts of who was responsible that came after, make them one of the most consequential series of events in Russia's post-Soviet history. They had huge implications for the possession of power in Russia, and also led indirectly to one of the most serious confrontations between Britain and Russia since the end of the Cold War.

The initial consequence of the attacks was panic and terror. The very ordinariness of the chosen targets meant that no one could feel safe until the attacks stopped, or at least were explained. The uncertainty as to who was behind them, and why, only added to the fear. Russia's new prime minister, Vladimir Putin, a former KGB officer who had cut his political teeth in the shark pool of post-Soviet Saint Petersburg, had only been in office since the previous month. He was in no doubt as to who had carried out the attacks. As a worried Russian public looked for answers, and some sense of security, he was on hand to provide a suspect, and a solution. Putin blamed Chechen 'terrorists'. He promised to pursue them and kill them, 'even in the shithouse'. Even so early in his political career, Putin was already demonstrating some of the techniques and characteristics which would be the foundations of his entire approach to political success and the exercise of power: decisiveness; toughness; and a readiness to use language more suited to the barracks or the beer hall than the offices of government and gilded halls of the Kremlin. He simplified a complex situation and showed that he knew what to do, and would do it. That autumn, Russia was again at war in Chechnya.

The first Chechen war had ended in the summer of 1996, with accords negotiated on the Russian side by Alexander Lebed, a general who had begun his career in the Soviet Army. Lebed came to enjoy political success, too. He stood as a candidate in the 1996 presidential election, coming third in the first round of voting. After his elimination, he pledged his support for Yeltsin in the run-off. He was later appointed governor of Krasnoyarsk, a vast, resource-rich region of Siberia. The agreement that ended the first Chechen war was known as the Khasavyurt Accords, after the town in Dagestan in which they were signed. The Chechen delegation was led by Aslan Maskhadov, who had been Chechen president since Dudayev's death in a Russian missile strike in April that year. Dudayev had been killed when Russian aircraft picked up the signal of a satellite phone he was using and used it to determine his location. Now the agreement and subsequent formal ending of hostilities that had brought relative calm to Chechnya were forgotten as the Russian government launched what it termed an 'anti-terrorist operation' against separatists in the region at its restive southern edge. If Putin had presented a simple case for war, not everyone was convinced. While a frightened populace seemed generally to accept his assertions, others – including Lebed and Maskhadov – did not.

Russia was entering a new election cycle, with a presidential vote due in the summer of 2000. Yeltsin, his ratings woefully low, would not stand again. As he later admitted in his memoirs, serious consideration had been given to postponing the 1996 presidential elections, dissolving the Duma and banning the Communist Party. Decrees to this effect had even been drawn up.[32] Yeltsin understood very well that he could not necessarily expect a successor that would be sympathetic. In a country still suffering dire economic hardship, stories of those around him reaping great financial benefit from their proximity to power were not seen well. Those targets of popular anger included the businessman Boris Berezovsky and Yeltsin's own daughter, Tatiana Dyachenko. Primakov had proved to be a popular prime minister but also close to factions in the Duma who were planning new impeachment procedures against Yeltsin. Combined with Primakov's own growing political profile, Yeltsin may have seen this as a risk. Primakov had formed an alliance with the powerful mayor of Moscow, Yuri Luzhkov. It was easy to foresee a new presidency that might seek to look into allegations of financial irregularities enriching members of the Yeltsin 'family' – a term that was expanded to include close members of the inner circle. For that reason, and for the fact that no Chechen link to the bombings was ever satisfactorily proved, there has always been a suspicion that the attacks were not what they seemed; that those the Kremlin blamed were not those who were responsible.

Lebed, who died in a helicopter crash in 2002, questioned the official version of events almost from the start. In an outspoken interview published in the French newspaper *Le Figaro* on 29 September, Lebed declared of Yeltsin: 'The president and "the family" [quotation marks in the original] find themselves isolated today. They have no political force that would permit them to win the elections. So, seeing the inextricable character of the situation, the power can only have one aim: to destabilize the situation so that there are no elections. Houses explode, there are already 294 dead, thousands of invalids, millions of traumatised.'[33] The correspondent, Laure Mandeville, then asked Lebed if he was saying that 'the hand of power was behind the attacks'. 'I am almost convinced,' Lebed replied, arguing that any Chechen commander seeking revenge would have 'taken to blowing up generals' or military or security targets, rather than attacking 'simple and innocent people'. Maskhadov himself had made a similar point in an interview with Sophie Shihab of *Le Monde* earlier that month: 'A true Chechen, even if he really wants to take revenge, could not do that, destroy a residential building'.[34] It is hard to imagine that, had his forces been involved, Maskhadov would have been keen to admit such involvement. Yet his denial is given greater weight by Lebed's analysis, and by the fact that the authorities never satisfactorily proved Chechen guilt.

There was another incident at the time that gave rise to suspicion of official involvement. It took place in the Russian city of Ryazan, where a number of sacks of what appeared to be explosives were discovered in the basement of an apartment block. As outlined in detail in the book *Blowing up Russia*, the Russian Federal Security Service (FSB) issued various contradictory accounts as to whether or not the 'explosives' were such, or sugar, and part of an exercise designed to test citizens' vigilance. The authors presented their book as the 'account of Vladimir Putin's secret election coup'. One of them, Alexander Litvinenko, himself a former FSB agent, was fatally poisoned in 2006 in London, where he had fled and where he was working for Berezovsky, who had also left Russia following Putin's election victory. At the time of his departure, Berezovsky was facing criminal charges in relation to his business activity – charges that he always insisted were politically motivated. In 2013, Berezovsky was found hanged at his house outside London.[35] Suspicion that he had been involved in orchestrating the Basayev-led incursion into Dagestan – the idea being that this was part of the planned operation to create instability and thus provide an excuse for the postponement of elections – first emerged in Russian media reports in September 1999, the month of the bombings.[36] Berezovsky strongly denied this and threatened to sue one of the newspapers, *Moskovsky Komsomolets*, that had published what it claimed were transcripts of phone conversations between Berezovsky and Chechen militant commanders.[37]

Russian officialdom never wavered from the version that Chechen militants were behind the bombings of 1999, though they never provided evidence beyond dispute that that was the case. Some suspects did stand trial. However, in his detailed study of the bombings, John B. Dunlop concluded of the judicial process, 'there is no reason to credit any of the information generated by these tainted and suspect trials which were held in camera'.[38] What is beyond dispute is that the events of late summer and early autumn did provide an opportunity for the largely unknown and untested new prime minister to show himself as a credible successor to Yeltsin, at least in the eyes of those who in that time in Russia still mattered most: the electorate. Polling published in the latter half of 1999 shows that Putin's popularity soared as the second Chechen war went on. In August, just 2 per cent of respondents to a poll conducted by VTsIOM who intended to vote in the 2000 presidential election said that they would vote for Putin. By January 2000, ahead of an election due in March, it was 61 per cent.[39]

Yeltsin, in poor health, and often absent from public view amid persistent rumours of heavy drinking, had one final surprise. He had started his presidential career as a hero, but his years in office came to be remembered mostly for a series of shocks. The last of those was his resignation, in a televised address on the last day of the twentieth century: 31 December 1999, before the end of his term in office. As the world waited to see whether the 'millennium bug' would cause havoc with computer systems, Yeltsin left the political stage for good. His words summed up his own political journey, and that of Russia and the USSR: 'I want to ask you for forgiveness, because many of our hopes have not come true, because what we thought would be easy turned out to be painfully difficult.'[40] Under the terms of the Russian constitution, the prime minister – Putin – became acting president until elections could be held, the following spring.

When Yeltsin resigned on the eve of the new century, one of the most bewilderingly unpredictable decades in Russian history had ended. Moscow had started the 1990s as the capital of a superpower. It ended the decade battling against insurgents on the territory of the Russian Federation, falling living standards, an unstable economy and growing tensions abroad. 'Abroad' now fell into two categories. The usual Russian expression, literally translated as 'beyond the border', now had an additional meaning, as parts of what had been the USSR and, before that, the Russian Empire became sovereign states. Ukraine was already a particular source of tension: 'the more Ukraine asserted its sovereignty, the more Russia questioned it,'[41] as Paul D'Anieri has written. Further abroad, as was discussed earlier in the chapter, the wars in Yugoslavia, and NATO involvement in them, almost led to direct confrontation between Russian and British troops – while NATO's own plans to take in new members continued to provoke opposition across the Russian political spectrum.

This was the Russia of which Vladimir Putin became acting president on the last day of 1999. The popularity he soon came to enjoy was based on his approach to the problems Russia faced: a feeling of lost respect abroad, and disorder at home. Through all the concerns about the state of Russian democracy, the US, Britain and other Western countries had stuck with Yeltsin. It was clear that the likely alternatives

– communists or nationalists – would be worse. There seems to have been a belief – a hope, at least – that Russia was generally heading in the right direction: that it would eventually stabilise at home, and not seek renewed confrontation abroad. There was also considerable evidence that might not be so.

For most of the Cold War era, and until the end of the twentieth century, the US government funded the United States Information Agency (USIA). It was established in August 1953, a few months after Stalin's death, and abolished in 1999, the year that Putin first became Russian prime minister. The agency was originally set up 'as a consolidation of all the foreign information activities of the U.S. Government into one program'.[42] In the last years of its existence, the USIA commissioned extensive polling in Russia. The data were collected for relevant offices in the State Department and other agencies. They are a remarkable resource for the historian today because of the insights they offer into Russian elite and wider public opinion during the country's decade after the collapse of communism. The pollsters sought views on a wide variety of subjects. One, on attitudes to the US, included a question on which brands of American cigarettes respondents had purchased.[43] There were also surveys on matters such as NATO enlargement, Kosovo and Ukraine. In the first decade after the end of the Cold War, with Russia and the US enjoying better relations than at any time since, the US government seems correctly to have identified the issues that would bring it once again into confrontation with Russia, two decades before that renewed confrontation reached crisis point in the February 2022 escalation of the war in Ukraine.

Polling on attitudes to NATO was carried out as far back as 1993. USIA hired Russian polling organisations to carry out the work on their behalf. In November 1993, one poll conducted among 'leaders of public opinion' (these were members of Russia's elite, according to the details of the sample included with the results, representatives of government, politics, business, science and the military) asked whether respondents trusted NATO. Only 28 per cent said they did, with only

3.4 per cent saying they trusted the alliance completely. Sixty-one per cent said they did not trust it. Sixty-three per cent were against Ukraine's joining the alliance, with 23 per cent in favour.[44] A similar survey was carried out among 1,878 ordinary Russians the following month. In that poll, 42 per cent opposed, to various degrees, the idea of Ukraine joining NATO – but the biggest single category was 30 per cent, for 'do not know'. Asked whether NATO had 'played a useful role' in the former Yugoslavia, 40 per cent gave the same answer. The relative lack of engagement with international affairs was perhaps a reflection of a population overcome with the daily financial struggles of the era. In the same poll, more than three quarters, 75.4 per cent, saw the threat to Russia as being from 'internal' rather than 'external force'.[45] Attitudes on Western military action appeared significantly to have hardened by the following April. A telephone poll conducted then in the Russian capital found that 79.2 per cent of those asked opposed 'somewhat' or 'strongly' recent NATO airstrikes in Bosnia.[46]

As the decade continued, the sense that the US was well-intentioned diminished. In April 1996, 27.9 per cent of residents polled in the Moscow region believed that the US wanted 'to help Russia revive'. Almost twice as many, 54.2 per cent, believed it was 'trying to reduce Russia to a second-rank power'.[47] The US is consistently identified by both elites and samples of ordinary citizens as the country posing the greatest threat to Russia. The US was named by 29.3 per cent of respondents in a March 1997 poll of the Russian elite (people from the Duma, government, the military, the media and science and culture). No other country reached double figures. The same poll asked, 'What might be the positive elements for Russia if Poland, Czech Republic, Hungary and some other European countries joined NATO?' Eighty-five per cent said, 'None'.[48] Four months later, those three countries were invited to join NATO. USIA also commissioned a poll among military personnel that year. Conducted in May, it gathered the opinions of 1,200 respondents of different ranks of the army, navy and air force. Eighty per cent of them favoured the idea of reunification with

Ukraine in the next five years. Eighty-five per cent agreed with the proposition that the USSR's leaders sacrificed the country's interests and got nothing in return. Eighty-eight per cent opposed NATO enlargement. Eighty-four per cent opposed NATO membership for Ukraine. These numbers – clear, if not astonishing, given the occupation of those surveyed – are even more clearly understood considering answers to one of the later questions. The respondents were asked when they had last received their full salary. For 38.7 per cent, it had been three months earlier, in February.[49] The perceived threat from a powerful foe, previously seen as an equal, was combined with the humiliation of poverty. It was a potent political mix.

To this polling data can be added stark diplomatic warnings. In February 1995, a diplomatic despatch from the British embassy in Moscow to the Ministry of Defence in London addressed Russian responses to 'NATO expansion'. It began: 'Dangerous to underestimate Russian opposition to NATO enlargement. Key MFA [Ministry of Foreign Affairs] with support from Kozyrev and probably Yeltsin, understand its inevitability: but they are negotiating to limit damage, not just to save face, against a domestic political background where most regard the process as a blow to Russian society, to relations with the west, and to the electoral prospects of Russian democrats.'

The copy of this very direct message that is held in the National Archives of the UK has the handwritten addition of the words, 'A very clear warning shot'.[50]

The USIA surveys' incisive questioning led to valuable insights into elite and wider public opinion. At this distance of time, the choice of subjects shows that those who commissioned the surveys understood very well the issues that might cause feelings of resentment or mistrust towards the US: NATO enlargement, Ukraine and military action in different parts of the former Yugoslavia. The information seems not to have driven any change in policy. Russian elite opposition to NATO enlargement was clear, yet it went ahead months later. The Russian military's distrust of the US six years after the collapse of the USSR, and even longer since Washington and Moscow had been bitter ideological enemies, endured, and arguably strengthened as their own financial hardships were a daily reminder of lost status.

The military personnel were also asked whether the Western allies should also have withdrawn their troops from Germany (as the USSR had). Ninety per cent of respondents agreed that they should. On 3 February 1990, Putin had made the journey back from his KGB posting in Dresden to the USSR. Having assessed the validity of the various versions of the reasons for his return before his posting would normally have finished, Philip Short concluded in his biography of Putin that it was a simple redeployment, not a direct consequence of the fall of the Berlin Wall.[51] All the same, Putin was not alone in making that journey and returning to a motherland in much reduced circumstances. He must have understood the officers' resentment. In *First Person*, a volume of interviews with him conducted by Russian journalists and published in 2000, Putin related how he had been offered a job with the KGB in Moscow but turned it down. 'Why? I knew there was no future to the system. The country didn't have a future. And it would have been very difficult to sit inside the system and wait for it all to collapse around me.'[52] He was part of a generation of loyal servants of the Soviet security state who suddenly felt that it had all ended in nothing. If the State Department did not fully grasp the possible longer-term consequences of the opinions the USIA surveys had uncovered, Putin saw the political potential of the humiliation and discontent they reflected.

3

Russia Knows What Terrorism Means

The autumn of 1999 was a time of tension because of the apartment bombings, political uncertainty as the Yeltsin era drew to a close, and bloodshed in Chechnya. Russian forces took up positions around Grozny in mid-October. At the launch of this new military campaign in Chechnya, there were no unwise boasts about victory being a matter of hours away. Having learnt not only from military mistakes in the first war but also from errors in the media war, the Russian authorities now kept journalists from the frontlines, and even, to a large extent, from the territory of Chechnya itself. Press accreditation that in theory entitled international journalists to report from the whole of the Russian Federation was not valid in the area that was declared a zone of 'anti-terrorist operation'.[1] More enterprising and risk-averse reporters did make it into Grozny and reported from there as the shells and rockets fell, their words and pictures widely shared around the world. But getting into Chechnya became so difficult and so dangerous, as well as technically illegal, for journalists that most were reduced to working in the neighbouring region of Ingushetia, where they gathered the stories of the thousands of displaced people escaping the war. That autumn, I was among those journalists based in Ingushetia and making furtive trips into Chechnya when opportunities arose.

In one sense, the second Chechen war was a continuation of the previous conflict. In another, it was a departure: a new kind of war. If the conflict of the mid-1990s had had a largely separatist, nationalist character – where a territory sought to break away from the larger state of which it was a constituent part – this new war involved a radical religious element. Referring also to the succession that was underway in Russian presidential politics, James Hughes characterised this renewed conflict as a 'dual radicalization', with the radicalisation on the Chechen side being 'a direct product of the experience and practice of violence in the first war, and the emergence of a new "meta-cleavage" within the Chechen national movement along a religious fault line'.[2] This change in their enemy's nature and motivation gave the Russian federal authorities the opportunity to reinforce their message that this was a war on international terrorism. The presence among insurgent commanders of fighters such as the Saudi Ibn al-Khattab allowed Moscow to claim additional justification for the war they had launched on the basis of the bombings of apartment blocks. Russian tactics also evolved. Not wishing to risk a repeat of the chaotic carnage that had characterised the storming of Grozny five years earlier, the Russian army prepared more carefully. 'Our predominant criteria remain the same – to fulfil our tasks with minimal losses among the forces,' the Russian defence minister, Igor Sergeyev, said as the assault progressed.[3] Its most intensive phase began on Christmas Day (in the Western Christian calendar), 25 December – the date perhaps chosen because Western media and public opinion might not be paying too much attention. At the end of January, the Chechen fighters defending Grozny took the decision to withdraw. They left at night. They found themselves crossing a minefield. They suffered many casualties. A Chechen surgeon who operated on some of the wounded later told the BBC's Steve Rosenberg that 300 fighters had been brought to his clinic outside Grozny. 'In 48 hours I performed 76 amputations and seven brain surgeries,' Khassan Baiev said in an interview in 2012.[4] Among the amputees was Shamil Basayev, who lost part of his right leg during the escape from the besieged and ruined city. Although the insurgency continued in the outlying mountainous areas of Chechnya, Moscow had re-established control over Grozny, though even that was not complete. Visiting as correspondents in March, my colleagues and I were only permitted to be in the city for a few hours during daylight. We were kept constantly under the protective and watchful eye of the Russian soldiers accompanying us. Still, the Kremlin's mission had been accomplished: both on the battlefield and in the opinion polls.

With poll figures such as those he came to enjoy by January 2000 (61 per cent approval rating), and absent any serious opposition, Putin was all but certain to be the next president. Western leaders hoped an era of greater stability and predictability would follow the Yeltsin years. One, in particular, was so keen to forge a relationship with the presumed successor that he made a significant departure from diplomatic convention. The British prime minister, Tony Blair, himself then a relative newcomer on the international stage (he had been elected in 1997), visited Putin before polling day – an unusual move given that Putin was at that time only head of state in an acting capacity. It was a short visit, although the two leaders and their wives did have time to attend a performance of Prokofiev's opera *War and Peace* at the Marinsky Theatre in Putin's home city of Saint Petersburg. Perhaps referring to the Napoleonic wars during which *War and Peace* is set, and almost certainly to the two countries' alliance with the US against Hitler during the Second World War, Putin said at the start of the visit that Britain and Russia 'always were together in history's critical moments'. He added, 'Thank God no such critical moments are taking place now.'[5] In diplomatic terms, though, the decision to visit Putin at this time 'was risky', Blair's then chief of staff, Jonathan Powell, said in 2023. 'There was a lot of criticism of Putin and the campaign and so the decision we made was to cut a bit of space on Grozny, and on Chechnya, in order to try and build a relationship with him.' Powell conceded that the desire to build this relationship was 'partly coloured by how odd Yeltsin had been as a partner' – citing as examples a plan he had suggested to Bill Clinton for 'a summit on a submarine in the middle of the Atlantic'[6] and an uncomfortably long bear hug that Yeltsin gave to Blair at an international meeting after the Kosovo conflict. Of the latter, Blair himself later wrote, 'The first ten seconds were, I thought, wonderfully friendly. The next ten began to get a little uncomfortable. The following ten started respiratory problems. I finally got released after about a minute.'[7] Such encounters as these – especially in the light of perilously tense moments in Russia's relations with NATO and its members during the Kosovo conflict – help to explain why Blair decided to see Putin before he was elected. As Powell recalled, 'We were distinctly worried about relations with Russia in those circumstances. And again, in Kosovo, it had been pretty tricky with the Russian forces coming in with nearly starting World War Three. So we're quite keen to see if we could start a relationship with a rational leader on a more stable and rational basis.'

Powell later judged it to have been 'a successful visit', one during which it became clear that Russia's presumed next president would differ from his predecessor. 'He struck us as a much lower key figure than Yeltsin, quite small, quite reserved, more like a clerk or bureaucrat.'[8] Roderic Lyne, who had taken up his post as British ambassador to Moscow very shortly after Putin had become acting president, formed an impression – based on his conversations in Russian political circles – that was similar. 'The consensus view of the Russian political class was that he was going to be a transitional figure who'd been put in there by Yeltsin to mind the shop because he was young and sober and quite an efficient bureaucrat.'[9]

Sobriety and efficiency were not words that had been readily associated with the Yeltsin presidency. As election day approached, the US embassy in Moscow hosted a lunch for pollsters 'to discuss the nature of the Russian electorate' – an electorate that seemed set to elect a president defined so far largely by these qualities alone. A report of the event was sent by diplomatic cable to the then secretary of state, Madeline Albright, reporting on information gleaned from the event. The names of the invited pollsters have been redacted from the copy of the cable available in the digital archive, but one 'argued that Putin's popularity was explained entirely by Chechnya. He said Putin was the right man at the right time, explaining that circumstances put him in a position where he could do things that would create a strong image of him as a person who would act.' On 26 March, with the Russian army still fighting in Chechnya – though by then having captured Grozny and gained the upper hand – Putin was elected president of Russia with 53 per cent of the vote. His rise to political prominence was built upon a faltering, if not unsuccessful, military campaign against internal separatism. As Bettina Renz has noted, when he spoke on the eve of the election, Putin referred to the fact that he would not only be head of state but also commander-in-chief. In consequence, 'the Russian military's fortunes changed with the election of Putin to the presidency'.[10]

The margin of Putin's victory – more than half the votes cast – obviated the need for a second round. This was an outcome that one of the pollsters invited to the US embassy lunch in Moscow had predicted, while regretting 'that it was "too bad" that there would likely be only one round because it would devalue the electoral process'.[11] Still, the embassy seemed satisfied that democracy had been served. A cable sent to Washington on 28 March, two days after voting had taken place, judged the election to have been 'reasonably free and fair'.[12] For the first time, power had passed peacefully from one occupant of the Kremlin to another as the result of a popular vote: peacefully, perhaps – but not without some help. Talbott later wrote of a conversation he had had with Yeltsin's daughter, Tatiana Dyachenko, during Clinton's last visit to Moscow as president, in June 2000. 'She leaned forward to me and whispered, "It really was very hard, getting Putin into the job – one of the hardest things we ever pulled off."'[13]

As Putin's first term as president began, there were already signs of the improvements in the Russian economy over which he would preside, and from which he would build political capital as his years in the Kremlin went on. GDP grew by 7.7 per cent in 2000, with industrial production up 9 per cent, as the economy continued to recover from the crisis of 1998. In another sign of what was to come, Russian earnings from energy exports reached a record level, accounting for 53 per cent of the total, as oil and gas prices rose.[14] As if to repay the faith that Blair had shown in him by meeting him in Saint Petersburg before the March election confirmed him as president, Putin visited London in April. This was his second foreign visit since the election – his first was to Belarus – and it took place even before his inauguration. On his arrival to meet Blair at Downing Street, Putin was met by demonstrators protesting against Russian conduct of the war in Chechnya. Though that conflict would not be officially declared over for years to come, it did not explode again on the scale of 1994 or 1999.

Putin did still face a stern test of his leadership during his first months in office. In August 2000, the Russian nuclear submarine *Kursk* sank in the Barents Sea. All of its 118 crew members died. Perhaps because of a mixture of shame and the Cold War mentality that still persisted in the Russian navy, offers of outside help were refused as the story of what had happened to the crew continued to change. There was even a suggestion that the vessel had collided with a NATO submarine, possibly British. It was not true. As the sailors' families waited at the dockside, distraught, Putin waited days before cutting short the holiday he was enjoying to come to meet them. Only a month later, speaking in a television interview, Putin admitted, 'From the point of view of PR, that could look better'.[15] While seeking to put right that public relations blunder, Putin committed another. The interviewer, CNN's Larry King, asked him what had happened to the *Kursk*. 'It sank,' Putin replied.

The new president had built the foundations of his political career on the war in Chechnya. His air of decisiveness and toughness – when he talked about wiping out 'terrorists' in 'the shithouse', he said it as if he were keen to pull the trigger himself – had taken him to the summit of Russian politics. Once there, he was cautious and hesitant. In seeking to avoid mistakes, in the case of the *Kursk*, he committed some. On the international stage, he had found a potential ally in Blair. The situation with the US was less straightforward. President Bill Clinton had enjoyed a good personal relationship with Yeltsin, but Yeltsin's presidency was over, and Clinton's soon would be, too – as the end of his second term in the White House drew nearer as the year 2000 went on.

Clinton's successor was George W. Bush. His victory in the 2000 election began a presidency that would coincide with Putin's first two terms in the Kremlin. In the summer of 2001, both still relatively new in office, the two presidents met for a summit in Slovenia. At the news conference that followed the meeting, Bush was asked whether he trusted Putin. He replied, 'I looked the man in the eye. I found him to be very straightforward and trustworthy. We had a very good dialogue. I was able to get a sense of his soul.' Michael McFaul, later a member of the national security team under President Barack Obama, and later still US ambassador to Moscow, had been invited – as a Russia expert – to brief the president prior to the summit with Putin. Two days after Bush's remarks, he told the *New York Times* that the president's words had been 'a rookie mistake', for Bush was dealing with an ex-KGB man 'who was trained to lie'. He was never invited to brief Bush again.[16] Condoleezza Rice, Bush's national security advisor, retained his trust – but was no more impressed than McFaul. 'I visibly stiffened', she wrote later, recalling the news conference. 'We were never able to escape the perception that the President had naively trusted Putin and had been betrayed.'[17]

Such sentiments were only to be expressed later, though – for just weeks after his meeting with Putin in Slovenia, Bush found himself facing one of the severest shocks, and one of the greatest security challenges, in American history. The attacks of 11 September 2001 took almost 3,000 lives. They also shook the sense of safety – and perhaps, in some quarters, secure superiority – that the US had enjoyed after decisive victory in the Cold War a decade earlier. Ten days after the attacks, Bush made an address to a joint session of Congress and to the American people. In it he declared, 'Every nation, in every region, now has a decision to make. Either you are with us, or you are with the terrorists.'[18] The man in the Kremlin whom Bush had already judged 'very straightforward and trustworthy' had already taken his decision, sometime before. After the attacks happened, Putin had been the first world leader to call Bush to offer his support. Bush later wrote that Putin had told him, 'Good will triumph over evil. I want you to know that in this struggle we will stand together.'[19] Publicly, Putin was equally forthright. 'Russia knows directly what terrorism means,' he said in a televised address. 'And because of this we, more than anyone, understand the feelings of the American people. In the name of Russia, I want to say to the American people – we are with you.' Putin's words – 'We are with you' – directly answered Bush's question even before it was posed. The Russian leader clearly sensed an opportunity to cement the relationship with his new counterpart in the White House. Yeltsin and Clinton, the leaders who had worked to define the Russia–US relationship in the first chaotic decade after the collapse of communism, had left the international political stage – given the sometimes comic nature of Yeltsin's public conduct, that is probably the best metaphor – and now these two new leaders would build a new relationship. For Putin, as his words 'Russia knows what terrorism means' clearly demonstrated, this was not only an opportunity to help a former Cold War foe in its hour of need. It was also an opportunity to portray Russia's war on separatists in Chechnya – an insurgency that had taken on an increasingly Islamist tone – as part of a similar struggle to that which the US must now face if it was to vanquish its Islamist enemies.

One challenging element was that this campaign of response and revenge must focus on Afghanistan, scene of a long Soviet military adventure that had ended in failure after almost a decade – thanks in part to the US's support for the armed groups, including the Taliban, who were fighting to drive the Soviets from Afghan soil. Unable initially to reach Bush, who was on his presidential plane, *Air Force One*, Putin spoke to Condoleezza Rice, then Bush's national security advisor, in the White House. Rice told Putin that the US had gone to DEFCON 3, a heightened state of military alert. In response, Putin called off Russian military exercises planned for the next day in the North Pacific, lest they should prove a distraction for a nation that sensed so strongly it was under attack.[20] As the US began to formulate its military response to 9/11, Russia's political elite wondered where the limits of cooperation might lie – insofar as that response would be more effective with US bases in Central Asia, on territory that had been part of the USSR a decade earlier. The debate within the Russian elite ended in favour of not opposing the establishment of US bases in the region, 'as long as it has the objective of fighting the war on terror, and is temporary', as Putin reportedly told Bush in a telephone call announcing the decision.[21]

This cooperation between the leaders of countries whose ideological confrontation, underpinned by a nuclear arms race, had been a rivalry that had defined the world in the second half of the twentieth century was like nothing that had been seen before. This was the high point of Russia's relations with the West after the end of the Cold War. Yet, as concerns over a US military presence in Central Asia showed, there was never a moment when the enmity of the Cold War entirely vanished. The elites both in Russia and its Western counterparts, political and military alike, had all spent their formative career years in the Cold War and could not all shed the attitudes that the experience had created. The same was true of the Russian electorate, as the expected strong showing of the Communist Party candidate, Gennady Zyuganov, in the 1996 presidential election demonstrated. Nevertheless, the mood of cooperation continued, most notably the following year when the NATO–Russia Council (NRC) was formally launched at a meeting in Rome.

Ever since the end of the Cold War and the disbanding of the Warsaw Pact, Russia's relations with NATO, the Cold War-era alliance that had survived the end of that confrontation, had been undefined. While Moscow no longer led a military alliance, Washington most certainly did (even if NATO headquarters were in Brussels). As it sought to find its new place in the international arena, one of the main relationships Russia needed to redefine was that with NATO. In the Yeltsin era, as noted in the previous chapter, the idea of eventual Russian membership of NATO was even talked of, though as Shea said in his 2023 interview, 'The idea was always to leave that particular door open without pushing it in a day-to-day policy sense.' At least from a NATO point of view, this seems always to have been a non-starter. Putin himself even raised the issue with George Robertson, NATO secretary general when Putin first became president and for three years after, on a visit to Brussels early in his presidency.[22] The idea seems never to have seriously been entertained by NATO itself, but that did not mean that the alliance did not realise that it too needed a new kind of relationship with its former Cold War foe. The formal launch of the NRC, in May 2002, was the solution.

The meeting was hosted by the Italian prime minister, Silvio Berlusconi. The Rome Declaration, the document made public at the end of the summit, placed great emphasis on consensus as a defining characteristic of the new body. 'It will work on the basis of a continuous political dialogue on security issues among its members with a view to early identification of emerging problems, determination of optimal common approaches and the conduct of joint actions, as appropriate.'[23] At their news conference, the leaders' words echoed and amplified this unprecedented message of cooperation. 'It shows that cold warriors can become partners in building a better world,' Robertson told reporters. Speaking after Robertson, and only eight months since his pledge of support for the US after 9/11, Putin said, 'The new situation in the world has forced us to accept and recognise our interdependence and the new threats to our stability and security although our common interests cannot be ensured if we act disparately.' Berlusconi, as host, also spoke, paying tribute to Putin, 'because in spite of the considerable domestic difficulties he has been facing, he was courageous enough to opt for this avenue, this path'. Despite those persistent misgivings in sections of Russia's military and security establishment, Putin wanted to see Russia back on the world stage, but not in isolation. Responding to a reporter's question, he recalled a time when 'Russia was on one side, and the other side was practically the whole of the rest of the world'. He continued,

'Nothing good came of that confrontation between us and the rest of the world. We certainly gained nothing by it.'[24] Where sometimes public statements and diplomatic despatches give wildly varying assessments of what has taken place, this was an exception. David Manning, then foreign policy adviser to Tony Blair, wrote an account of the leaders' meeting over lunch to Simon MacDonald, a senior official in the British Foreign Office, the following day: 'The meeting of the NRC was a notable event. Putin took his seat at the Council table in a scene unthinkable a very short time ago. He handled himself with skill and was one of the most impressive performers at the lunch – contributing fluently, confidently and candidly. As a further step in bringing Russia in from the cold, this was a remarkable event.'[25]

If Russia's immediate, supportive, response to 9/11 had been a contributory factor in the success of the Rome summit – Robertson said in his remarks, 'We are here because these attacks changed people's minds and perspectives about the world' – then the longer-term consequences of 9/11 were to have the opposite effect. While Russia had, despite concerns, accepted the invasion of Afghanistan, the later invasion of Iraq was quite a different matter. It was a more complicated issue from a Western policy perspective, too. While France and Germany declined to follow Britain into the invasion force, other European countries, including some who had been part of the Soviet bloc, supported the invasion. This led the then US secretary of defense, Donald Rumsfeld, to make the provocative distinction between 'old Europe' and 'new Europe' as he criticised those who would not join the war on Saddam Hussein. Russia was firmly opposed. By this time, Yevgeny Primakov had become an adviser to Putin. In that capacity, he had travelled to Baghdad in February 2003 in an attempt to persuade Saddam Hussein to resign, in the hope it might avert the war.[26] As Primakov wrote the year after the invasion, referring to Putin's attempts to work with France and Germany to avoid war, 'Putin's restraint and Russia's generally reserved policies in this crisis period were guided by the principle that a military solution to the problem of Iraq was unacceptable.'[27]

One factor in Russian policy was the debt that Iraq owed to Russia, much of it for weapons supplied to Saddam Hussein's regime in Soviet times. Later in 2003, the figure given in media reports was $8 billion[28] – a substantial sum for a country that had yet to recover fully from the shock of economic collapse in the preceding decade. Moscow feared that the downfall of Hussein's regime would mean the end of Russia's chance of that debt being repaid – and that the US did not care. 'Putin thought that Russia's interests were not going to be taken into account by Bush when it came to Iraq,' David Manning said in 2023. 'As I recall, he didn't really care very much what happened to Saddam Hussein, but he wanted Russia's debts repaid.' This was a world before the oil prices soared as they would later in the decade, bringing billions in revenue to transform a struggling Russian economy. In February 2003, the month before the invasion, oil averaged $31.54 a barrel.[29] As Manning later reflected, 'Putin is faced with this appalling economic situation in Russia. Critical for him is that, whatever happens, he wants to ensure that Iraq's debts to Russia are repaid, and that Moscow has some say in what happens in Iraq afterwards. Although the Americans said that they would take account of Russian interests, Putin thought that they did not. He may have had a case.' Manning saw this as a moment when Putin's views of the West began to change:

> I think this was a critical factor for him. He realised that it was going to be difficult securing a place at the top table. Despite Bush famously saying that he had looked into Putin's eyes and seen his soul, I think Putin concluded that this wasn't going to translate into Iraq's debts being repaid to Russia. He was resentful that Russian interests were apparently being disregarded – and this despite Moscow having cooperated closely after 9/11 with the US over Afghanistan.[30]

It was not simply a question of money, important though that may have been. In his book *A World Challenged*, also cited above, Primakov asked, based on the fact that the US and Britain went ahead with the invasion of Iraq without a United Nations (UN) resolution in support of the attack, 'Is this our first glimpse of a system that will supplant the UN-based world order we know now?'[31] Speaking in 2023, Jonathan Powell, who was working in Downing Street when Manning was foreign policy adviser, shared the view that the 2003 invasion of Iraq 'was really what broke it, for us with Putin'. He accepted that this was a 'British perspective', for 'The French and Germans, they saw this as a great thing. Putin was siding with them.' Powell, though, saw Iraq as a crucial moment – the point after which the relationship would never be the same: 'I put the fracture then. That's when they felt that this idea of sucking up to the West in the hope that we'll be taken seriously and put at the top table isn't going to work. We have to be tough and stand up to them.'[32]

As Powell himself said, this was a British perspective, and European division over Iraq actually created an opportunity for Russia, France and Germany to find common ground on a major foreign policy issue. For relations between Moscow, Washington and London, however it was a different matter. The decision to go to war without a UN resolution, against Russia's wishes and to Russia's financial detriment, may well have persuaded Putin that talk of a new world of cooperation was just that. Even if this was not the fracture that Powell and Manning see, there is a persuasive case that if Iraq was not the end of Russia's desire to work with the West, it contributed to it. It may even have led Putin to fear that one day his administration might be the target of another US-led attempt at regime change in another country.

Fiona Hill was national intelligence officer for Russia and Eurasia at the US National Intelligence Council from 2006 to 2009, under presidents George W. Bush and Barack Obama, and later, during President Donald Trump's first term, Senior Director for European and Russian Affairs at the National Security Council. In her 2015 book with Clifford Gaddy, *Mr. Putin: Operative in the Kremlin*, she and Gaddy wrote that the Kremlin knew that Saddam Hussein did not have weapons of mass destruction. They recounted a conversation between Alexander Manzhosin, a Putin aide, and a visiting delegation from the Brookings

Institution, a Washington think-tank. Manzhosin asked the visiting Americans, 'Do you not see he is bluffing? Our intelligence professionals know this. Don't yours?'[33]

When Hill joined the National Security Council three years later, it was, as she put it in a 2024 interview, 'in the aftermath of what I think is actually the most important event, which is the US decision to invade Iraq, because that really shifts thinking in Russia and many other places in that world about what the United States is up to'. Just as Powell put 'the fracture' then, Hill argued that Iraq, 'for Putin, it makes him start to think the US is a menace. So, when you start to think about everything else, it's really fed through a filter for Putin and Russia by Iraq. So everything is seen through that kind of dark, darkened lens.'

Seen from the Kremlin, the US-led invasion of Iraq was not about Saddam Hussein's weapons of mass destruction. It could not have been. He did not have any. The US must surely have known that. The non-existent weapons were therefore being used as a pretext for the true aim of the invasion: regime change. In Putin's eyes, Washington had become a threat seen through a darkened lens. Nor was there even complete unity between London and Washington, the two Western powers firmly committed to the war. Robertson also saw the attitudes of two of the American architects of the war in Iraq – the vice president, Dick Cheney, and the defense secretary, Donald Rumsfeld – as being a factor in the way relations broke down:

The American defense secretary and the American vice president really were not comfortable about getting closer to Russia. And that was one factor. The other factor is that I think that Putin was beginning to sort of increasingly look for the admiration and the respect that he thought the Soviet Union got, you know, with a very thin skin, and he had a very thin skin and was getting, you know, sort of insulted by the sort of dismissive attitude to Russia, that the administration at that time displayed.[34]

Russia's concerns over US-led military action against Iraq pre-dated the 2003 invasion. In December 1998, the Russian ambassadors to Washington and London had been withdrawn in protest against airstrikes carried out following Iraq's lack of compliance with UN resolutions and lack of cooperation with weapons inspectors.[35] As with Kosovo the following year, Moscow felt that, now weak, its views were being ignored. The scale and nature of the 2003 invasion seemed to Russia – as Primakov made clear the following year – to be just the latest and largest part of an attempt to 'supplant the UN-based world order'.

The launch of the NRC – a response to the question of European security after the Cold War, but also to the attacks of 9/11 – preceded the Iraq War. It is harder to imagine Putin's outlook on future cooperation with the West being quite so positive after the start of the Iraq War. This was perhaps the period – from September 2001 to March 2003 – when Russia's relations with the West were at their most cordial and constructive at any time since Washington, Moscow and London formed an alliance to fight Nazi Germany during the Second World War. Even then, the three allies were united by a common enemy. Their deep, bitter ideological divisions remained, as the coming of the Cold War would show. Ideological divisions – and the suspicions and mistrusts they bred – still lingered in this post-Cold War period. Rice herself hinted at that when she wrote, in early 2000, 'That we do not know how to think about what follows the U.S.–Soviet confrontation is clear from the continued references to the "post-Cold War period" '.[36] The elites on both sides of the relationship had acquired all their experience in the Cold War. It was the way that they understood the world. It was often said during this period that the world had changed. Not all attitudes had. For cold warriors on both sides, it must have been tempting to think that the Cold War was over, but the rivalry was not forgotten. Some wished to confine that rivalry to the past, with the conflict itself. Others saw themselves either as victors, now able to ignore their former foes and their interests, or as defeated, and compelled to reverse and avenge the defeat.

For some in the older generation of cold warriors, there was yet another view of the opportunities and risks of the decade after the confrontation ended. William Perry served as US defense secretary from 1994 to 1997, during the Clinton administration. In 1997, he gave a speech in Germany, commemorating the Marshall Plan, under which the US gave former wartime friends and foes financial assistance to build their economies after the Second World War. Perry himself had been in the US army in Asia during the conflict. 'Everyone who saw the devastation at first hand,' he said, 'was moved by the human suffering in ways that affected the rest of their lives.'[37] He expanded on his theme in May the same year, in another speech, to the United States Airforce Academy. Here, he emphasised the importance of rebuilding security in Europe after the Cold War, arguing, 'We should never believe that a failure of the experiment in democracy now underway in Russia would affect *only Russians*' (emphasis in original). Noting that the end of the Second World War had led to a divided Europe, he concluded, 'This time we must not fail.'[38]

Perry repeated his point during a 1998 discussion at Stanford, his alma mater, with George Shultz, who had been US secretary of state under President Ronald Reagan in the 1980s, and who was also a Second World War veteran. The moderator, reflecting on the chaotic decade Russia had experienced, put it to the two retired statesmen that 'the mess the Russians are in is a mess of their own making, isn't it?' Perry answered by talking of the massive reparations that were forced on Germany after the First World War, and arguing, 'If the Weimar Republic had been sustained, we could have avoided World War II. That's the analogy I would draw with present-day Russia.' Shultz responded that 'we've coddled the Russians. We've been too ready to excuse the negative aspects of what's taking place over there.' He concluded by warning that the US was 'creating a bailout mentality'.[39]

The US and its allies never seriously considered a modern 'Marshall Plan' for the former USSR, although there were elements of a late-twentieth-century equivalent in the programmes to educate a population brought up under Marxism-Leninism about the workings of business and democracy. It is a matter for speculation whether even greater financial aid might have prevented renewed confrontation. Certainly, poverty at home and perceived humiliation abroad seem to have had such damaging effects that, by the end of the Yeltsin era, many Russians had ceased to see the US and its allies as their friends or trusted partners.

Whenever the fracture came, however, there is no doubt that the NATO summit in Rome in 2002 suggested that another path – one which did not lead to the fracture – was possible. Putin did not disagree when one of the leaders offered the view that 'Ukraine is an independent sovereign state and it will choose its own path to peace and security'.[40] He hardly could. They were his words. Nothing then was inevitable.

With more than twenty years' hindsight, it is tempting to wonder whether Putin, nursing then the same deep resentment that burned inside the Soviet officers who had been sent home from Germany, was just waiting for his moment, believing one day it must come. It may also be that he was sincere then in his desire for cooperation with NATO, only to feel the following year – when the US invaded a Russian ally, Iraq, giving reasons they knew to be untrue – that Washington had deceived and ignored Russia once more.

The manner of Putin's coming to power was one of the most significant events in Russia during this period: not the election of a new president so much as the way that it happened. The electorate was presented with a favoured candidate and duly elected him. The vote itself may have been a fair reflection of the Russian electorate's choice, but the ground had been well prepared so that the political elite – Yeltsin outgoing, Putin incoming – knew exactly what the choice would be. As with every Russian presidential election since, nothing was really left to chance. There was no real choice. Because of the relief that accompanied the end of the Cold War, and the perception that Boris Yeltsin's Russia was no longer a threat as the USSR had been, there may have been a tendency to see Yeltsin's time in power as a better time – but the trend of elections in which there was no choice (in Russian, as numerous joke-tellers have subsequently observed, the word for 'election' and 'choice' is the same) began here.

While what came afterwards was not inevitable, nor was it as different as some might believe. For two important elements of the Putin era actually began under Yeltsin: managed elections, and war as a means of shoring up political power. Wherever one sees the blame for the apartment bombings of 1999, one of the consequences was to allow Putin the opportunity to build a political image that would ensure he secured the presidency. Another was the murder in London, years later, of a former Russian secret policeman – an incident that showed that Russian political violence could also reach the West.

4

Control

As Putin's first term as president continued, Russia changed dramatically once again. The sense of looming collapse, with flashes of feverish excitement and fear, that had characterised the late Soviet period was gone. The lawlessness and chaos of the first post-communist decade had not disappeared, but it had been elevated from the streets to the higher structures of political intrigue – where it affected the daily lives of ordinary citizens much less than in the wilder years of the 1990s. Putin remained popular and would face no serious challenger when he stood for re-election in 2004. Yet if Russia's relations with Washington and its ally, the UK, had been put under pressure by the so-called 'war on terror', Putin's opposition to the war in Iraq had not eased the deadly challenges that the wars in Chechnya continued to raise.

In the autumn of 2002, a night at a Moscow theatre turned to terror. On the evening of Wednesday 23 October, a group of heavily armed Chechens broke into the auditorium of the Dubrovka Theatre in Moscow, where the second act of the musical *Nord-Ost* – 'a wartime tale of love between a dashing Soviet pilot and the beautiful daughter of an Arctic fleet commander'[1] – had just got underway. The gang of some forty attackers, led by the Chechen rebel commander Movsar Barayev, prevented the audience from leaving. They told their captives that they would not be harmed if the Russian government stopped the war in Chechnya – clearly a request to which the authorities would not accede. More than 900 people were held hostage for more than 48 hours. Some of the hostages – including children and pregnant women – were allowed to leave as the siege went on. Others were shot in cold blood. On Saturday morning, 26 October, Russian special forces stormed the building, killing the militants and freeing most of the hostages. Not all of the hostages, though – some 130 were killed, the majority as the siege ended.[2] In order to weaken their enemy before the assault, the security forces had pumped gas into the theatre, through the air conditioning system, to render them unconscious. Many of the hostages, already weakened by an ordeal lasting more than forty-eight hours, were affected, too – and some of them died. While the authorities hailed the saving of more than 700 lives as a huge success, the secrecy that surrounded the rescue operation also demonstrated a cruel callousness. Medical staff tending to the hostages who had been affected by the gas were not informed what chemical compound had been used – severely limiting their ability to treat their patients.

In addition to the terrible loss of life, the incident illustrated three important points about the way that Russia was changing in Putin's first term: firstly, the man who had come to power thanks to his tough line against Chechnya was reminded that the war was not over; secondly, the authorities felt in no way accountable to those citizens they were supposed to protect (even though they did protect the majority of them on this occasion, they also bore some responsibility for the high number of deaths); thirdly, the nascent security state's ability to keep people safe was compromised by weaknesses in its system: a report from the *Sunday Times* correspondent Mark Franchetti quoted a Chechen commander as saying that the reason the gang had been able to reach their target was 'simple: money'.[3] Russia was a country where corruption was so widespread that practically anything – including the access needed to commit a murderous attack on a soft civilian target – could be bought if the right amount was paid to the right person.

Still Putin remained popular. However, as Russia entered another election cycle in the autumn of 2003, as in 2000, once again very little was left to chance. The make-up of the Duma that resulted from parliamentary elections on 7 December 2003 meant that even less would be left to chance thereafter. United Russia, a party that had technically existed since 2001, now truly came to the fore in its new role as a movement that really had no purpose other than to support Putin. He himself was not a member. His separation from the party meant he could remain a certain distance from any scandals that might be exposed within its ranks. The fact that United Russia supported Putin did not mean that Putin supported United Russia, unless it suited him to do so on any particular occasion. The 2003 Duma election significantly strengthened United Russia's ability to back the leader who was their sole raison d'être.

Having won a total of 221 seats in the December vote – the largest single bloc in the 450-seat parliament – by early 2004, their number had swelled to 310, a consequence of previously 'independent' deputies deciding to join them.[4] As a result, United Russia had a supermajority of more than two-thirds of deputies: enough votes in the Duma to pass legislation that would change the constitution. As support for Putin surged, tactical mistakes by parties still seeking to take Russia towards a more Western-style version of liberal capitalist democracy led them to commit a strategic error. With the threshold to gain seats in the Duma from the party lists set at 5 per cent, Yabloko, under the leadership of Grigory Yavlinsky, and SPS (Union of Right Forces – SPS being the first letters of these words in Russian) could not agree on a common programme. In consequence, they ended up with four and three seats respectively, the total of seven far lower than they would have had had they combined the 8.27 per cent of the vote they achieved between them.[5] This poor showing seemed to surprise even Putin himself, who called Yavlinsky on election night to congratulate him on his party having entered the new Duma.[6]

Putin himself suffered no such partial success. The electoral system was now timed to allow the Duma elections late in the preceding year to act as a kind of test run for the presidential vote the following spring. In the presidential election on 14 March 2004, Putin won comfortably in the first round, meaning there was no need for a second round of voting. On a turnout of 64 per cent, Putin won 71 per cent of the vote.[7]

Putin's popularity combined political skill and good fortune – and both he and those who advised him knew how to make the most of the good fortune that came their way. To begin with, he was not Yeltsin. It was impossible to imagine Putin drunk in public, or perhaps at all. In a society in which public drunkenness was a major problem, and alcohol consumption had soared following the end of restrictions Gorbachev had placed on vodka sales in the early *perestroika* period, Putin was sober. Most Russian men were not. In 2003, the year before Putin won his second term, 'half of all deaths in working-age men, in a typical Russian city' were 'attributed to hazardous drinking'.[8] It was a major factor in Russia's depressingly low male life expectancy: just fifty-nine in the years 2000–5.[9] Many voters must have seen the president as an island of sobriety in a sea of drunken despair. The economy was improving. Growth would have been expected from the depths of the debt default in 1998, but it continued and strengthened, averaging 6.7 per cent in the period from 1998 to 2006.[10] As the devaluation of the rouble that followed the default helped domestic manufacturing, to this was added 'an upturn in oil prices in 1999 and 2000'.[11] As with his tough words on Chechnya when he first emerged from relative obscurity as a possible successor to Yeltsin, Putin understood what voters wanted. His KGB background might have been a disadvantage in a society that had just endured more than seven decades of a police state of varying degrees of severity. In fact, it enabled Putin to portray himself as a guardian of order: something that had been lacking in the chaos of the previous decade. Here again, Putin combined an understanding of populist desire with an instinct for self-preservation. Even before he was re-elected in the spring of 2004, he had started to crack down on the perceived excesses of that minority who had not become poorer since the collapse of communism. They had instead become richer to a breathtaking extent.

Boris Berezovsky was one of them. He had gone into effective exile in the UK. Mikhail Khodorkovsky was in a league of his own. By 2003, after a career that had started during the years when small-scale capitalism was permitted to exist alongside communism and thrived as capitalism rapidly replaced moribund Soviet socialism, he was said to be Russia's richest man, worth a reported $15 billion.[12] His business activities had varied from selling computers, through banking, to oil. Thanks to the latter, he was now chief executive of the oil group, Yukos. Such wealth, acquired as it was in the chaos of the 1990s, would never endear its possessor to the wider Russian public, beset as they were with falling living standards and even life expectancy. Yet even if it could not deliver popularity, such wealth could deliver political influence, especially at a time when Russian democracy was still struggling to grow from the feeble roots it had been able to put down. Khodorkovsky was keen to support this. One way he did so was by donating money to liberal political parties, including Yabloko, with the aim of building what he hoped would be a Russia different from what had gone before and what he saw then, in the early Putin era.

For what he saw then – based presumably in part, at least, on his own experience of trying to build up his businesses – was corruption. From Chechen gangs paying their way past checkpoints, to errant motorists seeking to bribe their way past over-officious traffic police, most things in Russia in the 1990s could be bought. Transparency International's Corruption Perception Index for 2003 scored Russia at 2.7 out of 10, where a score of 10 suggested a 'clean' system. Russia came in joint 86th place out of 133 countries in that year's survey.[13] In February 2003, during a televised meeting in the Kremlin where Putin was hosting business leaders, Khodorkovsky alleged corruption among officials in a state oil company. The public nature of the charge, in the presence of Putin and in front of a television audience, probably sealed his fate. On 25 October that year, while his private plane was refuelling at Novosibirsk airport in Siberia, he was arrested by FSB agents who came aboard the aircraft.[14] He was taken into custody and charged with fraud and tax evasion. His arrest came just weeks before the 2003 Duma elections, and just a day after the Moscow offices of Yabloko had been raided by prosecutors from the Russian state's Agency for Strategic Communications. The account of that raid, which appeared in the *Financial Times* the following morning, was probably being printed as Khodorkovsky was being arrested. As the newspaper reported, the raid was carried out 'ostensibly as part of the growing investigation into the oil group Yukos'.[15] In an editorial three days later, the *Financial Times* reported Putin's insistence that Khodorkovsky's arrest 'did not signal any general assault on the oligarchs or privatisation'. The editorial welcomed this on the grounds that 'revisiting the 1990s would undermine the stability that Mr Putin has worked hard to create'.[16] The *Financial Times* is cited here because its opinion mattered as Putin's Russia took shape. As will be discussed later in this chapter, improving the country's international image became a priority for the Kremlin – principally in order to encourage foreign investors that they were putting their funds into a business environment that they could trust. A Western media adviser, working with Putin's communication team, once told me that the news organisations in which the Kremlin was keenest to get good coverage were the *Financial Times* and *Wall Street Journal*. They were seen as most influential with prospective investors. Khodorkovsky's arrest did not set off too many alarm bells, or, if it did, the rewards of doing business in Russia seem generally to have been judged to outweigh any perceived risk. World Bank data for 2003 give foreign direct investment in Russia as $7.93 billion. In 2004, it was $15.4 billion. By 2008, that had risen to $74.78 billion.[17]

When his trial concluded in May 2005, Khodorkovsky was found guilty and sentenced to nine years in a prison camp.[18] He and his fellow defendant, Platon Lebedev, were also ordered to pay $613 million in taxes and fines. It destroyed the finances of the business, the assets of which were sold off, with the largest production facility, Yuganskneftegaz, being bought by the state-controlled oil company Rosneft.[19] Khodorkovsky, who had always denied charges his supporters dismissed as politically motivated, was eventually released in 2013. He went first to Switzerland, before settling in London, where he remained an implacable critic of Vladimir Putin and his leadership of Russia, especially after the escalation of the war in Ukraine in February 2022. For all his skill at understanding the new, capitalist Russia, for seeing opportunity therein and making a fortune on the basis of his insight, Khodorkovsky had failed to judge correctly the situation in which he found himself in 2003, three years into the Putin presidency. He overestimated his own strength in new times. In consequence, he lost his liberty for a decade, much of his wealth and what political influence he had. While his arrest did cause rapid and dramatic falls on Russian financial markets, subsequent foreign investment figures showed that it was not enough to scare away those who wished to continue to speculate in what the liberal newspaper *Nezavisimaya Gazeta* ('The Independent Newspaper') called at the time 'capitalism with Stalin's face'.[20]

As the Duma election results of a few weeks later – and Putin's comfortable re-election as president the following spring – showed, the arrest of Khodorkovsky led neither to a surge of support for those parties he had funded, nor to any kind of protest against Putin. Rather, many Russians perhaps saw the jailing of one of Russia's new rich as a necessary corrective to the excesses and injustices of the way the wealth of the USSR had been shared in the 1990s. International investors were more focused on profits than prison sentences. Khodorkovsky had challenged Putin. Putin accepted the challenge. Putin won.

His power safely consolidated, and growing, Putin decided it was not the only battle he wished to fight. Russia's transition period from communism to capitalism had been one of extreme financial hardship for millions of those who lived through it. It had been a tough business environment, though some had thrived: some of them spectacularly so. For journalism, and the media in general, it had been a time of opportunity and liberty without precedent in Russian history. For television and popular entertainment, that meant everything from the import of programmes that would never have been permitted in Soviet times to hard-hitting discussions of issues facing a society in crisis. In the 1990s, the Mexican telenovela *The Rich Also Cry*, a series that followed the travails of Mariana, an orphan, making her way in the world, was a particular favourite. Satire flourished. There was even a Russian version of what was known in Britain as *Spitting Image*, where latex puppets of politicians and other prominent people mocked the real-life personalities on which they were based, often mercilessly.

For journalism, this was a special time. It was hardly the first time in Russian history that there was so much to write about. It was, however, the first time in Russian history that it was possible to write about it so freely. It had started in the *perestroika* era under Mikhail Gorbachev. His reform programme needed *glasnost* – usually translated as openness, the word comes from the same root as the Russian word for 'voice', so it includes the idea of voicing a fact or an opinion – to support it, not least against conservative, anti-reform elements in the Communist Party which he himself led. His solution was to allow the news media unprecedented liberty, thus getting the problems of the late Soviet system into the open. The approach had the additional benefit of gaining the support of the news media, who themselves became supporters of reform for the new opportunities the new times afforded. It was not all straightforward. During the coup by Communist hardliners in August 1991, the main Soviet TV channel had fallen back on the kind of arid news control they knew. A presenter read out the statement about the formation of a 'State Committee for an Emergency Situation' that was taking over from the supposedly unwell Gorbachev. The channel had also broadcast a recording of the Tchaikovsky ballet *Swan Lake* instead of news or discussion when a seminal moment in Russian history was unfolding on the streets of Moscow. Crucially – perhaps because times had already changed too much, or because, as with their reluctance to use violence to crush their peaceful opposition, they simply lacked the courage to take the action that a successful coup d'état required – they did not shut down all media or make any concerted effort to restrict the work of Russian or international journalists.

The post-Soviet era in Russia had begun with a genuine commitment to press freedom that came from the very top of the political elite. It is important to emphasise the reasons that this started. As Ivan Zassoursky has pointed out, 'A freed up (but still controlled) press was in essence the only reliable ally Gorbachev possessed in his struggle with conservative forces in the party apparatus'.[21] So this press freedom was still controlled, in the sense that it had been granted by a Marxist-Leninist government and could therefore be taken away again – but freedom it was, nevertheless. The importance of this freedom is difficult to exaggerate. In a country where the political systems of tsars and communist commissars alike had historically placed strict controls on freedom of expression, Russians had come to look to their writers – including writers who were journalists – for guidance in understanding the social and political issues of the day. The Russian media academic Elena Vartanova has argued of Russia in the nineteenth century, 'The Russian vision of literature presupposed a much broader social and cultural role for it than in other countries, thus often merging it with journalistic activity'.[22] In the late twentieth century, under Gorbachev, journalists also began to address the murderous episodes that had taken place earlier in the Soviet period, including the mass killings of the Stalin era, with the weekly *Ogonyok* (meaning 'little flame' in Russian) leading the way in shedding light for a readership who had been kept in the dark for decades, save for what family stories they dared whisper around the kitchen table. *Argumenty i Fakty* ('Arguments and Facts') similarly addressed pressing social issues, provoking such interest among readers that queues would form in anticipation of the arrival of new issues at newsstands. In 1990, *Argumenty i Fakty* was entered into the *Guinness Book of Records* for its print run of 33.5 million, the highest in the world.[23]

It was not all rosy. Just as the business climate of the 1990s involved contract killings, there were murders of journalists, too. One of the most shocking was that of Dmitry Kholodov, a twenty-seven-year-old reporter for the *Moskovsky Komsomolets* newspaper. In the 1990s, *MK*, as it was often known, served up a mixture of scandal, crime and dogged and dangerous investigations. Kholodov had been working on stories of corruption in the military. A source had told him to go to collect a briefcase from a luggage locker at the Kazan station in Moscow. When he opened it, it exploded. He was killed. At Kholodov's funeral, his editor, Pavel Gusev, said, 'We will avenge but we will not blow up and kill, we will write the truth about the cynics and scoundrels which exist in our state.'[24] That is what Russian journalists did in the early post-Soviet years, with remarkable success, and, as in the case of Kholodov, at great risk.

While investigative journalism often carries risk, reporting on armed conflict almost always does, and Russian journalists showed great courage here, too. Journalists and camera operators from NTV, set up by the media tycoon Vladimir Gusinsky as part of his Media Most holding company, excelled in their coverage of the first Chechen war, access to which was later described by Franchetti, the *Sunday Times* correspondent at the Nord-Ost theatre siege, as a 'free for all'.[25] The only limit then placed on journalists' access in that conflict was their sense of personal safety. 'NTV presented all points of view and let the audience decide what to think', concluded a study by Russian academics published in 1995.[26] It did not go down well with the authorities, a fact reflected in the much stricter controls on the media during the second war, from the autumn of 1999 onwards.[27] By that time, NTV had run into deeper trouble with the Kremlin, particularly over a television discussion programme that sought to establish the truth about the 1999 apartment bombings. It included an examination of inconsistencies in the official account of what had happened – this at a time when the Putin government, under the Yeltsin presidency, was trying to make the case to go to war in Chechnya. The following year, Gusinsky was arrested on what *The Economist* termed at the time 'a spurious-sounding allegation of fraud'.[28] Gusinsky ended up living abroad, periodically pursued by international arrest warrants from the authorities in Moscow in the early years after his exile.

Putin's Russia was taking shape. Freedoms in business and in self-expression were being curbed, especially where those freedoms were seen to threaten the interests of the Russian state as the political elite around Putin defined those interests. That is not to say that the restrictions so far were universal. It was more subtle than that. As the so-called oligarchs had learnt, there were new, unwritten, rules to the game. These definitely included keeping out of politics. Journalists – especially older ones who had worked in the Soviet era before *glasnost* – were able to fall back on experiences of times when they exercised self-censorship in the interests of self-preservation, at least in editorial terms. Businesspeople had no such template. All forms of capitalism had been technically illegal for more than seven decades. This was a time when the state sought to exercise more control over commerce – directly and indirectly. Here, growing corruption among state organs also played its part. Business owners, from the smallest market stall or corner kiosk to the largest conglomerate, came to dread a visit or phone call from the tax inspector or fire safety inspector, knowing that a thinly disguised threat of prosecution would likely follow. To avoid prosecution, the business owner would be expected to pay a bribe.

In terms of freedom of expression, there was a new trend alongside the experience of NTV, which, after Gusinsky's departure from Russia, ended up as part of the media arm of the Russian energy giant, Gazprom. For control of the message at home was not considered enough. Looking at the growing international influence of news channels such as CNN and BBC World News, and no doubt having noted the launch of an English-language version of the Qatari-owned Al-Jazeera network, Russia decided in 2005 to launch its own. Russia Today, as it was originally called (it later changed its name to the simple 'RT') claimed to acquaint 'international audiences with a Russian viewpoint on major global events'.[29] It was part of a drive by the Russian authorities to counter what they saw as negative international – particularly Western

– coverage of the country. In this respect, they had a point – at least to the extent that the images of empty shelves, and other signs of economic and social collapse, from the late Soviet period seemed to have left such an indelible mark in the West that they were still thought to be current more than a decade later, at least as far as anecdotal evidence goes. Preparing to leave London for a posting to Moscow in the spring of 2006, concerned neighbours asked me if I would be able to find in Russia sufficient food for my infant daughter. Still, RT had an inauspicious start, struggling to find audiences or influence. It did, though, benefit from support from the source that it mattered: the Kremlin itself. The station's founding editor-in-chief, Margarita Simonyan, was a twenty-five-year-old reporter for Russian state television. To the Kremlin's own efforts to influence international public opinion they added hired international expertise. Early in 2006, with Russia preparing to host the G8 summit of leading industrial nations the following summer, they signed a contract with Ketchum, a public relations company from the US, and GPlus, a Brussels-based public affairs company. With oil prices rising, the Kremlin had money to burnish its international image. Angus Roxburgh, who worked for GPlus on the Kremlin account, cited in his later memoir a US Department of Justice figure suggesting the Russians were paying Ketchum 'almost $1m a month'.[30]

There were aspects of life in Russia that Putin could not control. As he sought to consolidate state influence over business and the media, security continued to present deadly challenges. From Soviet times onwards, the first day of the school year, always 1 September, had been something of a celebration in Russia. Pupils would dress smartly, girls with ornate ribbons in their hair. Often accompanied by their parents, the children's walk to school for the first day of the new term would be a joyous procession. School Number 1, in the town of Beslan in North Ossetia, a region of the North Caucasus, at the southern edge of the Russian Federation, had typical plans that included a ceremony to mark the start of the school year. Beslan is only a little more than 50 kilometres from the Chechnya border, across Ingushetia, which borders both Chechnya and North Ossetia.

As the ceremony at School Number 1 ended, an armed gang of Chechen rebels burst into the school's courtyard, where the ceremony had been taking place, firing weapons as they went. They had soon captured around 1,000 hostages, pupils and parents alike. They forced them all into the school's sports hall. There were explosives hanging from the basketball hoops. As with the Dubrovka theatre siege, the attackers demanded an end to the war in Chechnya. For two days, they kept the hostages in the hall, tortured not only by fear but also by increasing thirst in the heat of the late summer. On the third day, two huge explosions rocked the sports hall. The security forces, who had been waiting to move against the hostage takers, went in. The majority of the hostages were freed. Some 330, including 186 children, were not. They were killed. From the moment that the siege ended with such high cost, families of the dead began asking whether more lives could have been saved. It seemed, though, that the authorities' priority had been to kill the attackers – only one of whom survived to stand trial – rather than free hostages.[31]

For Putin, Beslan was, like Dubrovka, not only a direct challenge to the Russian state's ability to keep its citizens safe. It was a direct challenge to him personally, in that his whole political career had been founded on his willingness to talk tough and to be tough on separatist and Islamist militancy in the North Caucasus – particularly when that was felt beyond the immediate area where the war was being fought. Putin made a surprise visit to Beslan early in the morning of 4 September. He visited the hospital where survivors of the siege, including children, were being treated. He did not go to the school itself.[32] Later on the same day, Putin addressed the nation, linking the tragedy of Beslan to the end of the USSR, 'the collapse of an enormous, great, state', as he termed it.[33] There was also a rare admission from the president who had made his political image on strength and decisiveness. 'We showed ourselves to be weak. And the weak get beaten.'[34] Putin also made reference to inadequate understanding of the 'complexity and danger of processes happening in our country, and in the world as a whole'.[35] The fact that the events in Beslan drew sympathy from across the world is attested to by the many telephone calls from world leaders that the Kremlin recorded as having been received while the siege went on. They included one from George W. Bush, late in the evening Moscow time on the day the attack started.[36]

Aside from the shocking loss of life at Beslan, the incident is important for what it also showed about Kremlin relations with business and the media. Anna Politkovskaya, the fearless and outspoken correspondent for *Novaya Gazeta*, which despite its relatively small circulation had become established as a reliable source of excellent journalism challenging and questioning official versions of events, believed that she had been poisoned en route to report on the siege. Having passed out on a plane to Rostov-on-Don, she regained consciousness in hospital. As she wrote later in the *Guardian*, 'The nurse tells me that when they brought me in I was "almost hopeless". Then she whispers: "My dear, they tried to poison you." All the tests taken at the airport have been destroyed – on orders "from on high", say the doctors.'[37]

Politkovskaya's article went on to identify another important consequence of Beslan, in terms of the Kremlin's attempts to control the so-called oligarchs and the media. After the newspaper *Izvestiya* led with the headline 'The Silence at the Top', its editor, Raf Shakirov, was sacked. Politkovskaya suggested that the newspaper's owner, wealthy businessman Vladimir Potanin, 'was afraid to share the fate of Mikhail Khodorkovsky'.[38] Putin may have confessed to a degree of weakness, but his security services showed themselves very willing to take very tough measures – and he had already done enough to Russia's highest-profile businessman to make others think twice about association with political controversy.

Later in 2004, Putin himself courted controversy in foreign affairs and suffered a setback that helped to inform future policy. In November, Ukraine held presidential elections. Ever since the end of the Soviet period, a significant section of the Russian political elite had found it difficult to accept that Ukraine was an independent, sovereign state. As Vladislav Zubok wrote of Gennady Burbulis, a close aide to Yeltsin, 'Burbulis recalled that, he and his colleagues were completely in favour of Ukrainian independence. "Yet it was inconceivable, for our brains, for our minds, that this would be an irrevocable fact".'[39] Yet fact it had become. Ukraine shared a border with Russia, but it was no longer run from Moscow. As noted in the previous chapter, Putin had publicly accepted, in very clear terms, Ukraine's sovereignty when he spoke at the 2002 news conference after the NRC in Rome.

The final two candidates for the Ukrainian presidency were Victor Yanukovych, a businessman from the east of the country, and Victor Yushchenko, an economist and sometime head of the national bank. Yanukovych was seen as much more likely to be friendly to Moscow. Putin had even publicly endorsed his candidacy. It was not a clean campaign. Media coverage was heavily skewed in Yanukovych's favour. On polling day, Yushchenko still bore the scars of what he said had been an attempt to poison him. Voting took place on Sunday 21 November. Contradicting the predictions of exit polls, the official results gave the presidency to Yanukovych by 49.5 per cent to 46.6.[40] Yushchenko's supporters were not impressed. Putin was. The following day, according to the Kremlin website, Putin phoned Yanukovych to congratulate him on a 'convincing victory' after 'a sharp, but open and honest, struggle'.[41] Many disagreed that it had been open and honest. As *The Economist* reported a few days later, 'The falsifications on November 21st were egregious. Russian observers were sanguine about the poll, but European and American monitors were outraged.'[42] So were Yushchenko's supporters. They took to the streets in bitterly cold winter weather to protest against the election that had been stolen from their candidate. It worked. Ukraine's supreme court ordered a second run-off on 26 December. Yushchenko won. He was sworn in as president the following month.

Yushchenko's securing the presidency brought to an end the Orange Revolution, as it came to be known after the colour that Yushchenko's supporters wore at rallies.[43] This was a setback for Putin, especially after his very public support for a candidate who had won by foul means that Putin had been happy to declare fair. Coming a little over twelve months after the 2003 Rose Revolution in Georgia – where a peaceful change of power had seen the removal of the former Soviet foreign minister, Eduard Shevardnadze, who was replaced by the younger, Western-facing Mikheil Saakashvili – it made the Kremlin very wary of the potential power of street politics.

There was little sign of unrest in Russia. Political protest, such as it was, was represented by the 'March of the Dissenters', who wanted a Russia without Putin. The former world chess champion, Garry Kasparov, was the most high profile of the leaders. Their rallies, at which a broad range of dissenting opinion from left, to liberal, to 'National Bolshevik' was represented, tended to attract perhaps only one or two thousand people. Sometimes there were as many police officers on duty as there were protesters. In a city the size of Moscow, where the population swelled as the economy stabilised and then continued to grow, the dissenters were significant mainly for their scarcity.

For despite the endurance in the West of images of shortages in the late Soviet period, food and consumer goods were no longer scarce – continuing trends that had begun in the 1990s. 'Private ownership of cars doubled, rising from 14 cars per 100 households in 1991 to 27 in 2000', according to figures from the state statistics service.[44] Car ownership was one of the most visible signs of post-communist prosperity, especially in the capital. In the autumn of 2000, transport officials in Moscow said that the number of cars on the city's streets had 'increased threefold' in the preceding decade to reach 2.5 million – with 180,000 cars on Moscow's roads at rush hour. The suggested solution was new roads to help the traffic keep moving.[45] Shopping and driving continued to grow in popularity. By 2006, the *International Herald Tribune* reported on plans for 'at least 17 new shopping centers' in Moscow and '11 large shopping malls with a total of two million square meters, or about 22 million square feet of new retail space' in Russia's other major cities.[46] Queues for basic foodstuffs, and years on a waiting list for a car or a washing machine, belonged to another time: not so long ago, but very different.

This was the Russia to which Putin proudly welcomed his fellow G8 leaders – the heads of state and/or government of the world's leading industrial nations – from 15–17 July 2006. Russia had been a member of the group since 1997. Putin chose to host the meeting in his hometown of Saint Petersburg. As often happens at major international summit meetings, the formal agenda is overshadowed by what is happening in the world at the time when leaders gather. In this case, it was Israel's invasion of Lebanon. In response to a cross-border attack by Hezbollah, Israel had launched a major military operation just days earlier. The G8 leaders issued a statement on the middle day of their meeting in which they said they were united in their 'determination to pursue efforts to restore peace'.[47] There were some lighter moments. Bush and Putin renewed their acquaintance with a joke for the press about the first cars they had had.[48] Putin later drove Bush in a golf cart from one area of the summit venue to another.[49]

The formal agenda of the summit was wide-ranging. Global energy security and the fight against infectious diseases were among the issues that the leaders discussed, and which featured in the official documents published at the summit.[50] So too did pledges on corruption and the protection of intellectual copyright. The leaders declared, 'Corruption by holders of public office can deter foreign investment, stifle economic growth and sustainable development, and undermine legal and judicial systems.'[51] Corruption plagues all political systems to a greater or lesser extent. Given that this was one of the matters discussed at the summit, it is interesting to note that problems for US investors with the Russian business environment and legal system had been highlighted in a diplomatic cable sent by William Burns, then US ambassador to Moscow, the previous month. The version available to researchers remains heavily redacted, with the names of individuals and companies removed. One, 'Claimant A', had had $940,000 awarded by a Russian court after a business venture had gone wrong. The judgement, however, had not been enforced to anything like the full extent. Bailiffs had only been able to impound property worth $15,000.[52] Similarly, the leaders noted 'the usefulness of international congresses and workshops devoted to effective protection and enforcement of intellectual property rights'.[53] Copyright theft was a particular problem in Russia, to the extent that counterfeit CDs and DVDs were not only easily available in the country itself but also seemed to have become an export business. As *Billboard* reported in 2003, 'Russian-originated pirate CDs have been found in 26 countries'.[54] The fate of a major cultural milestone in Russia months before the summit illustrated the problem in Russia itself. Boris Pasternak's novel *Doctor Zhivago* had been banned in the USSR, because of its portrayal of the revolution and its consequences for individuals. In his memoir, Kozyrev recalled the time when, as a junior Soviet diplomat at the UN, he bought a copy in Manhattan, before 'reading it until darkness fell' then leaving it on a bench in Central Park because he was afraid of taking it back to the Soviet mission where he was staying.[55] In 2006, Russian TV adapted it for the screen for the first time in Russia. Even before the first episodes aired (this was before streaming), pirated DVDs were on sale in kiosks across Moscow.

Incidents such as soured business relationships that ended in unsatisfactory court cases, and theft of intellectual property, could not inspire confidence among Western investors in Russia, yet the potential rewards of doing business there as the economy boomed were too great to ignore. As noted earlier in this chapter, foreign direct investment in Russia soared during this period. In 2006, the year of the G8 summit in Saint Petersburg, it was $37.59 billion.[56]

It was not just the year of the G8 summit. For 2006 was also the year of two high-profile murders – both of people who had been implacable Putin critics. In October 2006, Anna Politkovskaya was shot dead in the entrance to the Moscow apartment building where she lived. The following month, Alexander Litvinenko, the former FSB agent who had fled Russia after accusing the security services of being behind the apartment bombings in the autumn of 1999, was fatally poisoned in London.

Both were killed after having challenged elements of the key event in Putin's rise to power: the second Chechen war. For *Novaya Gazeta*, Politkovskaya produced some truly remarkable and original journalism. With a wide range of contacts and a courage and determination that took her where few other reporters went, she told stories others did not. She also offered opinions – based on the evidence she gathered – that the Kremlin did not want to hear. 'The only thing the methods of this war accomplish is to recruit new terrorists and resistance fighters, and to rouse hatred, calling for bloody revenge',[57] was the conclusion to one 2003 despatch from Chechnya. In another, typical of her ability to spot significant detail in order to illuminate a bigger picture, she chronicled the casual cruelty and folly of soldiers serving in the war. In this particular case, they had shot a cow belonging to an elderly villager for no reason other than that they could, blaming the fact that they had not had their pay. Their evenings were spent consuming vodka and hashish for which they had traded ammunition – ammunition likely to end up being fired back at them or their comrades. The realities of the 'counter-terrorist operation' were rather different from the Putin propaganda. Politkovskaya was killed for daring to point this out so effectively and persistently. In 2014, five men were sentenced to long prison sentences for Politkovskaya's murder.[58] The person or persons who ordered the killing have never been identified. Politkovskaya was murdered on 7 October. It was Vladimir Putin's birthday.

Litvinenko was killed the following month in London. He was poisoned with polonium-210, a radioactive substance. He was probably given it in tea. Two Russian citizens, Andrei Lugovoi and Dmitry Kovtun, both former KGB agents, were suspected. They had met Litvinenko in a sushi bar in London. Both denied any involvement in his poisoning. Both a British public enquiry and the European Court of Human Rights blamed Russia, the latter after a case brought by Litvinenko's widow, Marina.[59] In the immediate aftermath of the killing, British detectives travelled to Moscow to try to pursue their investigation but were not able to make significant progress. The Russian authorities refused to extradite the suspects, citing a clause in the Russian constitution that forbids the extradition of Russian citizens. Kovtun died in Moscow in 2022.

Giving his annual address to the Russian parliament in April 2005, Putin returned to the idea – expressed in the aftermath of Beslan – that the troubles facing Russia were a consequence of the collapse of the USSR. In his address, he declared the fall of the USSR to have been 'the greatest geopolitical catastrophe of the century'. This is the line that is most frequently remembered from that speech, yet there are other details that must be considered for a more nuanced view of how he saw the development of Russia some five years into his time as its leader. He referred to the time after the collapse of Soviet power when, he said, 'Oligarchic groups – possessing absolute control over information channels – served exclusively their own corporate interests'. It was a formal statement confirming policies that sought to extend Kremlin control over commerce and communication. However, Putin also spoke of the fact that Russia 'had been, is, and of course will be, a great European nation'. His country's history and identity as part of Europe, rather than as the possessor of some unique destiny granted by its geography, was key to Putin's understanding of his country. So, too, was this: his conviction that, 'for contemporary Russia, the values of democracy are no less important than the aspiration for economic success'.[60]

In this period, there were signs – greater control over business and the media; the dismay over aspects of western foreign policy, especially the US and UK over Iraq – of what was to come in later years. To say, though, that what came next was inevitable is to take too simplistic a view. What can be said is that Putin showed the characteristics he could come later to rely upon: an ability to learn from mistakes, and try again more successfully. His image, in his response to Beslan, of the weak being beaten, offers an insight into his view both of domestic politics, and international relations.

In the latter sphere, the key event of this period was the Iraq War. The way it was launched convinced the Russian leadership of three things that would come to influence policy approaches to the West. Firstly, that Russia was not so much of a 'great European nation' that its views over the wisdom or otherwise of the US-led invasion of Iraq could not be ignored. Secondly, and particularly in this case, there were divisions in Western policy that Russia could seek to exploit, as on this occasion finding common ground with the French and German governments. Putin personally also learnt from mistakes in international affairs. His open endorsement of Yanukovych in Ukraine in 2004 backfired, and would not be repeated. Thirdly, and related to the second point, the Russian political elite believed that the West's real motive in invading Iraq was regime change. If Britain and America would remove a leader in one part of the world, they might try to engineer a similar process in another – even including Russia.

This was a crucial period in Russia's post-Soviet history. The country's future course was not yet set. There were signs Russia could return to some form of autocracy, and reasons to believe that it would not. From one point of view, the moves against the oligarchs were a worrying development that threatened the rights of people to set up and build businesses, especially strategically important ones, whether in the energy sector or the media. On the other hand, the chaos of the 1990s, when even the law itself – a curious mixture of communist-era legislation, and new rules for a spectacularly unruly form of capitalism – was unclear, meant that there was every reason for the state to try to introduce some order. The more worrying element of that was the order that Putin was bringing in increasingly included a prohibition on political activity unless the would-be activist was on an unwritten, unpublished, Kremlin-approved list.

Khodorkovsky always denied the charges against him. He also understood the anger against him. 'We must accept that 90 percent of the population considers the results of privatization to be unjust, and its beneficiaries not to be legitimate owners,' he wrote the year after his arrest, in an article that admonished Russian liberals for their failures in the preceding decade.[61] Putin understood this too. He understood how to communicate to his constituency that he shared their views. He spoke to the people in a way that the liberal leaders of the 1990s had not. In the process, he steadily accumulated political capital as the oligarchs had once amassed financial capital. The starting point of Putin's political fortune, the second Chechen war, still cast a deadly shadow over his presidency. There was one notable success in that respect. Just days before the start of the G8 summit, Shamil Basayev was killed in Ingushetia. The insurgency continued, but at a low level. In 2009, Moscow declared the 'anti-terrorist operation' to be over. Other wars lay ahead.

5

Petroleum Power

The rivalry between Mikhail Gorbachev and Boris Yeltsin contributed to the chaos that accompanied the collapse of the USSR. Their views on the country's future began sharply to differ, especially after the failed coup of August 1991. On one matter, however, they were of the same opinion: Ukrainian independence was all but inconceivable. As the historian Serhii Plokhy has put it, 'Both believed that the second-largest Soviet republic could not be allowed to go its own way.'[1] Ukraine had gone its own way, though – or at least spent most of the 1990s trying to do so. Putin's blatant and unsuccessful attempt at election interference in the Ukrainian presidential election of 2004 showed, however, that the Russian political elite, whether under Gorbachev, Yeltsin or Putin, had never really accepted Ukraine's independence – whatever they might have said or been obliged to appear to agree with publicly. Condoleezza Rice's description of the Russian experience of Ukraine's independence helps to explain: 'It has been said that, for Russia, losing Ukraine was like the United States losing Texas or California. But that doesn't begin to capture it; it would be like losing the original thirteen colonies.'[2] In fact, once Ukraine began to seek to emulate Western democracies and also seek closer ties with the West, it became more like losing the original thirteen colonies to a former foe.

All the same, the major issues that had caused tension between Moscow and Kyiv in the aftermath of the end of Soviet power – principally the future of the Soviet navy's Black Sea Fleet and the status of Crimea – 'largely receded as issues'[3] in Putin's first term as president. These issues were not resolved. They were, though, mostly left undiscussed – although the return of Crimea to Russia was a subject that Russian nationalists were keen to raise whenever the opportunity came. The future of the Soviet navy's Black Sea Fleet, and how its ships and bases would be divided now that Russia and Ukraine were separate countries, was difficult – but not dangerous. Relations were generally cordial. The Ukrainian president, Leonid Kuchma, met Putin eighteen times between 2000 and 2002.[4]

That cordiality started to disappear after the Orange Revolution for two main reasons. Both contributed to tension between Russia and Ukraine and Russia and the West. The first was political. Putin's humiliation was not just a wound to his pride. Victory for Yushchenko, following the Rose Revolution in Georgia a year earlier, came to be seen as a strategic threat to the kind of Russia that Putin was trying to build. It is very possible Putin began to fear he too might one day be driven from power. The second factor was decisively in Putin's favour: the continuing rise in global energy prices. At home, this meant that Putin and his administration enjoyed the political benefits that came with presiding over better standards of living. Beyond Russia, this wealth could be transformed into political power. Ukraine may have been seeking a different political path than that offered by close ties with Putin's Russia. Soviet-era gas pipelines meant, however, that when it came to energy supplies, Ukraine's journey away from Moscow's orbit was much more complicated. The West was affected too. Much of the Russian gas consumed in the rest of Europe reached its destination by way of Ukraine. While Russo–Ukrainian relations were working well enough, the system as a whole functioned well enough, too. There was one other lingering legacy of the Soviet-era that did not sit well with new political realities: since the Soviet period, Ukraine had imported

Russian gas at subsidised rates. Payments were not always made on time, especially as the vicissitudes of the transition to the market economy affected the Ukrainian economy, and the government's coffers. That kind of laxity was not tolerated for long after the Orange Revolution.

Soon after Yushchenko's win in the re-run presidential election, Russia complained that Ukraine was not paying its bills, and further alleged that 'it was diverting gas from the pipelines supplying western Europe'.[5] At the time, Ukraine was paying $50 per 1,000 cubic metres of gas – far below the world price. This was a legacy of the times of the Soviet planned economy, but it was also an attempt by the new Russia to keep former Soviet satellites within what Moscow saw as its sphere of influence. The Orange Revolution suggested that had not worked. In late 2005, Russia demanded that Ukraine pay a new rate of $230 per 1,000 cubic metres. The Russian state energy company, Gazprom, said the increase was for economic reasons – although, at the time, Belarus, with its Kremlin-friendly government led by Aleksandr Lukashenko, was being charged only $46 per 1,000 cubic metres. Even Georgia, which had also dismayed the Kremlin with its own 'colour revolution' in 2003, was at the time paying only $110.[6] Ukraine rejected Gazprom's characterisation of the price hike as being for economic reasons and accused Russia of raising the rate for political reasons. Yushchenko accepted the principle of paying market rates but only after a transition period. With both money and political power in play, the negotiations deteriorated into an ill-tempered dispute. On 1 January 2006, Russia reduced the amount of gas it sent to Ukraine to the amount it was contracted to provide for onward transit to Western Europe. Deprived of domestic supply, Ukraine reduced the amount it was sending onwards. In consequence, some of Russia's customers further West did not receive all the gas they were due. As the coldest time of year in Europe approached, this naturally caused alarm. The EU's High Representative for Common Foreign and Security Policy, Javier Solana, urged the two sides to come to an agreement so that normal supplies could resume.[7] They did so, on 4 January.

The consequences for energy supplies were relatively small, because the dispute was resolved relatively quickly. The political consequences were more serious. Russia's gas customers in the EU worried that they were dealing with a partner on which they could no longer rely. Gazprom and the Russian government naturally argued that any interruption in supply was the fault of Ukraine. Russia could not – this argument held – be blamed for Ukraine's breach of contractual obligations and refusal to send on supplies destined for the EU. Other assessments held that Russia was so keen to punish Ukraine for being insolent enough to seek closer ties with Western Europe that it did not care whether others were affected, too. Russia had shown that its energy resources were a source of diplomatic as well as economic strength, and Western powers had no obvious answer. As Condoleezza Rice later concluded in her memoir, 'The Kremlin had fired a warning shot that the colour revolutions were vulnerable to pressure by playing the "energy card". And we didn't really have a good response.' Rice also regretted the fact that, despite the crisis, 'there were simply too many conflicting interests' for European nations 'to develop a common energy policy to lessen their dependence on Moscow'.[8] Perhaps the starkest example of those interests was Germany's increasing reliance on Russian gas supplies. Rice admitted later, 'we were stunned', when shortly after leaving office, the German chancellor Gerhard Schröder became chairman of Nord Stream, the gas pipeline crossing the Baltic Sea from Russia to Germany.

As prices continued to rise during the first decade of the new century, the Kremlin's power grew with them. With negotiations taking place towards the end of each year, and the commercial nature of those negotiations increasingly taking on an additional political character, the question of who would blink first came to be posed annually as the New Year holiday drew near. In early 2009, Gazprom turned off supplies to Europe through Ukraine. Gazprom and the Ukrainian national gas company, Naftogaz, blamed each other – though in the short term, at least, European consumers were less interested in who was at fault and more concerned about when the gas would flow normally again. The supplies were cut for thirteen days, including to countries in south-eastern Europe that relied entirely on Russia for gas.[9] Gazprom, and by extension Russia, had decided that letting customers in the EU down was worth it to make the desired commercial and political point to Ukraine. As John Lough (the NATO official of the 1990s worked for energy companies later in his career) has noted, 'Gazprom had enjoyed an unblemished reputation with its European (primarily German) customers for reliability of supply'. It no longer did. That did not mean seeking alternative supplies, but seeking alternative means of delivery. The incident 'reinforced the case in Germany for building the new Baltic gas pipeline to deliver gas directly to Germany'.[10] At this stage in Russia's post-Soviet relations with the West, the idea that it might one day be politically unacceptable (and, to an extent, environmentally questionable) in the West to take as much fossil fuel supply as possible from Russia was unthinkable.

Eagerness on the part of Germany and other Western European countries to take Russian energy to fuel their economies helped to bring Europe, East and West, together in what seemed to be a mutually beneficial commercial arrangement. For Putin, closer commercial ties with Germany were an opportunity for a different kind of relationship with the country where he had been stationed as a KGB operative, and whence he had returned to his native city after the fall of the Berlin Wall. In *First Person*, Putin described the German Democratic Republic (GDR) as 'harshly totalitarian'.[11] All the same, for Putin, the end of communism in Germany had involved the traumatic experience of angry crowds gathering outside the building where he worked in Dresden. When Putin sought assistance from Russian forces based nearby, he 'was told: "We cannot do anything without orders from Moscow. And Moscow is silent."' This gave him, he said later, the feeling that 'the country no longer existed'.[12] The wealth and consequent power that flowed east to Moscow as the oil and gas flowed west helped to change that. Nor did Putin forget where he came from as his political fortunes changed along with the fortune of the country as a whole. In research published in 2003, based on their study of the backgrounds of the political elite forming around Putin, the scholars Olga Kryshtanovskaya and Stephen White concluded that 'every fourth member of the Russian elite has a military or security background, and their numbers are continuing to grow'.[13] Igor Sechin, who in 2024 was the chief executive of the Russian oil company Rosneft, is likely to be among a number of that group who has influence in both energy and security circles. Like Putin, Sechin came from a working-class background in Leningrad. The two men worked closely together for decades. Sechin has never publicly admitted, or denied, that he served in the Soviet intelligence services. He did reportedly work as a military translator for Soviet forces in Angola and Mozambique – a role in which, according to diplomats quoted by the *Financial Times* in 2018, 'he began working with the KGB'.[14] Sechin's official biography on the Rosneft website includes no details of his life from his birth in 1960 to his appointment to the executive office of the Russian president in 2000, save the fact that he was awarded his PhD in 1984.[15] It may be that Rosneft's communications team does not consider Sechin's life up until the age of forty relevant for his role at the company. It may also be – as with others who have served as intelligence officers – that his CV is not for publication.

Rising energy prices were not only a new source of strength in dealing with countries in 'the near abroad' (a term Russians sometimes use for former Soviet republics) and further afield. They were also an incentive for Russian business to flex its muscles at home. Whatever worries international investors may have had about doing business in the 1990s in a country where executives could end up face down in grubby snow if a deal went wrong, they largely evaporated in the face of a burning desire for profit. As capitalism spread where communism had once dominated, it brought with it new expertise, drive for profit, and, of course, cash. The incentive was there. In 1991, the year that the USSR collapsed, Russia held 6.52 per cent of the world's oil deposits, and just less than a third of its gas.[16] When, in 2003, the oil company BP put $8 billion into a deal with the Tyumen Oil Company (known as TNK from its initials in Russian), it was the largest-ever foreign investment in Russia.[17] The relationship that followed was a story of financial success and hair-raising risk. At one point, in 2008, Robert Dudley, chairman of TNK-BP (as the joint company was known) even fled Russia, after what he described as 'sustained harassment' from Russian shareholders.[18] In August 2011, 'black-clad special forces' raided BP's offices in Moscow, as Reuters reported at the time.[19] In 2013, BP left the joint venture – receiving $12 billion and a stake in the giant Russian oil company Rosneft, of which Igor Sechin was chairman.[20] John Lough, who began working at TNK-BP in 2003, remembered in a 2024 interview joining the company 'just at the time when oil prices were rising again, and the revenues were coursing into the Russian system'. He compared the effect to 'an adrenaline spurt'. In Lough's assessment, 'this sense of greater prosperity didn't create so much a sense of wellbeing' as much as 'it strengthened feelings of resentment, and a desire to settle scores'.[21] A similar conclusion might be drawn from the experience of Royal Dutch-Shell. In 2006, Shell agreed to hand over to Gazprom control of the huge, $20 billion, Sakhalin-2 oil and gas project.

Foreign investors and others doing business in Russia had concluded that continuing colossal profits merited continuing and even increasing their presence after the conviction of Khodorkovsky. Now, even as Russian companies, with the full support of the state, sought to renegotiate deals to their advantage, the potential revenues for foreign investors were still more than attractive. For this was an era in which Putin's devastating conclusion that the country no longer existed was beginning to be reversed. His former comrades in the security services – if former is the right word; a saying in Russian, using the word for an agent of the Cheka, a forerunner of the KGB, has it that 'there is no such thing as a former Chekist' – were increasingly powerful. They were influential in the top echelons not only of politics but also business, including in an energy industry that was taking on a strategic role in international relations, too. Some parts of the successor organisation of the intelligence services of the solidly atheist Soviet state were even moved to see divine intervention behind their good fortune. In a 2007 article that mentioned a recently restored church near the FSB's building in central Moscow, *The Economist* quoted a priest there as saying, 'Thank God there is the FSB. All power is from God and so is theirs.' The article continued, 'A former KGB general agrees: "They really believe that they were chosen and are guided by God and that even the high oil prices they have benefited from are God's will." '[22] The belief that God favoured the direction that Russia was taking was important. Of course, success in Russian business in the 1990s had involved a willingness to take risks. It had required the cultivation of political contacts and the careful calculation of how to use them. As the Putin presidency continued, that included an understanding of the influence of the Orthodox Church.

Officially suppressed during the Soviet period, with members of the clergy among those shot during the Stalinist purges of the 1930s, the Russian Orthodox Church's re-emergence into public prominence was an important part of Russia's new identity after the collapse of communism. There had been times – especially during the Second World War, when Stalin encouraged religious faith in the hope it would help to inspire resistance to the invader – when the state had tolerated the church more than at others. There were also persistent rumours that the KGB recruited some members of the clergy to inform on those who insisted on observing their faith despite the state's official atheism – and even that senior members of the church worked closely with the KGB. This went right to the top. In 2023, Swiss newspapers reported that Patriarch Kirill, head of the Russian Orthodox Church, had worked for Soviet intelligence in the 1970s, while living in Geneva as the church's representative.[23] The priest's praise for the FSB, cited above, suggests that these two important forces in Russian history were able to reach an accommodation on at least some occasions. In the 1990s, one priest,

Gleb Yakunin, took advantage of the short-lived opening of the KGB archives to investigate. He concluded that the Moscow Patriarchate was 'practically a subsidiary, a sister company of the KGB'.[24]

One consequence of Russia's opening up to the West after the fall of capitalism was the influx of Western people, money and ideas. That included missionaries spreading the word as interpreted by Western evangelical churches. This caused concern among the Russian church hierarchy. Church leaders were worried that just as the pressure of the Soviet state was being lifted, the moment of opportunity might be lost as incomers seized the chance to fill the spiritual void caused by more than seven decades of communism. In the 1990s, the head of the church, Patriarch Alexei II, wrote to Yeltsin to ask that he legislate to protect 'the individual from the destructive, pseudo-religious and pseudo-missionary activity that has brought obvious harm to the spiritual and physical health of people, to the national integrity of our people, and to stability and civic peace in Russia'.[25] This was a spiritual appeal which also encompassed a patriotic political meaning. Orthodoxy distinguished Russia from Western Christianity. That distinction, in the view of the church, should not be lost as the political distinction between East and West was supposedly dissolving with Russia's acceptance, or even cautious embrace, of democracy.

The church's quest for a post-Soviet role was not just a simple story of spiritual renewal. There was controversy, too. Like most institutions in early post-Soviet Russia, the church found itself short of money. One solution to this impecunity involved the church in an odd scheme that showed it was capable of dealing with the seedier side of Russia's nascent capitalism, even if it did so in the hope of supporting the country's renewed faith. In 1996, Irina Rykovtseva of the *Moscow News* reported that the church had been importing cigarettes and alcohol as humanitarian aid, under an agreement with a government agency. The cigarettes were sold to wholesalers and the profits returned to the church's department of external relations. The state was reckoned to have lost some $40 million in tax revenue.[26]

In the following decade, such scandals faded into the background. The church came to occupy an increasingly central role in Russian life. The Moscow skyline had already changed to reflect this renewed religious influence. The white walls and golden domes of the Cathedral of Christ the Saviour had occupied a prominent place on the bank of the Moskva River, close to the Kremlin, since 1997. This was a striking physical manifestation of Russia's spiritual turn away from the atheism of state socialism. Yet it was not only that. For the cathedral was in fact a reconstruction of one blown up by the Bolsheviks in 1931 as Stalin sought to sweep away the old religion in favour of the new one he and his followers were forging. Plans to replace the cathedral with a colossal 'Palace of the Soviets' were never realised (an open-air swimming pool was built on the site instead). In the 1990s, the cathedral was rebuilt. It had originally been conceived as a monument giving thanks to God for Russia's deliverance from Napoleon after the invasion of 1812. That such a monument was recreated and reopened a little over two years before the start of the Putin era is somehow apt. It could not have been known at the time that Russia's next president would make Orthodox Christianity, and memories of Russia's victories over invading armies, cornerstones of his political vision for Russia – but the cathedral's reconstruction presaged very well what was to come. It also witnessed events that showed that Putin's embrace of Orthodox ritual resonated with the people whose president he had become. During the first years of his presidency, and ever afterwards, Putin was regularly seen on television celebrating the holiest days in the church's calendar: Christmas, Easter and Epiphany – which in Russia involves plunging into cross-shaped holes cut into the thick ice that has formed at the very coldest time of the Russian winter. Even if social surveys suggested that church attendance did not actually rise during this period, the strength of Orthodox Christian identity definitely did. Between 1991 and 2008, the number of Russians identifying as Orthodox Christian rose from 31 per cent to 72 per cent, though actual observance was much less than that, with about 10 per cent of Russians saying they went to church at least once a month.[27] It was a contradiction commented upon by Patriarch Kirill, when he became head of the church in early 2009: 'Millions of people have been baptised, and consider themselves Orthodox Christian', he told the Russian newspaper *Trud* then. 'But the degree of their observance leaves much to be desired.'[28]

There were exceptional occasions beyond Christmas and Easter that did draw the crowds to church. In June 2006, thousands of people queued for hours to see the right hand of John the Baptist when it was displayed at Christ the Saviour. It was an astonishing turnout in the capital city of a country that had been officially atheist for decades – and where for periods the state had enforced that atheism with deadly violence and destruction of sacred sites – until just fifteen years earlier. That the relic proved such a popular draw suggests that Putin's increasing readiness to be seen in public observing religious holidays had a political as well as a spiritual significance.

In April the following year, crowds gathered once more outside Christ the Saviour – though they were not as great in number as those who had waited patiently to see the hand of John the Baptist. They had come not to marvel at a holy relic, but to mourn. Boris Yeltsin died of heart failure in Moscow on 23 April 2007. His funeral was held two days later, at Christ the Saviour – the cathedral rebuilt during his presidency. The two US presidents whose time in office had coincided with his – George H.W. Bush and Bill Clinton – both attended, as did many other international leaders. A photograph provided by the Russian presidential press service and printed the next day in the *New York Times* showed Bush and Clinton standing behind Putin.[29] Obituaries wrote of Yeltsin's mixed legacy: his leading role in ending communism in Russia, and the economic chaos and Chechen wars that shamed his presidency.

His era was already long over, though. Russia's relations with the West and with its neighbours were changing as the country's economy continued to improve, and the Kremlin's confidence both at home and abroad grew in consequence. Tensions grew not only with Ukraine over energy and political ideology, but also with other former Soviet states, sometimes called in Russia the 'near abroad'. The term may be geographically correct in the sense that the countries it describes border Russia. It is also politically loaded to some in those same countries for its suggestion that there are degrees of being 'abroad', and therefore, in the Kremlin's view, limits on sovereignty. If the Yeltsin era had been characterised by generally cordial relations with these neighbours and an acceptance – however reluctantly reached, especially in the case of Ukraine – that their independence was a reality, in a newly rich and assertive Russia, attitudes began to harden. There was one issue in particular where Russia was especially angered by any perceived insolence or disrespect from their former Soviet subjects: the Soviet role in the Second World War.

As would become increasingly apparent as the war in Ukraine escalated in February 2022, the Putin administration would accept only one version of history from the Second World War: Soviet forces liberated lands that had been conquered by the Nazis and thus – as gilded letters that adorn the Soviet war memorial in Treptower Park in Berlin proclaim – saved European civilisation. The Soviet role in the victory, even as the Soviets lost some 26 million of their own citizens in the war, is beyond dispute. For those – in the Baltic republics, western Ukraine, Poland and other countries of Eastern and Central Europe – who found themselves at the end of the war in the Soviet bloc or even in the USSR itself, such an account does not tell the full story: far from it. The 'liberation' that came with the Red Army's victory soon turned for them into another occupation. In the 1990s and afterwards, with the USSR gone, they moved to change their urban landscapes to reflect a new political reality. Countless monuments to Lenin fell with the fall of the USSR. The leaders and people of post-Soviet Russia accepted this – grudgingly, in some cases, joyfully in others – as being part of the nature of new times. Some statues to Soviet heroes were even removed in Moscow itself. Estonia's decision in April 2007 to move a Soviet war memorial from the centre of the capital, Tallinn, provoked a very different response – a response that included an early form of cyber warfare.

The Estonian authorities' plan was to move the Soviet war memorial, which was in the form of a bronze statue of a soldier, from the city centre to a military cemetery on the outskirts. The move was prompted by the fact that, for many Estonians, and other peoples of the Baltic states, this was a monument that – considering what followed – recalled not liberation from Nazi occupation so much as forced incorporation into the USSR. Yet not all citizens of the country saw it that way. The Estonian population included a significant ethnic Russian minority. To the majority of them, the memorial was as it was described by an official statement posted on the website of the Russian foreign ministry: 'the Monument to the Liberator Soldier'. The statement expressed the hope that the Estonian authorities would 'show a respectful attitude towards history and the memory of the fallen soldiers'.[30] The decision to move it led to two nights of rioting in which one person was killed and more than a hundred and fifty people injured. There were some thousand arrests.[31] It also infuriated the Russian political establishment. The Russian foreign minister, Sergei Lavrov, abandoned diplomatic nicety to call it 'disgusting'. Perhaps more revealing of the way that Russian officialdom viewed the incident, he even borrowed the language of religion to call it 'blasphemous'.[32] In the days that followed, the websites of Estonian ministries, media organisations and others were taken offline by distributed denial of service (DDoS) attacks that originated from Russian IP addresses. DDoS attacks render websites inaccessible by overloading them with traffic from multiple origins. As with subsequent instances of internet-based attacks that evolved as technology did, direct Russian official involvement was never acknowledged, or proved, publicly at least. The incident was significant for the way it started with a dispute over Soviet history of the last century and escalated to making the most effective and destructive use of technology in this one. These two characteristics were increasingly to become part of Russia's relations with the West in the Putin era.

If the involvement of the Russian state was strongly suspected, if never conclusively proved, in the unrest and cyber attacks relating to the bronze soldier, there had been no such uncertainty earlier that year when Putin spoke at the Munich Security Conference. His speech was a direct and forceful verbal attack on the foreign policy of the US, on NATO, and, to a lesser extent, on the EU. Jamie Shea, the former NATO official, was in the audience. 'It took everybody by surprise,' he recalled in a 2023 interview. 'Nobody was ready for the sharpness of the tone, or the consistency of the denunciation.'[33]

Putin began by recalling the Cold War, and a world that was 'economically and ideologically divided'.[34] He went on to lament a world in which 'there is one master, one sovereign'. In the early part of his speech, Putin had provoked laughter with a nervous edge when he suggested that what he was about to say might lead to the moderator cutting him short after two or three minutes. As he went on, his enthusiasm for his subject grew – as did the signs of a frustration that approached fury with the current state of power in the world. Not yet having named that 'one master, one sovereign', he offered the following analysis of what he termed 'the unipolar world':

And this certainly has nothing in common with democracy. Because, as you know, democracy is the power of the majority in light of the interests and opinions of the minority.

Incidentally, Russia – we – are constantly being taught about democracy. But for some reason those who teach us do not want to learn themselves.

The target of his anger now obvious, if still unnamed, Putin continued. 'Today we are witnessing an almost uncontained hyper use of force – military force – in international relations, force that is plunging the world into an abyss of permanent conflicts.' This was a world in which the US and its allies were still occupying Afghanistan and Iraq, having been fighting insurgencies since Washington had led the invasions of those two countries earlier in the decade. Putin summarised the situation as follows: 'The United States has overstepped its national borders in every way. This is visible in the economic, political, cultural and educational policies it imposes on other nations. Well, who likes this? Who is happy about this?' If, in Putin's assessment, the US had overstepped its borders, Russia's own frontiers were under threat as a consequence of NATO enlargement. With the alliance's then secretary general, Javier Solana, in the audience, Putin turned his rhetorical fire on NATO. Referring to the Conventional Forces in Europe (CFE) Treaty, Putin referred to troop withdrawals he said Russia had made from bases in former Soviet territory, while accusing NATO of having 'put its frontline forces on our borders, and we continue to strictly fulfil the treaty obligations and do not react to these actions at all'. If Russia had apparently accepted NATO's recent addition of new members, it no longer did so willingly. 'I think it is obvious that NATO expansion does not have any relation with the modernisation of the Alliance itself or with ensuring security in Europe. On the contrary, it represents a serious provocation that reduces the level of mutual trust.'[35]

In the hall as Putin spoke that day, Shea later assessed this as a moment when 'there is no longer this kind of common view of the world, this common language'. Tony Brenton, then British ambassador to Moscow, later saw the Munich speech as 'the first explicit statement of how angry they were at the West's behaviour in the Balkans, NATO expansion, and all of that'. David Manning, by then British ambassador to Washington, remembered that after Putin's Munich speech, 'It did feel like a change of mood and tempo'. Reflecting in 2023 on events then, Manning also saw a connection with Putin's domestic political plans: 'At this point, he starts to talk about foreign relations in a much more antagonistic and confrontational way. This helps him justify what he wants to do domestically which is to exert tighter political control. He becomes more repressive and bears down on democratic institutions.'

Putin's Munich speech did contain some conciliatory notes. He referred to President George W. Bush as his 'friend', adding, 'when I talked to him he said: "I proceed from the fact that Russia and the USA will never be opponents and enemies again". I agree with him.'

Nevertheless, Putin articulated plenty of points on which he bitterly disagreed with his 'friend' – plenty of areas in which he was vehemently opposed to the foreign policy of the country that 'friend' led. In our 2023 interview, Brenton contrasted the Munich speech with Russian policy under Yeltsin, when, 'The NATO enlargement stuff, they seem to have bought it very supinely.' Putin, leading a Russia no longer supine, now stood to challenge an alliance he accused of being all but poised to invade Russia. A crucial moment in the decline of Russia's relations with the West was to occur the following year, 2008, when NATO held a summit in Bucharest.

Putin's questioning of the alliance's motives deterred neither NATO from accepting new applications for membership, nor countries of the former Soviet bloc from seeking to join. These included Georgia and, even more sensitively for Russia (remember Rice's words about losing the original thirteen states), Ukraine. In her memoir, Rice recalled the situation as the alliance prepared for the Bucharest summit, which would be the last of President Bush's time in office. Putin's words had clearly been heard. 'As the alliance moved steadily east,' Rice wrote, 'Moscow's tolerance was being tested.' By 2008, Georgia and Ukraine were the next countries due to be considered for NATO's Membership Action Plan (MAP).[36] With the Bush presidency nearing its conclusion, Rice assumed that 'we would not push this plan' before Bush left the White House. When she explained that to Yushchenko, she later wrote, he 'almost cried'.[37] Balancing the competing diplomatic and security demands was a challenge: one to which NATO proved incapable of finding a successful solution.

Rice later conceded that 'there didn't seem to be a good way out'.[38] The discussion at the summit dinner when the allies tried to solve the problem was 'the most heated'[39] debate she saw in her entire time as US secretary of state. Heat did not produce light. For while the summit declaration said, 'NATO welcomes Ukraine's and Georgia's Euro-Atlantic aspirations for membership in NATO. We agreed today that these countries will become members of NATO', it did not formally offer the MAP. Instead, it declared, 'MAP is the next step for Ukraine and Georgia on their direct way to membership. Today we make clear that we support these countries' applications for MAP.'[40] In consequence, this satisfied nobody. Russia saw an attempt by NATO to encroach further on territory that had been part of the USSR – some of it part of the Russian Empire, too. Ukraine and Georgia had not got what they had come for. Rice declared herself 'happy with the outcome', because membership for Georgia and Ukraine was 'a matter of when, not whether'.[41] Speaking in 2023, and pointing out that neither Ukraine nor Georgia had in fact become NATO members, Lyne referred to the section in the summit declaration as a 'dreadful paragraph, probably the worst bit of diplomatic drafting ever'. It was, in his view, 'the biggest mistake that's been made on the western side, in the whole of the Putin period'.[42]

In her book, *Freedom: Memoirs 1954–2021*, the German chancellor, Angela Merkel, defended the decision not to offer Ukraine and Georgia a clear path to membership. Merkel's memoir was published in 2024, so she was writing with the benefit of much greater hindsight than Rice had enjoyed. Merkel argued that 'it was unprecedented for a NATO candidate to be so entangled with Russian military structures', adding, 'What's more, only a minority of the Ukrainian population backed NATO membership at the time: the country was profoundly split.'[43] Her first point does not adequately answer Lyne's accusation. While the intention may have been to avoid further antagonising Russia, it did not work. The second point is well made. Polling from 2008 suggested that only around 20 per cent of Ukrainians supported NATO membership, with more than half opposed, and the rest undecided.[44]

The short-term diplomatic fix was to be a factor in Russia's coming confrontation with the West, and, more seriously, in wars that cost tens of thousands of lives. The first of those, as will be discussed in detail in the next chapter, came in the summer of the same year in Georgia. By then Russia had a new president, Dmitry Medvedev. The Russian constitution as established in late 1993, after the October events, invested great power in the presidency – but it did limit the president to two four-year terms. Having won elections in 2000 and 2004, Putin was obliged to stand aside in 2008. This he did. But such was his influence and popularity, as living standards continued to grow, that whomever he endorsed – perhaps 'appointed' might be more accurate – as his successor was certain of victory in the upcoming election. Because of Putin's popularity – there is little doubt that he would have won the 2008 election had he been eligible to stand – there had been speculation that he might try to find a way to remain in the Kremlin. In the end, he respected the constitution and stood aside, but his choice of candidate – from two who had long been spoken of as Russia's possible next president – suggested that Putin certainly did not see his political career as over. In the weeks before polling day, on 2 March 2008, one Russian politician with good connections to the Kremlin told me that 'the Putin era is just beginning', making the comparison – presumably for the benefit of a British journalist – with Britain's wartime prime minister Winston Churchill and his eventual return to 10 Downing Street despite having lost the election that followed soon after the war.

Putin's choice of preferred successor had been a matter of intense speculation for more than a year before he actually named Medvedev on 10 December 2007. Dmitry Medvedev was forty-two, and a lawyer from Saint Petersburg. He had been a Putin protégé. 'I have known him for more than 17 years, I have worked with him very closely all these years, and I fully and completely support this candidacy,' Putin said.[45] The other possible contender was Sergei Ivanov, who, like Putin, but unlike Medvedev, was a former KGB officer. He was more like Putin in other ways, too. As defence minister, a post he held from 2001 to 2007, he echoed his boss's tough talk on Chechen insurgents, whom he referred to as 'bandits'. In 2001, as the conflict in the Caucasus continued, he warned those who had been responsible for the death of Russian servicemen: 'We forget nothing, and for people of that type we will find a final resting place one by two meters in size.'[46] Meeting Ivanov at the summit between presidents Bush and Putin in Ljubljana in 2001, Rice remembered 'a former KGB officer with extraordinary linguistic capability [. . .] Sergei was tough and somewhat suspicious of the United States, but he was dependable'.[47] He may also have been too tough for Putin's liking. As he prepared to step aside, Putin – who as Medvedev's prime minister for the duration of his protégé's presidential term retained significant power – wanted someone in the Kremlin who would not, or could not, seek to dominate him. Medvedev's survival as Putin's chief of staff in the Kremlin's political shark pool of competition, conspiracy and betrayal showed that he was no pushover, but nor could he necessarily be expected to mount a serious challenge to the authority of his mentor and former boss. The same could not be said with certainty of Sergei Ivanov. In consequence, he lost out.

Election day on the first Sunday in March went as expected. Facing three other candidates – none of whom presented a serious challenge – Medvedev won comfortably in the first round of voting, with 70.3 per cent per cent of the vote on a turnout of 69.7 per cent. His nearest rival, the veteran communist leader Gennady Zyuganov, won 17.7 per cent.[48] Medvedev was sworn in as president on 7 May. Within hours, he had appointed Putin to the post of prime minister – the leadership of the government guaranteeing Putin a seat at the heart of Russian power. Two days later, on 9 May, Medvedev looked over Red Square from the balcony on Lenin's Mausoleum as the parade to commemorate the 63rd anniversary of the USSR's victory over Nazi Germany passed before him, other assembled dignitaries, diplomats, and Russian and international media. The presence of the media was especially significant on this occasion because there was an important difference in the ceremony. For the first time on Red Square in the post-Soviet era, the Victory Day parade that year included contemporary military hardware (vintage vehicles from the Second World War had previously been involved). Tanks, rocket launchers and missiles all rolled across the cobblestones of the Moscow landmark. The parade concluded with a display of military aircraft: helicopters bearing state and military flags; bombers; and fighters.[49] Later that summer, oil prices would reach their all-time record high of $147 a barrel. Russia felt rich as a result, and Victory Day 2008 was an occasion to remind the world that it also wanted to be powerful militarily – recapturing some of the fearful respect that the USSR had inspired for so much of the previous century. Later the same year, it would become clear that this demonstration of martial might was not simply for show. For the first time since the end of Soviet power, Moscow would seek to settle a dispute with a neighbour by military force.

While in this period NATO enlargement, plans for its continuation and Russia's response undoubtedly provoked disagreements between Russia and its Western partners, it was nevertheless correct to speak of partnership. For example, remembering discussions between Putin and Bush after Bush took Putin fishing off the Bush family house at Kennebunkport, Maine, in the summer of 2007, Rice wrote of 'relatively good cooperation on Iran – far better than the public perception'. So it is important to set the relationship in its wider context. As Catherine Ashton would note of a later era, during her time as the EU's High Representative for Foreign Affairs and Security Policy, when tensions over the Maidan Revolution (also known the Revolution of Dignity) in Ukraine put great strain on Russia's relations with the EU and the US, cooperation on Iran continued. 'We had a regular place where we were collaborators with Russia on a good project.'[50] There were still parts of the relationship that worked well to the benefit of all parties.

With the seeds of renewed confrontation between Russia and the West having been sown in the 1990s, the first two terms of Putin's time as president were the time when the causes of that confrontation became clearer. However Western governments might plausibly argue that Russia had not opposed NATO enlargement with particular vehemence when it began, this did not mean it was not seen as a threat. The fact of the alliance having, in Putin's words, 'put its forces on our borders' became a matter of very public challenge and contention. For a domestic audience, it fuelled a smouldering sense of grievance that Western countries and NATO had humiliated and mistreated Russia after the end of the Cold War. It was not only Western ones: Rice remembers meetings with

Russian delegations at NATO in Brussels during her time as US secretary of state when 'the East Europeans never let the Russians forget that they'd lost the Cold War, and they sometimes treated the Russians in a manner that bordered on ridicule, which made me uncomfortable'.[51]

Such playground-style mockery may seem a relatively trivial matter in the world of international diplomacy and military alliances. For a country in which the most powerful politician was Vladimir Putin, it was more serious than that. This was a man who explained to his interviewers for the 2000 book *First Person* that he had not been in the Pioneers (an approximate Soviet equivalent of the Cub Scouts, but linked to the Communist Party) because he 'was a hooligan'.[52] In a 2024 interview, Fiona Hill contrasted Putin's approach with the eras of his Kremlin predecessors, Yeltsin and Gorbachev. 'What he does want to do is to get rid of the humiliations and put the country back on his feet', she said. 'For him personally, it becomes a sort of extension of self, I think, over time, and he sees himself in a very different light.' She added, of the Russian elite, 'They're insulted actually is a better way of putting it because if you think about the Russian word – kind of being insulted – "*obidelsya*" – means, I've taken on this insult.'[53] Ridicule in a NATO meeting hall would not be taken well by any international delegations – and certainly not by representatives of a leader who described himself as having been a 'hooligan' at school.

Lough's successor in his NATO public affairs role in Russia was expelled after NATO bombed Serbia during the Kosovo crisis. Despite having been deployed to Russia to promote the alliance, Lough is critical of the decisions taken at the Bucharest summit. 'I don't think it was a genius move in 2008 to signal that Ukraine and Georgia would join NATO when neither country was ready for it, when NATO didn't really mean it in the first place.' He believed that it 'gave the Russians an opportunity to say that, "our interests are being threatened here." And I think to invest in those sort of public narratives was very important for the consolidation of the regime around certain ideas. I think that was very rash and unnecessary.'

Contrast this with Putin's visit to Brussels in 2002, when he and the then NATO secretary general, George Robertson, spoke to reporters after their meeting. 'I have already explained our vision of future cooperation between Russia and NATO', the Russian president said. 'We believe that we have found a good tool to meet our mutual concerns and to work together and we are quite satisfied with the way we work in the Council.'[54] This was just ten days before the NATO summit in Prague, when the former Soviet republics of Lithuania, Latvia and Estonia, along with Bulgaria, Romania, Slovakia and Slovenia, would formally be invited to begin accession talks. Putin's calm words in Brussels then were very different from his anger at NATO in Munich less than five years later.

The increasing tensions between Russia and NATO over the alliance's enlargement in this period, and especially the suggestion that Ukraine might join, were further fuelled by the Russian assertiveness that came with the increase in oil prices. In his 2023 interview, Lyne, British ambassador to Moscow from 2000 to 2004, saw this as a crucial factor in the eventual breakdown of Russia's relationship with Western-led international organisations: 'I would say that one of the things that went wrong was the oil price went up.' In consequence, he suggested, 'As you went through towards the end of 2003, you had this sort of mood of saying, well, we don't actually have to listen to the IMF and Western governments and all the rest of it any more, we can do it our way. And we can kind of take the money. And that's when the Putin administration turned its face against reform.'

Whether or not the Kremlin shared the view of some in the FSB that the rise in oil prices was a gift from God, it was certainly a gift that brought the opportunity to begin to abandon democratic reform at home, and to use military force to achieve foreign policy objectives, too. The return of military vehicles to the parade on Red Square in 2008 had not just been for show.

6

War in the Near Abroad

The unsatisfactory statement at the end of the NATO summit in Bucharest was yet another source of division and mistrust between Russia and the alliance in their post-Cold War history. But confrontation over Russia's 'near abroad' had already been looming. When Russia attacked Georgia in August 2008, in a conflict over the separatist Georgian territories of South Ossetia and Abkhazia, the war was the consequence of tensions that had been building for years: unfinished business from the end of the USSR; Russian anger at perceived Western double standards, especially over Kosovo and NATO attacks on Serbia; and Georgia's Western-leaning government, under President Mikheil Saakashvili. Russia's attack on Georgia followed both the NATO summit and the show of military strength in May in celebration of Victory Day. There was one important staging post on the road to Russia's war on Georgia that pre-dated both of those events, and which deserves more attention than it has tended to receive.

Saakashvili had been a leader of the so-called 'Rose Revolution' in Georgia in late 2003. Early in the following year, he was elected president by a massive majority. He set about the task of reforming the country, with the longer-term aim of preparing it for membership not only of NATO but also of the EU. His policies included re-establishing

Georgia's territorial integrity. That meant bringing the separatist regions of South Ossetia and Abkhazia back under the control of the central government in Tbilisi. They had been beyond Tbilisi's reach since wars in the late Soviet and early post-Soviet periods. In the words of the Caucasus expert Thomas de Waal, the conflict in South Ossetia was the 'darkest legacy of Zviad Gamsakhurdia', Georgia's nationalist leader in the early 1990s. After coming to power, Saakashvili sought to restore Gamsakhurdia's reputation by bringing his body back from its resting place in Chechnya to be 'reburied in a grand ceremony in the national pantheon overlooking Tbilisi'.[1] As well as dismissing large numbers of police officers – the force was rotten with corruption – and ditching their Soviet-era uniforms, as a visible sign of change, Saakashvili also placed much larger resources at the disposal of a reformed army. If in 2003 spending on defence was just 1.1 per cent of GDP, by 2006 that had risen to 5.2 per cent, before soaring to 9.2 per cent in 2007.[2] It was not simply about sending a message to potential Western allies that Georgia was ready to be their partner. By 2006, Georgia was already training troops for deployment alongside those of the US and other allies in occupying Iraq: a military campaign that had both angered and worried the Kremlin. It was hard to think of a set of policies that had less in common with those of Georgia's much bigger neighbour.

In September 2006, relations between the two countries deteriorated sharply when Georgia accused Russian military officers stationed in Georgia of spying.[3] Direct transport links between the two countries were soon cut, and hundreds of Georgians living in Russia were deported, accused of breaking immigration law.[4] The expulsions caused economic hardship for those Georgians relying on remittances from Russia to make ends meet.

Such was the atmosphere between Russia and Georgia when, in November 2006, the separatist government of South Ossetia decided to hold a referendum on independence from Georgia. The vote was to be combined with an election for the president of the territory, in which the incumbent, Eduard Kokoity, was the candidate considered most likely to win. Polling day was set for Sunday 12 November. Kokoity had made his views on Saakashvili's Western-leaning reforms very clear shortly before the vote. Denying that South Ossetia and Abkhazia's conflict with Georgia was based on ethnicity, Kokoity argued that instead it was 'clearly politico-legal – Georgia would like to impose the norms of Western democracy [on us], while these can never be above our Caucasian [traditional] laws'.[5] South Ossetians are ethnically distinct from Georgians, emphasising instead their ties with North Ossetia, on the other side of the Caucasus mountain range, which is part of the Russian Federation. The Russian Federation did not comment on the comparative validity in the region of Western democracy or Caucasian tradition, but Moscow was keeping a very close eye on the vote. Two days before polling, the Russian foreign ministry issued a press communiqué that spoke of 'the tough line of Tbilisi', which, 'seeking to fan up tensions in relations with South Ossetia while demonstratively refusing to fulfill the current agreements and understandings, has forced Tskhinvali to take reciprocal measures, to which the referendum apparently belongs'.[6] When, to no one's surprise, the referendum result indicated 99 per cent in favour of independence, and 96 per cent for Kokoity to continue as president, a further statement hailed the result: 'And no matter how hard Georgia and a number of western states may try to downplay the significance of these elections, it is a milestone event. And not to reckon with this is short-sighted at the very least.'[7] As events two years later, in the summer of 2008, would show, that was true. And in justifying Russia's military action against Georgia, President Medvedev would cite the precedent of Western countries' recognition of Kosovo, which formally declared independence from Serbia on 17 February 2008.[8] Putin would do the same years later in the case of Crimea, though Russia would annex that latter territory rather than simply recognise its independence.[9]

Russia's invasion of South Ossetia needs to be seen in the wider context of relations between Russia and the West, and the US in particular, that unfolded in the twenty-one months between the referendum and the outbreak of war. To explain is not to excuse, but there were bigger factors at play. The war was about much more than Moscow's support for a separatist cause in a region of its southern neighbour's territory. Continuing Russian concern over NATO enlargement was one factor, as Putin had made clear in his 2007 speech at the Munich Security Conference. Another was Washington's plan to build components of a missile defence shield in Poland and the Czech Republic. Earlier that year, media reports citing US government officials had appeared, outlining plans to build the system against 'possible attacks by rogue states or terrorist groups'.[10] Given the proposed location of the planned installations – missile interceptors in Poland, and a radar in the Czech Republic – Russia soon protested that the system was designed as a defence against it in a possible future confrontation. Michael McFaul, who was US ambassador to Moscow from 2012 to 2014, wrote in his 2018 memoir that 'the Russians complained with good reason that such a radar in this location was capable of tracking Russian ICBMs'.[11] As the *New York Times* noted in one of the earliest media reports on the plans, both Poland and the Czech Republic had sent troops to support US forces occupying Afghanistan and Iraq.[12] In consequence, the two countries were seen as staunch allies. Their governments' enthusiasm for hosting a US missile system was not shared by the Czech and Polish people. In April, an Associated Press report published in the *Washington Post* cited opinion polls that suggested 57 per cent of Poles, and 68 per cent of Czechs, were opposed to the plans, with just 25 and 26 per cent respectively in favour.[13] Despite this opposition in the member states in question, NATO did not raise any objections to the plan – seeking only to ensure that 'any US system should be complementary to any NATO missile defence system', as a news release cited the alliance's then secretary general, Jaap de Hoop Scheffer, as saying. The NATO news release specifically identified 'Iran and North Korea' among the 'missile threats'. De Hoop Scheffer added that the plans 'would not affect the strategic balance with Russia'.[14]

Russia was absolutely not convinced but did initially appear to show some willingness to discuss the plans. The subject came up after Putin and Bush's fishing trip off the coast of Maine that summer. Rice recalled the two presidents 'agreeing to find a way to cooperate', although, as she wrote later, 'I believe now that there was some miscommunication between them but I didn't catch it at the time. The President was trying to make clear he wouldn't reverse the decision to place sites in Poland and the Czech Republic. Putin was offering alternative sites.'[15]

Finding a way to cooperate in fact proved impossible, although the issue continued to come up in discussions between the two presidents even as they both approached the end of their terms in office. Both would step aside for their successors following elections in 2008. Bush had come to the end of the two terms permitted by the US constitution. He was succeeded by the winner of the 2008 presidential election, the Democratic candidate, Barack Obama. Putin, who, as the conduct of the war in South Ossetia – to mention but one major international issue – showed, retained the real political power in Russia even while in the nominally subordinate role of prime minister. While the US would not, as Bush insisted, 'reverse the decision', considerable diplomatic effort was expended to try to find an acceptable solution on missile defence before the two men met for the final time as leaders of their respective countries. After the meeting in Kennebunkport, Rice and the US defense secretary, Robert Gates, made two trips to Russia before Bush and Putin met in Sochi in April 2008.[16] The 'U.S.–Russia Strategic Framework Declaration', issued after that last meeting of the Bush and Putin presidencies, seemed to acknowledge the diplomatic effort that had been expended, while being frank that there was no agreement. 'Russia has made clear that it does not agree with the decision to establish sites in Poland and the Czech Republic and reiterated its proposed alternative. Yet, it appreciates the measures that the United States has proposed and declared that if agreed and implemented such measures will be important and useful in assuaging Russian concerns.'[17]

Rice certainly seems to have tried. But if Putin 'demonstrated a willingness' at least to listen, a meeting with Lavrov and the military 'pushed us further from resolution'. In an attempt to reach an agreement, Rice, Gates and Stephen Hadley, then national security advisor, even came up with the idea of allowing Russia to station military personnel at the bases, though Rice later admitted, 'The Czechs and Poles themselves were none too happy with the idea of Russian soldiers on their territory.'[18]

The issue of missile defence was an outstanding source of discord when Putin's second term as president came to an end in the spring of 2008 and Medvedev became the third president of Russia. Bush was frank about the problem but also defensive, telling reporters after that final meeting, 'You can cynically say it's kicking the can down the road [. . .] I don't appreciate that,' and emphasising, 'We spent of a lot of time in our relationship to get rid of the Cold War [. . .] It's over.'[19]

A different kind of conflict was coming, however. In July 2008, the Russian foreign ministry issued a response to the news that an agreement had been signed between the US and the Czech Republic for the deployment of part of the missile defence system. Any sense of 'agreeing to find a way to cooperate' had disappeared. The statement dismissed any threat from Iran as 'imaginary' and argued that the agreement did not 'add to the security of either the Czech Republic or Europe as a whole'. Russia expressed its disappointment at its objections being ignored. 'All our arguments had merely been heard out but by no means taken into account.' The statement made direct reference to the declaration after Bush and Putin met in Sochi three months previously: 'the transparency and control measures we had proposed, which could somehow have reduced Russian fears, were called off by the US side, thus undermining the relevant accord of the Russian and US presidents, confirmed in the Declaration they adopted at Sochi on April 6, 2008'.[20]

To this sense of being sidelined and ignored was added warning of a coming conflict. Just four days before the statement criticising the agreement between the US and the Czech Republic, another accused the Georgian army of firing mortars at residential areas of Tskhinvali, the main city in South Ossetia. The statement concluded by charging the government in Tbilisi with 'committing undisguised acts of aggression against South Ossetia'.[21] Five days later, the day after the statement criticising the agreement on missile defence, the Russian foreign ministry issued another news release, this one accusing Georgia of stoking tension in both Abkhazia and South Ossetia, warning, 'The actions of Tbilisi pose a real threat to peace and security in the Southern Caucasus and could place the region on the brink of new armed conflict with unpredictable consequences.' Now Russia directly accused US State Department officials of making remarks that strengthened the Georgian leadership's 'belief in all-permissiveness'.[22] On 14 July, Lavrov met Kokoity. The foreign ministry in Moscow declared afterwards that the two were of the 'unanimous' view that stability in the region could only be ensured with the resumption of dialogue. Moscow also expressed 'serious concern over the escalation of tension in this region as a consequence of the aggressive policy of Georgia, aimed at destabilizing the situation in South Ossetia'.[23] This criticism of Washington's missile defence plans and its support for the Georgian leadership, and Moscow's accusations that the Georgian leadership was risking wider armed conflict in the region, were all published within less than a week. Russia was about to react in a way that the West could not ignore.

On the night of 7–8 August 2008, Georgia sent troops into South Ossetia. The advance was preceded by an artillery barrage. Russia soon responded, sending troops through the Roki tunnel, beneath the Caucasus mountains, that joins South Ossetia to North Ossetia. The arrival of these troops, supported by air and naval forces, halted the Georgian advance. Russia's far greater military strength soon showed. In addition to the ground advance into South Ossetia, Russia also launched airstrikes against Tbilisi and the Georgian city of Gori – both of them beyond the administrative border of South Ossetia – and blockaded the port of Poti on the Georgian coast. They also took part in an Abkhaz attack on the Kodori Gorge, 'the one area of Abkhazia that Georgia controlled before the war'.[24] Russian forces advanced to within 40 kilometres of Tbilisi, leading to fears that Moscow intended to take the Georgian capital, and depose Saakashvili.[25]

The main period of fighting lasted until 12 August. A ceasefire negotiated by Nicolas Sarkozy, president of France, which then held the EU's rotating presidency, brought an end to hostilities. The short war was a significant strategic victory for Russia. If Saakashvili's government, with its very public desire to join NATO and the EU, had expected any kind of Western military support, it was gravely mistaken. While there was widespread condemnation in Western capitals of Russia's military intervention, there was no attempt to offer any kind of military backing for Georgia. For the first time since the war in Afghanistan in the 1980s, Moscow had deployed combat forces beyond its border to secure a political strategy – and won.

Although the main phase of the war lasted only a few days, its consequences were immense. The Georgian army, beneficiary of nearly a tenth of Georgia's GDP, and seen within the government as a vanguard of Western-facing reform, had been routed. Saakashvili's plans to reintegrate the separatist territories of South Ossetia and Abkhazia had not only failed: their realisation had become all but impossible to foresee for years, if not decades – especially when, later in August, President Medvedev signed decrees recognising the two territories as independent countries. Medvedev's pen stroke may have established that new diplomatic reality, but the way this brief, bloody resolution of Russia and Georgia's differences had unfolded had made it clear that the real power in Russia remained in the hands of his predecessor in the Kremlin. By 9 August, the second full day of the war, Putin had flown back from the Beijing Olympics, where he had represented the Russian government at the opening ceremony, to North Ossetia, the area of the Russian Federation bordering South Ossetia. There, in casual clothes rather than prime ministerial suit and tie, he toured tent encampments and other temporary facilities set up to receive refugees who had fled from the fighting. He was back in Russia and, for a senior politician, close to the war zone, as the Russian army achieved its objectives.

Those objectives were both short and long term. In the short term, the idea that Russia would seek to remove Saakashvili from power remained just an idea – although a senior diplomatic adviser to Sarkozy, present at the negotiations in Moscow, later claimed that Putin had threatened such a move in the most undiplomatic of terms. Jean-David Levitte said that, with Russian tanks drawing ever closer to Tbilisi, Putin had declared, 'I am going to hang Saakashvili by the balls.'[26] According to Levitte's account, Sarkozy dissuaded Putin from such a course of action by reminding him of Bush's reputation after the war in Iraq, when Saddam Hussein had been deposed and hanged. Saakashvili and his government survived for the time being. Their ambition to join NATO did not.

Georgia's international aspirations were not the only casualties. A report commissioned by the EU, and published the following year, concluded:

> Human losses were substantial. At the end, the Georgian side claimed losses of 170 servicemen, 14 policemen and 228 civilians killed and 1 747 persons wounded. The Russian side claimed losses of 67 servicemen killed and 283 wounded. The South Ossetians spoke of 365 persons killed, which probably included both servicemen and civilians. Altogether about 850 persons lost their lives, not to mention those who were wounded, who went missing, or the far more than 100 000 civilians who fled their homes.[27]

The report, often referred to as the Tagliavini report after Heidi Tagliavini, the Swiss diplomat who led the team that compiled it, concluded: 'Open hostilities began with a large-scale Georgian military operation against the town of Tskhinvali and the surrounding areas, launched in the night of 7 to 8 August 2008. Operations started with a massive Georgian artillery attack.'[28] In that sense, Georgia was judged to have started the war that began on 8 August. However, the report also concluded that 'much of the Russian military action went far beyond the reasonable limits of defence'.[29] In addition, 'Georgian forces, Russian forces and South Ossetian forces – committed violations of International Humanitarian Law and Human Rights Law'.[30]

The news media – outside Georgia, at least – highlighted the conclusion that Georgia's artillery assault had started the five-day war.[31] And the media's opinion mattered, for this conflict was one in which – even more than is always the case in a time of armed conflict – the belligerents invested heavily in winning the media war, too. Both Russia and Georgia had public relations agencies working for them, seeking to influence, from their cool offices on the boulevards of Brussels, the coverage of a war in the unforgiving heat of a Caucasus summer. For Georgia, once it became clear that there would be no NATO or other cavalry riding to their rescue, the media war became the main front. Saakashvili, who spoke near-perfect English after studying and working in the US, spent what seemed a surprising amount of time on international television news channels, considering he was leading a country at war with its more mighty neighbour. The Kremlin, on the advice of its Western public relations executives, made a series of senior officials, including Sergei Lavrov, available to the international media for interview.[32] As BBC correspondent in Moscow then, I was among the journalists invited to the Russian foreign ministry on Saturday 9 August to interview him. Lavrov robustly justified Russia's actions and even said there were alleged cases of Georgian soldiers shooting dead Russian prisoners of war. 'That's the reports we are getting, and we are verifying them.'[33] Though the Tagliavini report concluded that 'all sides to the conflict – Georgian forces, Russian forces and South Ossetian forces – committed violations of International Humanitarian Law and Human Rights Law', this particular allegation was never proven. True or not, it was significant as an indication of the great importance the belligerents placed on their propaganda war.

The time that members of both the Russian and Georgian political elites – especially the latter – devoted to making their case in the media marked this conflict as a new departure. In an academic paper on their findings from a study of the Russian, Georgian and English language news media during the conflict, Rick Fawn and Robert Nalbandov wrote, 'The intensive communications and information networks now available risk becoming not sources of objective information but weapons in the war.'[34]

That Russia prevailed militarily was beyond question. The Kremlin also achieved its strategic aim of preventing Georgia from joining NATO. The victor in the propaganda war was harder to decide upon. Neither side came out of the conflict having done especially well in the eyes of international public opinion. If Georgia initially benefited – especially in the international English-language media – from making more officials available to make their case, that success did not necessarily last. The conclusions of the Tagliavini report tended to undermine the David against Goliath story that the Georgian government had told. Georgia was seen as having acted rashly, albeit in the face of major provocation. Writing the year after the war, Andrei Illarionov, who from 2000 to 2005 had been an economic adviser to Putin, argued that 'Russian authorities had been making serious preparations for war over the span of nearly one decade'.[35] Even if that were so, not everything went as Russia planned. Despite being a much larger country, with far greater resources, extensive armaments manufacture and a much larger army, Russia did not win the war as easily as might have been expected. Instead, problems with equipment and communication meant that Russian forces were at far from full effectiveness. As my co-author Alexander Lanoszka and I concluded in a 2021 article, 'Russia appears to have won ultimately by dint of enjoying significant numerical superiority over an adversary in a conventional war'.[36] A similar – perhaps exactly the same – conclusion had been reached in the defence ministry and the Kremlin. On 14 October, just two months after the end of the main phase of the war, the defence minister, Anatoly Serdyukov, announced the start of a major reform programme that was due to last until 2020. The proposed reforms placed a strong emphasis on personnel, with one of the ultimate aims being 'to gradually increase the share of professional soldiers and decrease the share of conscripts'.[37] As Vasilii Kashin wrote in a 2021 article on the reforms, and with reference to the 2008 war, 'Using such a military in conflict with a more potent opponent would inevitably end in disaster.'[38] Wanting to flex its muscles in the near abroad and, eventually, on the wider international stage, Russia needed armed forces that would enable it to do so. The war with Georgia exposed the gap between ambition and reality, and the Kremlin set about closing it should it one day decide to take on a stronger enemy.

Nor were the lessons learned confined to the purely military sphere. During the war with Georgia, techniques first tried during the dispute over the bronze soldier in Estonia the year before were also deployed. Military force was accompanied by cyber attacks on Georgian internet servers and government sites.[39] And even if the winner of the propaganda war was a matter of opinion, Russia also understood the important role played by the media in modern conflict. Lavrov had given interviews to international broadcasters such as CNN and the BBC. Russia Today were reduced to asking the latter to broadcast their interview with the minister as they were not granted their own. The still newly established and relatively insignificant outlet would, in the following decade, be boosted by a massive budget increase and allies on the international media battlefield, in the shape of Sputnik News. The literal meaning of the word '*sputnik*' in Russian is a person accompanying one on a journey, a fellow traveller. Its choice for a new squadron of media platforms was a reference to a great Soviet achievement in the space race of the Cold War era. As such, it also suggested future intent. By 2015, the budget for Russian foreign language media platforms had soared to almost £350 million.[40]

Such was the Russian response to the war. That of the US and its allies sought to balance the competing interests of supporting an ally, and not antagonising to too great an extent that ally's larger neighbour. In early September, President Bush announced $1 billion in humanitarian and economic assistance for Georgia but 'stopped short of committing the United States to re-equipping its battered military', as the *New York Times* put it.[41] The British politician David Cameron, then leader of the opposition Conservative party, and who would later be prime minister from 2010 to 2016, had visited Georgia just after the main phase of the war. In the *Sunday Times* on 17 August, he wrote, referring to a leading department store in central London, 'Russian armies can't march into other countries while Russian shoppers carry on marching into Selfridges.' Cameron added that NATO 'should offer Georgia a clear pathway to membership'.[42] In fact, Russian shoppers did carry on marching into Selfridges, at the same time as the country's wealthy carried on beating a path to Britain's purveyors of luxury goods, high-end estate agents, elite schools and law courts. Georgia, on the other hand, got no clear pathway to NATO.

If Russia was using Georgia as an experiment in testing its own military and propaganda resources, as well as the West's will to support allies, the West's response cannot be seen as anything other than inadequate. Fiona Hill, at the time national intelligence officer for Russia and Eurasia at the US National Intelligence Council, said in a 2024 interview, 'If we were going to be serious about this, we'd have had a stronger response about Georgia being invaded. And the Russians thought we were going to have a strong response by the way, they were terrified.'[43]

Reflecting later on the events of August 2008, Lyne was critical of the fact that the Sarkozy plan did not force Russia to withdraw its forces from South Ossetia (although in October, Russian troops did leave some territory they held beyond the region's administrative boundary with the rest of Georgia). 'He comes up with a really lousy deal under which effectively leaves Russian forces in control of – I mean, they're already in Abkhazia – but of South Ossetia. It effectively legitimizes their presence.'[44] He was also critical of Saakashvili, who, he argued, obligingly fell into a trap set for him by the Russians. Laurie Bristow, then minister (deputy head of mission) in the British embassy in Moscow, sees the war as important. 'Why did this come as a surprise? Well, it kind of didn't actually,' he said in a 2023 interview. Bristow saw in the way the war unfolded 'an absolutely classic example of Russian controlled escalation [. . .] If you provoke a guy like Saakashvili long enough, he'll do what you want to do, which is rise to the bait, and then you smash him.'[45] In her memoir, Rice wrote that she had warned Saakashvili against just such an outcome. She had visited him in Tbilisi on 10 July and asked him to sign a pledge that he would not use force in his dispute with Russia. According to Rice's account, Saakashvili 'stubbornly refused'. 'Finally,' Rice wrote, 'I thought I'd better get tougher. "Mr President, whatever you do, don't let the Russians provoke you. You remember when President Bush said that Moscow would try to get you to do something stupid. And don't engage Russian military forces. No one will come to your aid, and you will lose." '[46]

So it turned out. The 2008 war did not at the time have major short-term consequences for Russia's relations with the West. Taking up her post as the EU's first High Representative for Foreign Affairs and Security Policy the following year, Catherine Ashton remembered Georgia being down the agenda when EU foreign ministers met. 'We would talk about Georgia, but never as number one item or as the dominating issue. And I think that was in part because Saakashvili, who was then the president, was highly regarded in lots of parts of the West.' Saakashvili's earlier reputation as an energetic, Western-facing reformer survived – in the short term, at least – his catastrophic miscalculation in sending troops into South Ossetia. The Georgian president's reputation aside, the war was a hugely significant milestone in Russia's relations with the West – and it was an episode in the history of those relations in which the Kremlin came out on top.

In a sense, the timing of the war also worked in Putin's favour – though how much credit he can take for this, given that the outbreak of fighting depended more on Saakashvili than Putin, is another matter. Western governments were dealing with the effects of the 2007–08 global financial crisis. Russia, where people had seen their savings wiped out twice in a decade, first by the sky-high inflation that came with the economic chaos at the end of the USSR, and secondly by the default on debt repayments of 1998, was shielded from the worst excesses. The finance minister, Alexei Kudrin, whom the *Financial Times* described in a 2008 article as being 'in the sometimes uncomfortable position of gatekeeper to the oil tax windfall stashed in Russia's Stabilisation Fund', had sagely set enough aside as energy prices soared to shield Russia from the direst consequences of even such a rainy day as fell in 2008.[47] Even if only the wisest had seen the financial crisis coming and prepared accordingly, political change in the US was no surprise. His second term drawing to a close, Bush was about to leave office. With Barack Obama emerging as a strong candidate for the presidency, there was no guarantee of a new Republican administration in the White House.

'The Russian-Georgian war compelled our campaign to develop a comprehensive policy toward Russia',[48] wrote Michael McFaul of his work on the election campaign that would end with Obama becoming president of the US. McFaul, a political scientist by profession, had spent years in Russia in the late-Soviet and early post-Soviet period. Early in 2007, he had been asked to join the Obama campaign. The war in Georgia brought his Russia expertise to the fore as part of that campaign. Following Obama's victory, McFaul became senior director for Russian affairs in the new administration. McFaul's 2018 memoir, *From Cold War to Hot Peace*, told the story of his engagement with the country during its time of transition, and of his own progress from graduate student to US ambassador to Moscow. As might be expected of someone who enthusiastically welcomed Obama's election victory, 'a tremendous moment of celebration for me, my family, and millions of other Americans',[49] McFaul was critical of aspects of the policies of the preceding administration. In his view, 'Surprisingly, the Bush administration did little to punish Russia for invading Georgia', a response he adjudged 'feeble'.[50] Further, McFaul argued, by the end of the Bush administration, the era of relations between Washington and Moscow that had begun with cooperation between Gorbachev and Reagan, an era characterised by 'the belief that engagement and cooperation served both Russia and U.S. interests', was over, having 'finally died in the

Caucasus in August 2008'.[51] McFaul was a leading part of the Obama administration's attempt to improve that, with a policy that came to be known as 'the reset'.

The policy had an unfortunate public debut, a public relations embarrassment for which McFaul was honourable enough to take responsibility in his later memoir. Hillary Clinton had been appointed secretary of state following Obama's election win. She was due to meet Lavrov for the first time in Geneva, on 6 March 2009. On Clinton's plane, en route to Geneva for the meeting, a member of Clinton's team asked McFaul how to spell 'reset' in Russian. He came up with *'pere-gruzka'*. 'None of the other Russian speakers on board disagreed.' Only later did he discover why the word was needed. It was to appear, alongside 'reset' in English, on a button that Clinton produced from a box as a gift for Lavrov at a photo opportunity for the media before the meeting.[52] 'We worked hard to get the right Russian word,' Clinton told Lavrov. 'Do you think we got it?' 'You got it wrong,' Lavrov replied in his flawless English. 'It should be *perezagruzka*, and this says *pere-gruzka*, which means "overcharged".'[53] Another possible translation, as McFaul noted, was 'overload'. Either way, when Lavrov pointed out the error, McFaul was 'mortified'.[54] It might seem a trivial incident, but, in a world where media image mattered so much in international relations, it seemed to betray a lack of attention to detail; a gap in expertise. For this was, after all, a serious attempt to rebuild relations that already – for a number of reasons, with the war in Georgia being the latest, and one of the most high profile – were at risk of returning to the cold confrontation of the previous century. This lack of attention to detail was embarrassing, especially as it concerned the foreign minister of a Kremlin in which, as Tony Brenton, British ambassador to Moscow from 2004 to 2008, noted, Putin was always 'very well briefed'.[55]

The core principle of the 'reset' policy held that 'improved relations with Russia should not be a goal of U.S. policy, but a possible strategy for achieving American security and economic objectives in dealing with Russia'.[56] The policy's broad assumption was that 'the United

States and Russia had some common interests, especially regarding our biggest security challenges'.[57] McFaul, having come from academia, admitted that while he 'was comfortable thinking and writing,' he 'was less adept, at least initially, at translating conceptual ideas into concrete policies'.[58] Despite the recent war in Georgia, over which Washington and Moscow had irreconcilably different views, the atmosphere in which the 'reset' began was in some senses auspicious. George W. Bush and Vladimir Putin had made way for younger, newer faces. Obama and Medvedev first met in London in April 2009, during the G20 forum for international economic cooperation. Progress during this meeting on the matter of cooperation over Iran's nuclear programme, and a Russian offer to allow the US to fly military aircraft through Russian airspace to assist operations in Afghanistan, led to hopes of a substantial improvement in relations.[59] That meeting was followed by summit meetings in Moscow in July 2009, and in the US the following year. During that visit, Medvedev travelled to Silicon Valley, and the two presidents enjoyed fast food at a burger joint in Arlington, Virginia, outside Washington, DC. Alongside the cheery photo opportunities that such events provided, some real progress was made in this era. In Prague on 8 April 2010, the two leaders signed the New START (Strategic Arms Reduction Treaty), which 'reduced limits on U.S. and Russia deployed strategic war heads by approximately one third'.[60] There was cooperation on policy on the Iran nuclear programme – though McFaul was frank when he wrote later that, on this issue, Putin, despite his nominally less powerful role in the new structure at the summit of Russian politics, 'was *the* key decision maker'.[61] This would remain the case throughout the reset, and the Medvedev presidency. Still, cooperation over Iran remained a major achievement in relations between Russia and the West in this era. Ashton would later write, of her time in office as the EU's foreign policy chief, 'Relations with Russia went downhill over these years, but in the Iran talks we kept our focus.'[62]

The indecisiveness, the lack of clarity, of NATO's statement on Georgia and Ukraine at the end of the summit in Bucharest casts a shadow over this period of Russia's relations with the West. If Putin and the rest of the Russian political elite had appeared to accept – reluctantly or not – the admission of new members into NATO, his 2007 speech at the Munich Security Conference made it clear that was no longer so. The time when, in Brenton's words, Russia accepted NATO's enlargement 'supinely' ended verbally with that speech. It ended militarily in the summer war of 2008. Putin had given his Munich speech more than a year before the NATO summit at which it was stated that Ukraine and Georgia 'would become NATO members'. As with the somewhat angry foreign ministry statement of July 2008, responding to the news that the Czech Republic and the US had signed an agreement on Washington's missile defence plans, Putin's Munich speech proved to be another occasion in which Russia's 'arguments had merely been heard out but by no means taken into account'. Apparently tired of being ignored, in Georgia in the summer of 2008, Russia decided to make its point with force of arms. The campaign exposed shortcomings in the Russian armed forces. Yet this was no unthinking military adventure. Russia chose its moment carefully, setting a trap that the Georgian leadership helpfully walked into. Saakashvili, not Putin, was the military adventurer. The Kremlin had also correctly calculated that – however much Georgia aspired to join Western institutions, and however much the Bush administration in particular saw Saakashvili as an ally – it would face no Western military response. Rice may have been, as she later wrote, 'happy with the outcome' at Bucharest, however difficult the drafting of the statement had been. Her admonition of Saakashvili shows that she was not happy with the conduct of the government that had been told it 'will' join NATO. 'The Western response was inept', Brenton argued in 2023. 'The instant western reaction was that the Russians have invaded Georgia. Eventually they did, but that wasn't the first thing that happened. So I was sent in to protest at this act of international aggression', he recalled of his visit to the Russian foreign ministry in Moscow. 'How can you do this?', Brenton says he asked of the Russian official who received him, a diplomat who had previously been posted to

London, and whom Brenton knew. 'But Tony, they fired first', came the reply. 'At which point,' Brenton conceded, 'it became quite difficult to pursue the conversation.'

The Russian diplomat's response was over-simplified for the purpose of being direct. It ignored the wider context of relations between Russia and Georgia; Russia and South Ossetia; and Russia and the West, in which the events leading up to the outbreak of war had unfolded. Yet the answer Brenton received when he had been sent to protest also reflected the fact that Russia could plausibly present a version of events in which it was not primarily to blame for the start of the fighting. It also reflected a Russian confidence that there would not be serious consequences. McFaul was then drafting policy ideas that would go on to be principles of the 'reset'. In his 2018 memoir, McFaul recognised that 'critics of the Reset have argued that we would have achieved better results with the Russian government in 2009 had we sought to punish it for invading Georgia'. He disagreed, on the grounds that Russian cooperation was needed on international issues such as START, Iran and Afghanistan. The common ground that Washington and Moscow found on these issues during the Medvedev presidency and Obama's first term, and the progress they made, support that view.

Saakashvili might have been solidly and predictably pro-Western, but he was less predictable in his actions. Rice's warning to Saakashvili, and Brenton's feeling of being stuck for a response in the exchange with the Russian foreign ministry, show the problems this unpredictability caused for Western policy. Saakashvili's judgment was deeply flawed. His decision to seek to take back control of South Ossetia by military force could never succeed, as Rice later claimed she had made clear. That he tried to do so anyway greatly undermined his reliability as a Western ally. It made it harder for the West to justify or formulate a more robust response to the Russian conquest of Georgian territory that followed Saakashvili's military adventure. Even with the benefit of hindsight, and the war on Ukraine that would begin five years later, a case can still be made that a muted response to the Kremlin's seizure of

South Ossetia and Abkhazia was wise because of wider circumstances. There were a lot of other issues at stake, and Saakashvili had not helped his country's cause by his rash actions. That being said, a stronger warning from the West – with sanctions of the kind and scale eventually imposed following the escalation of the war in Ukraine in 2022 – might have been more effective for the future.

The absence of a more forceful reaction meant there was no adequate deterrent against future Kremlin conquest – especially if, as Hill suggested, from her perspective as an intelligence official, the Russians expected a response and 'were terrified' of it. In Georgia, Russia drew a red line for NATO: one NATO dared not cross. In that sense, the Kremlin's strategic aim had been achieved. As Ukraine would show, although only in 2022, eight years after Russia first began military operations in that country, there were other occasions on which the West would support more forcefully those whom Russia attacked. For Putin, even though this was the era in which he completed the second of the two presidential terms that the Russian constitution allowed, it was only the end of the beginning of his power in Russia. As his rapid return to be close to the fighting during the Russian invasion of South Ossetia showed, he never left the scene. His step back gave him time to formulate longer-term plans and identify what he saw as longer-term threats, and the reasons behind them. Brenton, who was British ambassador to Moscow at the time of the 2008 war, said in his 2023 interview:

Putin, from what I have seen of him, when something untoward happens, his instant reaction is 'Who did this to us?' And on Georgia, the Georgians obviously wouldn't do this unprompted. Therefore, they were put up to it by someone. Obviously, it was the Americans.

That 2007–2008 period is a big shift. And it's when we start to see Putin getting really frightened about, quote, 'colour revolutions', democracy, the challenge, you know, which he sees as a regime change.

Combined with the conviction that the invasion of Iraq had been about regime change, not weapons of mass destruction, Putin saw the war with Georgia as a chance to show that Russia had returned as a military power. It was a chance to show NATO that he was willing to use military force as a means of stopping its further expansion. On both of those counts, by his own reckoning, and by that of many in the West, he had succeeded. The short-term consequences of the war with Georgia were few outside the immediate region. The longer-term ones would shake Europe's post-1945 security structure.

7

The Return of Russian History

The war in Georgia was not only about the present, but also about the past and how Russia saw its own military history. The idea that territory that had once been part of the USSR, and, before that, the Russian Empire, could become an independent country that sought membership of a Western-led military alliance was unacceptable. Such moves had to be resisted, by force of arms if necessary. Saakashvili's miscalculation in seeking to seize back South Ossetia by force contributed to Georgia's defeat. Saakashvili started a war he could not win. That did not undermine the justice of his desire to bring the breakaway territories back under the control of the government in Tbilisi. It undermined the possibility of achieving it. Russia's reaction may not have been justified, but it was predictable. If the war had the strategic aim of stopping Georgia joining NATO, it also played to narratives about Russia being attacked from the West, as it had been by Napoleon in the nineteenth century, and Hitler in the twentieth.

Having been, as an officer of the KGB, part of the system of Soviet power that stretched far beyond the USSR's borders in the second half of the twentieth century, Putin had served his country in a very different Europe: a Europe where the political and military alliances of the West were much further from Russia's borders, even if not so far from the borders of the USSR's satellite states. During the Cold War, this was where Soviet power ended and enemy territory began. In *First Person*, Putin recalled of his time in Germany, 'we were working from the territory of East Germany. We were interested in any information about the "main opponent" as we called them, and the main opponent was considered NATO.' In the next answer to his interviewers, Putin said he had never travelled into West Germany while he was in East Germany.[1] Of course, that may not be true. But the way in which the answer is given seemed to reinforce the idea that what lay beyond was 'the main opponent', the land from which, during the Second World War, a massive military force had come to conquer Russia and been heroically driven back.

The Soviet war memorial at Treptower Park in Berlin is a monument to the Soviet war dead killed fighting for Berlin. It is also a monument to the Soviet version of the history of that conflict. Arriving, the visitor passes between two vast marble monuments. At the base of each, a huge statue of a Soviet soldier kneels, his bare head bowed in tribute to the fallen, his helmet – no longer needed now victory is his – held in his hand. In the centre, another bare-headed warrior holds a child in the crook of his muscular left arm. In his right hand, a sword points downwards to where it has sliced through a swastika, cracked and broken under his solid Soviet army boot. Beneath the statue is a small space that houses a magnificent mosaic. A group of ordinary people stand respectfully behind two soldiers kneeling to lay a wreath. A ribbon on that wreath bears the single word '*slava*', Russian for 'glory'. The word, in gilded tiles, has been meticulously placed to catch whatever sunlight there is, on however dull a day, so that it shines for the eyes of the onlooker. The inscription above the whole scene gives thanks to the army that 'saved the civilization of Europe from the fascist *pogromsh-chiks* [those who organised a pogrom or massacre]'. A short distance away, on the approach to the memorial, there is a noticeboard with photographs of the occasions when prominent people visited the site. One of them, in black and white, perhaps prepared for publication in a newspaper before colour photographs were the norm, shows Vladimir Putin, relatively young, thin, in a suit that looks a little on the large side. Two Russian officers walk before him, carrying a large wreath. His eyes look slightly downwards. Perhaps he wants to be sure not to stumble on the steps on such an important occasion. Perhaps he is also thinking of the great feat of arms that saved European civilisation and how he, newly president, is now guardian of that glorious martial legacy.

During the Medvedev presidency, Putin – as diplomatic protocol demanded – took something of a back seat in international affairs, outwardly, at least. With the Obama administration realising that Putin was still '*the* key decision maker' as far as Russian policy on Iran's nuclear programme was concerned, McFaul came up with the ruse of seeking to arrange a call for Obama to seek Putin's advice on an Olympic bid. 'When Obama gently turned the conversation to Iran,' McFaul later wrote, 'Putin offered the president a brief lesson on the Russian constitution'. Having reminded Obama that foreign policy was not the responsibility of the prime minister, Putin handed the phone to Medvedev, whom he happened to be with.[2] If the Putin era was indeed 'just beginning', as a pro-Kremlin politician had told me in the spring of 2008, this was how it continued: with Putin, constitutionally, no longer the leading power in the country; in fact, very much the leading power in the country.

The pretence is important for the direction in which Putin would later take Russia. As Charles Clover put it, 'Putin has correctly surmised that lies unite rather than divide Russia's political class. The greater and more obvious the lie, the more his subjects demonstrate their loyalty by accepting it'.[3] Clover also noted Putin's references to 'civilization', and Russia's duty to protect it: 'The Great Russian mission is to unite, bind civilization. In this type of state-civilization there are no national minorities, and the principle of recognition of "friend or foe" is defined as common culture and shared values.'[4] There are echoes here of the inscription at the Treptower Park war memorial, dedicated to those who 'saved the civilization of Europe' – a feat beyond even that of defeating the colossal military might of Hitler's forces. Yet it was not Russia alone that achieved that. It was the USSR, the fall of which had been, in Putin's view, such a catastrophe. Before that collapse, the 'main opponent' had been NATO. After the collapse, NATO had expanded eastwards; the US had placed parts of its missile defence system on territory that had once been part of the Warsaw Pact; and very possibly, in Putin's view, as Brenton suggested, the US had also encouraged Georgia to go to war for South Ossetia. The USSR had not been ignored, its 'arguments not taken into account', as the Russian Federation now found its were. The glorious history of Soviet military might was remembered at Treptower Park. The war in Georgia was a small step on the road to recapturing some of that glory for Russia, and putting it on the path to once more being treated as an equal, a worthy adversary, for the superpower against which Moscow had contested the Cold War.

One area in which Russia was still treated as an equal, or at least as a fellow member of an elite group, was nuclear weapons. The final summit meeting between George H.W. Bush and Mikhail Gorbachev, the last Soviet leader, had focused on reducing the nuclear threat. However weak Russia became after the fall of the USSR, this was one area in which it could not be ignored. Bush senior and Gorbachev signed the treaty referred to as START I when they met in Moscow on 31 July 1991. It came into force on 5 December 1994. It had been the subject of lengthy negotiations. It was, though, a high point of cooperation between the Cold War foes, and a sign that conflict was reaching its conclusion. The White House news release, published on the day the treaty was signed, hailed it as 'the first agreement between the two countries in which the number of deployed strategic nuclear weapons will actually be reduced'.[5] The agreed reductions limited each side to 1,600 'strategic nuclear delivery vehicles'[6] (launchers, submarines, bombers) and 'represented levels approximately 30 percent below currently deployed forces'.[7] Both the US and the USSR (which would only last until the end of the year in which the treaty was signed, its obligations then taken on by the Russian Federation) met these commitments by the agreed deadline of 5 December 2001.

In May the following year, presidents George W. Bush and Putin signed the Strategic Offensive Reductions Treaty (SORT), also known as the Moscow Treaty because the two leaders met in the Russian capital. This committed the two sides to 'reducing their deployed strategic nuclear forces to 1,700–2,200 warheads apiece'. The agreement also kept START I in force.[8] Giving testimony on the treaty before the US Senate Foreign Relations Committee in July of the same year, Colin Powell, then secretary of state, reflected the spirit of cooperation in which the two former foes were now working. Reporting what Bush had told Putin of the numbers of warheads the US intended to retain, he said, 'This is what the United States needs. And it does not need it because you are an enemy; it needs this because of the nature of the world we live in, and we see you as a partner.'[9] Addressing Senator Joseph Biden, then chair of the committee (and later, of course, president), Powell put the treaty into the context of his own career as a cold warrior: 'Mr Chairman, this is a different treaty in a different world than the world I knew so well as a soldier.'

START expired in December 2009. In April the following year, presidents Obama and Medvedev met in Prague, where they signed the New START treaty. This committed both sides to '700 deployed intercontinental ballistic missiles (ICBMs), deployed submarine-launched ballistic missiles (SLBMs), and deployed heavy bombers equipped for nuclear armaments'.[10] At the news conference after the signing ceremony, Medvedev, speaking in Russian, borrowed an English phrase to help him describe the achievement. He hailed the treaty as a 'document that fully strikes a balance between Russian and American interests. The main thing is that there are no winners and losers. Rather, this is what they call a win–win situation.'[11] The treaty came into force on 5 February 2011. Both sides had complied by the agreed date of 5 February 2018.[12] In 2021, the treaty was extended until 2026. In February 2023, however, during his annual address to the Federal

Assembly, and accusing the US of 'trying to refashion the international order to suit exclusively its own needs and selfish interests', Putin said, 'I am compelled to announce today that Russia is suspending its membership in the New START Treaty. To reiterate, we are not withdrawing from the Treaty, but rather suspending our participation.'[13] Putin's criticisms of the US were a reminder of his desire for Russia to be seen always as an equal of the US, however much it was also a rival. Both the tone and the content of his announcement – towards the end of a lengthy speech – were striking for the way they contrasted with the sentiments expressed by Powell earlier in the arms reduction negotiation process, when he remembered his earlier career as a Cold War general. Putin's words were also very different from Medvedev's 'win–win situation' when the treaty was signed. 'Win–win' was not, in general, something that Putin believed possible: a 'win' for the other party in a negotiation meant a defeat for you, even if the nature of the defeat was not obvious. That was particularly the case by the time Putin suspended Russian membership of New START in 2023.

Putin's decision to suspend Russian participation in New START came in the context of the war in Ukraine, but it was not an isolated incident. Russia had already suspended participation in the CFE Treaty, signed by the USSR in 1990, after the fall of the Berlin Wall, and as the Cold War was coming to an end. In 2007, the year before the war in Georgia, Russia announced that it was pulling out of the treaty. In 2015, 'Russia finally withdrew from the Joint Consultative Group (JCG), the regular body responsible for the CFE accords'.[14] At midnight on 7 November 2023, the foreign ministry in Moscow published a statement saying Russia had completed the process for withdrawal from the treaty, which had thus 'become history for Russia once and for all'.[15]

This decision followed Western support for Ukraine in the face of Russia's full-scale invasion of 2022. It was the conclusion of a process during which Russia had considered the CFE Treaty unfit for its requirements in a world in which it was preparing to use military force, rather than diplomacy, to prevail in international disputes. Russia was not alone in withdrawing from international agreements. In late 2001, following the attacks on the US on 11 September, President George W. Bush announced that the US would withdraw from the Antiballistic Missile (ABM) Treaty signed with the USSR in 1972. Announcing the decision, Bush said he had 'concluded the ABM treaty hinders our government's ways to protect our people from future terrorist or rogue state missile attacks'.[16] In a sign of the more cordial relations that pertained then, Putin said in a television address that he believed the decision to be 'mistaken', but added, 'I can say with full confidence that the decision made by the President of the United States does not pose a threat to the national security of the Russian Federation.'[17]

There was no such cordial language when, in 2019, the US decided to withdraw from the Treaty on the Elimination of Intermediate-Range and Shorter-Range Missiles, known more usually as the INF Treaty. It had been signed by the US and the USSR in 1987. It required the destruction of cruise and ballistic missiles with a range of between 500 and 5,500 kilometres.[18] President Donald Trump had signalled Washington's intention to leave the treaty the year before. Speaking in October 2018, he accused Russia of having been 'violating' the agreement 'for many years'.[19] The following year, Trump's accusations were repeated by the US secretary of state, Mike Pompeo, when he announced that Washington would indeed withdraw. 'Russia is solely responsible for the treaty's demise', Pompeo said, accusing Moscow of having 'developed, produced, flight tested, and [. . .] now fielded multiple battalions of its noncompliant missile'.[20] Moscow's response was predictably sour. A statement from the Russian foreign ministry accused the US of 'launching a propaganda campaign based on deliberately misleading information', further charging that the US had itself violated the treaty. There was even a reference to Washington's earlier decision to withdraw from the ABM Treaty, 'despite insistent calls by the international community not to do so'.[21] The polite suggestion that a partner in international relations was making a mistake had given way to accusations that a would-be opponent was acting purely to suit itself.

The rhetoric of this propaganda campaign reflected spreading suspicion which in turn reflected a divergence of priorities during the period. There was one important contrast with the Cold War, when Washington and Moscow, bitterly divided by ideology, had not even pretended to see eye to eye. In a 2018 article, Sarah Bidgood noted that even at the height of the Cold War, 'US and Soviet leaders were able to overcome political challenges to cooperate closely on major non-proliferation and arms control achievements'.[22] This was not so in the less predictable times of the Putin era. It was not all about confrontation. At times, a genuine desire to leave behind the age of the Cold War arms race was celebrated. In 2005, it was possible to read a despatch from the ITAR-TASS news agency that began, 'A launch silo for an RS-20B Voyevoda (Satan in Western classification) ICBM was blown up in Chelyabinsk Region today.'[23] This was not, of course, the result of an enemy strike, but part of a programme to destroy the infrastructure built in case the Cold War became nuclear war. Trust took time to establish and was never fully consolidated, as an example from the 1990s shows.

In the summer of 1997, the *New York Times* reported, 'The Clinton Administration said today that Russia might have detonated a nuclear weapon on a remote Arctic island less than two weeks ago, in spite of its support for an international moratorium on nuclear tests.'[24] The island in question was Novaya Zemlya, off Russia's north coast, beyond the Arctic circle. Denials from Moscow swiftly followed, but they were not readily accepted. Only in October, after the director of the CIA, George Tenet, had 'commissioned a special panel to provide an independent assessment', did US intelligence conclude that 'the 16 August seismic event, which occurred approximately 130 kilometres southeast of the test site itself, was not nuclear in nature, and was almost certainly not associated with the activities at Novaya Zemlya'. However, Tenet also noted, 'there is strong evidence that weapons-related experiments were [redacted] performed in August'.[25] This conclusion duly appeared in the news media some days later. On 5 November, the *New York Times* printed an Associated Press wire that reported, 'Reversing itself, the

C.I.A. said today that a tremor detected in August near a Russian atomic test site was not a nuclear explosion.'[26] The incident, and the fact that the director of the CIA rapidly ordered an assessment, showed how potentially grave the consequences of the 'seismic event' might have been had it indeed been a Russian nuclear weapons test.

Such a test would have laid open to question Russia's signing of the Comprehensive Test Ban Treaty (CTBT), the 1996 international agreement that 'bans all nuclear explosions, whether for military or peaceful purposes'.[27] Both Washington and Moscow were signatories to the treaty, although only Russia subsequently ratified it.[28] The treaty is not only a framework for cooperation between the holders of the world's two biggest nuclear arsenals. It has also been a forum for unity, as in the case of condemnation of the nuclear tests carried out by North Korea.[29] Along with India and Pakistan, North Korea has not signed the CTBT. In October 2023, Russia withdrew its ratification of the treaty. On the day the Russian parliament passed the legislation revoking the earlier ratification, Reuters reported, 'Deputy Foreign Minister Sergei Ryabkov said Russia was not prepared to resume discussing nuclear issues with the U.S. unless Washington dropped its "hostile" policy.'[30] The statement on the Kremlin website on 2 November, when Putin signed the de-ratification into law, accused the US of 'the most destructive approach' of all countries that had not ratified the CTBT, and described Russia's decision as 'a response measure'.[31]

By that time, another nuclear weapons agreement, signed in less confrontational times, had come under scrutiny and criticism. When the USSR broke up, there were Soviet nuclear weapons on the territory of four of the newly independent countries that had once been republics of the USSR: the Russian Federation, Belarus, Kazakhstan and Ukraine. To limit the risk of parts of the Soviet nuclear stockpile falling into the hands of states desirous of establishing their own nuclear arsenals, or of terrorist groups, Belarus, Kazakhstan and Ukraine agreed to give up nuclear weapons. Ukraine's commitment to disarm was enshrined in what came to be known as the Budapest Memorandum, after the city in which it was signed by the US, the UK, the Russian Federation and Ukraine. In the agreement, the US, UK and Russia undertook to 'respect the independence and sovereignty and the existing borders of Ukraine'. The three also reaffirmed that 'none of their weapons will ever be used against Ukraine except in self-defense or otherwise in accordance with the Charter of the United Nations'.[32] It was a document drawn up in a time when the idea that Russia would seek to conquer Ukraine, and the US and the UK would arm Ukraine against the invader, was all but inconceivable.

One occasion during the Medvedev presidency when Putin really did leave responsibility for foreign policy to Medvedev proved to be especially consequential. In 2011 Western powers launched military action in Libya. That year, across the Middle East and North Africa, there had been uprisings against authoritarian and dictatorial regimes that were failing both to deliver a decent standard of living or to countenance any meaningful reform. While the causes of the uprisings – sometimes referred to collectively as the 'Arab Spring' – were many and longstanding, the immediate catalyst was unrest in Tunisia in late 2010. After Mohamed Bouazizi, a street vendor, set fire to himself (he later died of his injuries) in protest at police corruption and his treatment by law enforcement, large-scale political unrest followed. Zine El Abidine Ben Ali, president of Tunisia, was eventually forced from office. Demands for change spread to other countries, including Libya, ruled since 1969 by Muammar Qaddafi. There, the city of Benghazi – neglected by the regime, and a centre of opposition – saw widespread protests. In the words of Alison Pargeter, 'the years of systematic neglect meant that, by the time the Arab Spring arrived, Benghazi was on a knife-edge, ready to explode'.[33] When the protests did erupt, security forces fired on the crowds, killing more than 100 people and 'causing strong condemnation across the world'.[34]

Fearing that Qaddafi would send troops to suppress the rebellion and cause huge civilian casualties, Western governments, particularly those of France, the UK and the US, sought UN support for military action. On 17 March, the UN passed resolution 1973, allowing 'all necessary measures [. . .] to protect civilians and civilian populated areas under threat of attack in the Libyan Arab Jamahiriya, including Benghazi, while excluding a foreign occupation force of any form on any part of Libyan territory'.[35]

Russia did not vote for the resolution – but nor did it exercise its right, as a permanent member of the UN Security Council, to veto it. Such a move would have greatly undermined the legitimacy of military action. The Russian abstention removed a huge potential obstacle to Western powers going ahead with airstrikes on Libya.

The following week, Obama spoke on the telephone to Medvedev. The White House readout of the conversation reported that 'the two presidents discussed developments in the Middle East at length, with a particular focus on Libya. President Obama expressed his appreciation for Russia's support for the implementation of United Nations Security Council Resolution 1973 and subsequent positive statements that President Medvedev has made regarding the resolution's mandate.'[36]

The diplomatically worded White House statement, prepared for public consumption, did not tell the full story of what had gone on. Ashton later wrote that 'President Medvedev agreed with some of the analysis, but not all, sufficient to abstain but not to endorse'.[37] McFaul was even more frank. He recalled in a 2021 interview that he and then vice president Joe Biden had gone to Moscow ahead of the vote. 'We met with President Medvedev, and, shockingly to us – we were completely surprised by this – he agreed to abstain.'[38] It later became apparent that even this was a step too far. The Russian abstention on the Libya resolution was to have damaging and long-lasting effects on relations between the Kremlin and the West. It may also be seen as crucial moment in Medvedev's own political career: the moment when it started heading downwards.

Medvedev's decision not to veto the resolution infuriated Putin. As Brenton later put it, when recalling key points at which Russia's post-Cold War relations with the West had deteriorated, 'the Russians abstained on the Libya resolution in the security council, which Putin was incensed about'. It is not hard to see why. If the disastrous and bloody invasion of Iraq had in Putin's eyes destroyed any sense that he could really trust a US-led West, then Libya looked like it might be more of the same. If so, he was not alone in this analysis. In a 2024 interview, Ashton remembered, as Europe and the US sought a coordinated diplomatic and military response to the situation in Libya, 'a lot of opposition from the European member states, a lot of opposition, who saw all kinds of echoes of Iraq, and who feared that we were kind of moving into a war that we had not really thought about'. With two leading members of the EU, France and the UK (still then in the EU), at the forefront of the drive for military action, these misgivings were overcome – even if what followed in Libya, with no clear plan of what was to follow the military action, did vindicate the views of those who were wary and sceptical. Western military intervention did prevent Qaddafi's forces launching a major assault on Benghazi. It also emboldened his opponents. He was driven from power. In October 2011, after a convoy in which he was travelling was attacked by French warplanes, his enemies discovered him hiding in a drainage ditch and killed him. Video pictures of his final moments, and of his corpse being defiled, were widely shared. The Russians, and Putin in particular, felt that the US and its allies had deceived them, that the purpose of the operation in Libya had actually, from the start, been regime change. As Ashton said later: 'The Russians blamed the Americans, and specifically Hillary,[39] for persuading them to abstain: their argument being that the Americans had been clear that it was going to be stop Gaddafi taking Benghazi, and no further, that there will be no attempt to do anything to Gaddafi; that there would be no attempt to make dramatic changes in Libya. And on that basis, they say, Medvedev abstained.'

What unfolded was very different from what the Russians thought they had been led to expect. Within months of the passing of UN resolution 1973, not only was Qaddafi's regime finished, but he was dead – killed in an uncontrolled outbreak of political violence born of the rage his repressive regime had provoked. In telling Russia's UN representative to abstain, Medvedev had exercised his constitutional prerogative to decide on major matters of foreign policy – perhaps without seeking the approval of his mentor, and the man still widely seen as the real power in Russia. As Ashton said later of Medvedev, 'I don't know if he consulted Putin or not. But Putin was always furious about this. Always. It was visceral with him, he hated it. He hated the fact this had happened. And he felt betrayed by the West.' As Ashton pointed out, it had major consequences for cooperation between Russia and the West within the Security Council. In 2024, she estimated, 'they have vetoed more Security Council resolutions from that day to this than in the entire history of the UN from when it was created.' She added, 'The first ten years of that was mainly to do with Libya.'

Putin said nothing in public the day that the resolution passed. Four days later, with the first airstrikes having already been carried out, he was sharply critical of what had happened, and where he thought it might end. Speaking at a ballistic missile factory (the visit had presumably been planned before the UN Security Council debate, but the location suited Putin's message) in Votkinsk, some 1,200 kilometres east of Moscow, Putin said, 'The resolution is defective and flawed. It allows everything', Reuters reported. 'It resembles medieval calls for crusades.' Putin's evocation of war clashed with the mood of cooperation described in the White House's thanks to Medvedev days later. 'This is becoming a persistent tendency in U.S. policy', Putin added. 'During the Clinton era they bombed Belgrade, Bush sent forces into Afghanistan, then under an invented, false pretext they sent forces into Iraq, liquidated the entire Iraqi leadership – even children in Saddam Hussein's family died.'[40] The Clinton era, which was in its twilight when Putin actually came to power, cast a long shadow over his understanding of how Russia's relations with the West had unfolded since the fall of the USSR.

His remarks repeated Russian anger over regime change in Iraq – showing that, despite the 'reset', that anger had not been left in the past. It perhaps reflected Putin's fear that regime change was the US's true objective not just in Libya but everywhere it decided to intervene. Perhaps one day that might include Russia itself. Putin had known the Libyan dictator. The Russian journalist Mikhail Zygar wrote in his 2023 book *War and Punishment* that 'the footage of Gaddafi's death leaves a lasting impression on him. He becomes even more convinced that he must defend his power, or else the same fate beckons.'[41] Certainly, Putin seemed to hint at an eventual desire of the US's to remove him from power when he made reference to the military reforms launched after the war with Georgia. 'Today's events, including in Libya, confirmed our decisions on strengthening Russia's defense capabilities were correct.'[42] Putin's anger was not only directed at the US. By giving the US the opportunity to pursue this 'persistent tendency', as he called it, Medvedev too had fallen short. As Ashton pointed out, it is all but impossible to know from the outside whether or not Medvedev consulted Putin before authorising the abstention. Putin's first public remarks after the vote strongly suggest that he did not. In any case, this had happened when Medvedev was in charge, in name at least.

Just a couple of months later, in May the same year, there was a G8 meeting in Deauville, a resort on the Normandy coast of France. Missile defence was still a source of diplomatic tensions between the US and Russia. With both the Russian and US presidents due to attend the G8 summit, there was an opportunity to make a show at least of some kind of common approach. Russian and American teams worked hard to formulate one in the run-up to the meeting.[43] The furious work did not achieve the desired result. In the end, the US delegation decided to postpone making a statement. McFaul remembered 'real disappointment' from Medvedev when he heard the news. 'We had just handed the Russian president a defeat at the very moment when Medvedev believed Putin was deciding his fate.'[44] It may be that Medvedev's fate had already been decided. Putin's words in response to the start of the bombing campaign in Libya suggested he was dismayed with his protégé as well as the US. He could do little to change US policy, but he could once again take Russia's foreign policy very firmly into his own hands.

Towards the end of 2008, the year that Medvedev became president, the Russian constitution was amended to change the lengths of terms served by the head of state and of the parliament. A matter-of-fact statement appeared on the Kremlin website the day Medvedev signed the changes into law, 30 December, on the eve of Russia's long annual holiday for New Year, and Orthodox Christmas, which falls on 7 January. The amended constitution set 'the Presidential term as being six years, and the State Duma as five years (previously both the Presidential and Duma terms in office were four years). These changes affect any President and State Duma elected after the law is in force'.[45]

As Medvedev neared the end of his first, and only, four-year term, the significance of the change was made clear. In September 2011, addressing the United Russia party congress on the subject of upcoming elections, Medvedev announced, 'I think it's right that the party congress support the candidacy of the current prime minister, Vladimir Putin, in the role of the country's president.' There was no doubt Putin would win the election. Victory would give him at least six, and almost certainly twelve, more years as president. Medvedev's audience greeted his announcement with applause, which, he said, gave him the right to refrain from further elaborating on Vladimir Putin's experience and authority.'[46]

Putin prepared to return to the Kremlin in a Russia where living standards continued to rise. Russian government statistics covering this period show increasing numbers of Russians moving into higher income brackets.[47] Especially after the high inflation, unpaid salaries and general economic unpredictability that had made life so hard for millions of Russians in the decade after the collapse of communism, Putin's presiding over better times had delivered him reliably high popularity ratings and electoral success. There was an implicit deal with the electorate: give up some of the freedoms you enjoyed, and you can enjoy greater security and greater wealth. For Putin's first two terms in office, that worked. Putin had shown he understood what his electorate wanted, and had given it to them. The reaction to his intention to return to the Kremlin must therefore have surprised, if not shocked, him.

There was a warning when, in November 2011, Putin appeared in the ring of a martial arts contest in Moscow to congratulate the winner. Shortly after he began to speak, he was booed by large sections of the crowd – to the extent that their jeers were heard on the live television feed of the event. Even if Russian television did not dwell on the episode, it was widely viewed afterwards on YouTube, giving people who might have missed it live a chance to see the incident, whether Kremlin-wary editors on state television wanted them to or not.[48] Both Putin's public image and his administration's ability to control it had been damaged. These two factors were to be crucial in the Russian election season that lay ahead.

On 4 December, there were elections to the State Duma. United Russia received the largest share of the vote: 49.32 per cent, according to official figures, although this was down from the 64 per cent it had won in 2007. While it would be normal in many countries for an incumbent party to lose vote share, even while still winning the election, United Russia's Kremlin backers had left little to chance. A report by election monitors from the Organization for Security and Cooperation (OSCE) in Europe, published the following month, said of polling day, 'the quality of the process deteriorated considerably during the count, which was characterized by frequent procedural violations and instances of apparent manipulation, including several serious indications of ballot box stuffing'.[49] Interestingly, this seems to have had little effect on the overall result. Polling carried out by the Levada Center, respected for its surveys of Russian public opinion, carried out two weeks after the elections, came up with findings close to the official results. For example, 46 per cent of their respondents said they had voted for United Russia.[50] Those who had not cast their ballots for United Russia were not deceived. Even if the later findings of the Levada survey were accurate, it may be assumed that if the election observers saw ballot box stuffing, voters may well have done so, too.

The martial arts fans were not the only people ready to go public with their disapproval of Putin.

Earlier in 2011, Alexei Navalny, an anti-corruption campaigner, had described United Russia as a 'party of crooks and thieves'.[51] His phrase in Russian may also be translated as 'swindlers and thieves'. It was the perception that the political establishment had not only swindled the voters out of a fair election, but were also preparing to steal their right to have a real choice in the vote for president, that provoked widespread discontent. That was combined with the fact that even if living standards still continued to rise, members of the ruling party were increasingly seen as being out to line their own pockets. That is why Navalny's slogan found such a receptive audience. Its effects were felt beyond the websites and social media platforms where free expression in Russia continued to thrive, even as established media became less adventurous. In the wake of the election on 4 December, the activism spread from social media to the streets.

The following weekend, demonstrators gathered in towns and cities to protest against what they saw as an unfair election, and the fact that the next president had been in effect nominated by the current one, months before the vote was due to take place. They had four demands: the cancellation of the Duma election results; new elections; the resignation of the head of the central election commission, Vladimir Churov; and the release of protesters who had previously been detained. The biggest protest took place in Moscow. Perhaps not realising the strength of feeling, the authorities gave permission for the rally, held under the slogan 'For fair elections'.[52] They did, though, take the precaution of refusing the request for the rally to take place in Revolution Square, right in the city centre and very close to the Kremlin. Instead, the demonstrators were allowed to assemble only on condition that they did so on Bolotnaya Square, on an island in the Moskva River. The location meant that the police had the ability to control entry and exit from the area more easily. The authorities took the further precaution of deploying 'at least 50,000 police and riot troops'.[53]

Exact numbers at demonstrations are always hard to establish. As the BBC reported at the time, the organisers claimed a crowd of 100,000, with the police saying the number was a quarter of that.[54] What did seem to be beyond dispute was that this was the biggest demonstration Moscow had seen since the end of the Soviet period. Russia's middle classes had been stirred from the complacency that had come with better salaries, and access to consumer goods and foreign travel on which to spend those better salaries. These newly politicised professionals joined a range of other activists who had been leading the longer-term, if much smaller, movement for political change in Russia. The leader of the fringe National Bolshevik Party, 'Eduard Limonov, bitterly complained that his revolution had been stolen', *The Economist* reported.[55] The protest was on a scale, and over a social and geographical expanse, quite unlike anything that had occurred in the Putin era. If Zygar's words about Putin's response to the deposing and death of Qaddafi are to be believed, then this demonstration, coming only weeks after the killing of Libya's former dictator, may have alarmed him as he prepared to return to the Kremlin.

The demonstrators had in effect broken their side of the deal Putin had implicitly made with the people of Russia: accept limits on your political freedom, on your freedom of expression, and, in return, you can expect security and good salaries. The numbers who took to the streets that afternoon suggested that the discontent was not a passing phase. It was a clear and very public rejection of the kind of political system Putin was still in the process of constructing for Russia. It happened right when he was preparing for a key stage in that process, his own return to the Kremlin. Putin's own remarks at that time showed that he did not believe that this was the popular protest it seemed to be. Even before the Bolotnaya Square demonstration, he had drawn his own conclusions, deciding that the US was behind the protest. On 8 December, he accused Hillary Clinton directly. 'She set the tone for some actors in our country and gave them a signal', Putin said of the US secretary of state. 'They heard the signal and with the support of the U.S. State Department began active work.'[56] When, two days later, tens of thousands of people came out to protest, Putin must have felt that his suspicions – and his fears of regime change – were confirmed.

Alexei Navalny was not on Bolotnaya Square that afternoon. He was in gaol. There had been a smaller demonstration on 5 December the day after the Duma elections. While those taking part had been given permission to gather, they had not been allowed – as they subsequently tried to do – to march on the headquarters of the Central Election Commission. Police detained three hundred of them. Navalny was sentenced to fifteen days, but he was aware of what happened on 10 December. His blog post on his release radiated his trademark energy, enthusiasm, wit and defiance. 'We were inside for 15 days in one country, and came out in another', he wrote on LiveJournal. He was scornful of the state media, and the riot police, known in Russian as the OMON. 'The TV doesn't impress anyone, the OMON especially don't scare anyone.' The phrase in Russian had the ring of a jaunty rhyme.[57] He concluded by urging his supporters to attend the next demonstration, due to take place on 24 December.[58] They listened. That protest, on Sakharov Avenue (named for the Soviet-era dissident Andrei Sakharov) gathered an even larger crowd than the one two weeks earlier, despite temperatures well below freezing as the Russian winter was near its coldest. Navalny's biographers cited figures of 30,000 as the police estimate, and more than 100,000 according to the organisers.[59] The demonstrations were not confined to Moscow. They included people with a wide range of political opinions. Many had not protested before. 'This was so amazing,' remembered one, Tanya from Perm, 'you saw that there are so many like-minded people.'[60]

It was not enough to effect change. The elections were not re-run. Putin did stand for president again when the election took place the following March. The month before polling day, he addressed a large crowd at Luzhniki Stadium. The police said 130,000 people were there – perhaps a rare case of the authorities overestimating the numbers at a political meeting. Media reports suggested that the stadium was almost full, however (although some present told the BBC that they had either been paid or told they were being offered a free trip to a concert). For the rally, Putin chose a national holiday, 'Defenders of the Fatherland Day', when the nation's men, especially those who serve or have served in the armed forces, are honoured. He returned to his theme of Russia being under threat from outside forces. 'We will not allow anyone to interfere in our affairs, to force their will on us', he said, adding, 'Because we have our own will. We are a victor nation. It's in our genes.' He reinforced his historical patriotic theme by quoting verses from the nineteenth-century poet Mikhail Lermontov about the Battle of Borodino, during the Napoleonic wars.[61] The 200th anniversary of the battle would fall later that year. Putin was keen to reinforce the message of triumph over foreign invaders, for he saw the hand of their contemporary equivalents behind the protests that challenged his right to rule Russia.

When the presidential election took place on 4 March, Putin won comfortably, avoiding the need for a second round of voting. He received 63.6 per cent of the vote. His closest rival was the seasoned communist leader Gennady Zyuganov, with 17 per cent. Mikhail Prokhorov, a billionaire businessman who ran as an independent candidate, came third with just under 8 per cent.[62] Having attended the 24 December rally, he was the closest there was to an opposition candidate – although he had to deny suggestions that Kremlin spin doctors had persuaded him to run. In an interview with Radio Free Europe/Radio Liberty in the January before the election, he outlined some of his campaign promises, including commitments to pardon Khodorkovsky, re-instate direct elections for governors (this reform did actually follow) and cancel the extension of the presidential term to six years.[63]

More protests followed the results, but Putin had survived the most serious challenge to his authority since he first became president in 2000. Not everyone was convinced by the manner in which he did so. The OSCE report wrote of the conduct of the election, 'The process deteriorated clearly during the count, which was assessed negatively in nearly one-third of polling stations observed due to procedural irregularities.'[64] The US State Department issued a statement congratulating the Russian people on the completion of the election but also noted 'the OSCE's concerns about the conditions under which the campaign was conducted, the partisan use of government resources, and procedural irregularities on election day, among other issues'.[65]

Nothing in the international observers' report, or the US's muted congratulations on the result, suggested that the outcome of the election had not been a true reflection of the will of the Russian people. The demonstrations were large – by the standards of Russia's post-Soviet history, the largest seen – but did not achieve the kind of mass or impact to change Putin's plans. As one research paper published in 2013 by the political scientists Paul Chaisty and Stephen Whitefield noted, 'the Russian protests took place in the absence of significant elite defection – a fact that of course may explain why protest has to date failed to dislodge the regime'.[66] Putin still remained genuinely popular and would almost certainly have managed to win a free election had one been held, but already little was being left to chance. The election of 2012 did represent an interesting change in Russia's political geography. 'The area of electoral support for Putin in 2012 was finally shifted to the sociocultural periphery of Russia, where public life, mass media, and political activity were suppressed by the authoritative style of governance', wrote the Russian geographer Dmitry Oreshkin, noting that this was the 'antipode' of the support that Yeltsin had enjoyed in 1996, when he 'was mainly given the highest level of support in large cities'.[67] The excitement that the protests inspired among those Russians most wanting change allowed them to believe that it must come. 'In the winter of 2012 I am absolutely certain that Putin has only a few months left in power: civil society in Russia is getting stronger, and he will not be able to crush it', wrote Zygar in his 2023 book on Russia and Ukraine. He compared his feeling then to that which he 'first felt in Kyiv on the Maidan in 2004'.[68] Zygar was referring to the Orange

Revolution: inspirational to Putin's opponents; the stuff of nightmares for Putin. When Putin returned to the Kremlin in 2012, that revolution turned out to be unfinished. Its next chapter would draw Russia and the West into confrontation as never before since the end of the Cold War.

8

'Crimea Is Historically Russian Land'

On 21 May 2008, Moscow hosted the final of the UEFA (Union of European Football Associations) Champions League. For the first time, it was contested between two English teams, Manchester United and Chelsea. Because of the time difference (kick-off time was fixed with European television schedules in mind), the match, which went to extra time and penalties, did not finish until the early hours of the next morning. The English supporters were welcomed to the Russian capital by unusually polite riot police. Visa restrictions were relaxed to make the trip easier for travelling fans. They did not all go home happy. Chelsea supporters were naturally disappointed to see their team lose. But the Russian capital had proved a welcoming venue for a major international sporting occasion.

It was a test run for what was to come. The previous summer, Russia had been awarded the right to host the 2014 Winter Olympics. The venue, perhaps surprisingly, was Russia's warmest city: Sochi, on the coast of the Black Sea. More normally known as a summer holiday resort, Sochi had won for a bid that combined indoor facilities in the town itself with venues for skiing, snowboarding and other events at a resort some 50 kilometres away in the Caucasus mountains. The International Olympic Committee had come to see the facilities the year before. They had been impressed enough to make the award. Days before their February 2007 visit, Putin himself turned up to test out the ski slopes. Such obvious public support from the most powerful man in the country cannot have harmed the bid. The following July, the games were duly awarded to Sochi. The Champions League final served as a rehearsal for Russia's biggest international sporting event since the USSR hosted the Olympics in Moscow in 1980. By showing up in Sochi to demonstrate his commitment to the bid, Putin had also made it clear how important the Olympic games were to Russia as he was rebuilding it: strong, confident and respected. Weeks after the Champions League final, much of this soft power success was squandered, in Western eyes at least, when Russia went to war in Georgia.

The Olympics took place as planned in Sochi in February 2014. Despite the games going way over budget, and reportedly costing over $50 billion,[1] making them the most expensive Olympics ever, they were a sporting success. Russia topped the medals table, with twenty-nine.[2] But the attempt to polish Russia's international image was tarnished by protests around the world at legislation Russia had passed the previous year that made it illegal to provide information on homosexuality to people under eighteen. Putin himself was untroubled by criticism. The month before the games opened, the BBC reported that he had told a meeting of volunteers who were preparing to work at the games, ' "We don't have a ban on non-traditional sexual relations [. . .] We have a ban on promoting homosexuality and paedophilia among minors." '[3] Human Rights Watch argued that such remarks by 'Russian officials embolden homophobes and their violent attacks by persistently equating homosexuality with pedophilia'.[4] Yet this kind of discourse, like the legislation on which it was based, was the beginning of another of the elements of Russia's Putin-era identity that Putin was seeking to build. His use of the term 'non-traditional' was instructive. Russia was to define itself as the guardian of conservative values as opposed to the – in Putin's view – decadent tolerance of the EU and wider Western world.

A more serious form of confrontation was soon to follow. The 2008 Champions League final had been followed weeks later by war in Georgia. The 2014 Winter Olympics had not even ended when political tensions in Ukraine exploded. The events that unfolded in the first part of 2014 changed Ukraine's government and its de facto borders. It also placed the country at the centre of a conflict between Russia and the West that eventually and irrevocably marked the end of post-Cold War good will and cooperation.

During the autumn of 2013, Ukraine had been moving towards signing an association agreement with the EU. This would not offer Ukraine membership, at least in the short term, but it would, as the agreed text stated, 'promote gradual rapprochement between the Parties based on common values and close and privileged links, and increasing Ukraine's association with EU policies and participation in programmes and agencies'.[5] There would be increased trade. There was the prospect 'in due course' of visa-free travel for Ukrainians to EU countries. It may not have been an offer of membership, but it was a step along that road. It was also a clear indication, on the part of this country at the crossroads of Europe, of the direction in which it saw its future. The agreement was due to be signed at an EU meeting in Vilnius in late November. When the time came, the president of Ukraine, Victor Yanukovych, refused to put his name to the agreement. He said he needed more time.

Yanukovych was in a difficult situation. The political challenge he faced mirrored his country's geography within Europe: bordered on one side by the EU; on the other by Russia. In a less confrontational international environment, this might have been a blessing. In the twentieth century, it had been a curse. Ukraine lay in the 'bloodlands', as the historian Timothy Snyder's book so aptly put it.[6] Since the end of the USSR, Ukraine had tried to turn its location to its advantage. The gas wars with Russia, and consequences for European supply, showed just how difficult that was. Especially imaginative leadership might have managed to find a solution. Yanukovych failed to do so. He could not balance the desire of many in his country to move towards eventual EU membership with the loss of trade with Russia that might mean. Ashton, who in her capacity as the EU's High Representative for Foreign Affairs and Security Policy was at the summit, remembered a sense that Yanukovych 'was more and more looking to Moscow. He was not a strong character in that sense. And I was always told that the Russians didn't think very highly of him.' There is certainly evidence of indecisiveness. A special report by Elizabeth Piper of Reuters news agency, published in December 2013 in the aftermath of Yanukovych's decision not to sign the agreement, revealed a meeting that the Ukrainian president had called of his political party some months earlier, in September. When Yanukovych was faced with protests from businessmen worried about the consequences for trade with Russia, Piper reported, ' "We will pursue integration with Europe," he barked back, according to three people who attended the meeting. He seemed dead set on looking west.'[7]

When news reached Ukraine of Yanukovych's refusal to sign, there were protests, initially in the capital, Kyiv, and the western city of Lviv. The protesters' demands grew with time to include a demand that Yanukovych and the government resign. The protests became known as Euromaidan, after the central square, Maidan Nezalezhnosti (Independence), in Kyiv where the demonstrators gathered. As the protests continued, in the face of the president and government's continuing refusal to agree to their demands to quit, the security forces tried by force to break the demonstrators' will. 'The protests were characterized by violence and excessive use of force by the police and other law enforcement agencies', a UN report later concluded. In January and February 2014, '108 protestors and other individuals and 13 law enforcement officers' were killed.[8] Eventually, facing impeachment on 22 February, Yanukovych fled. Putin later said that Russia had helped him to escape.[9] In the view of both Putin and Yanukovych, the Ukrainian president had been driven from office by a coup d'état. To the victorious protesters, it became known as the 'Revolution of Dignity'.

Ashton, who in her capacity as the EU's High Representative was a frequent visitor to Kyiv during the period of revolutionary unrest, remembered 'a real sense of impending chaos. And an absolute feeling that Yanukovych had no sympathy with what was happening.' The US was also keeping a close eye on events as they unfolded. While the EU and the US generally had much common ground, there was uncertainty over which Ukrainian opposition figures to support in the confusion that followed Yanukovych's flight. At one point earlier in February, the US assistant secretary of state, Victoria Nuland, had apparently expressed her frustration with the EU in a telephone conversation with the US ambassador to Ukraine, Geoffrey Pyatt. An alleged recording of the conversation, the authenticity of which the State Department did not dispute, was later leaked and published on YouTube. 'Fuck the EU,' Nuland, exasperated, was heard to say.[10]

There was no such confusion as far as Russia was concerned, even as events unfolded with head-spinning speed. 'Things were disintegrating. And we weren't, we weren't able to stop it,' Ashton recalled in a later interview. 'Because in order to stop that, you need a government, you need people willing to stop it. And he [Yanukovych] wasn't prepared to. And you moved quite quickly onto the shooting of people in the square, then Yanukovych disappearing.' It was, she said, 'that turmoil in which I think Russia saw an opportunity'. It was an opportunity that Putin took.

After the bloodshed in Kyiv, and Yanukovych's escape, many of those members of the security forces who had used violence to protect his presidency fled the capital too, among them, members of the Berkut, a force of riot police that had grown out of the Soviet-era OMON (their Russian counterparts having retained that name). Some of them returned to their base in Crimea. They arrived in Sevastopol on 22 February. 'Their bus stopped in the middle of town, where they were treated as heroes and given flowers.'[11] In the coming days, they appear to have formed a majority of the masked men who took over the Crimean parliament.[12] The takeover of the parliament was the start of a much larger military operation. On the night of 27–28 February, troops, without insignia, moved in to take over Crimea. One source from March 2014 claimed that, the day before, 'Russian naval ships, which had returned from Sochi to Sevastopol, landed more than one thousand men on the peninsula'.[13] If so, the ships must have been returning from security duty at the Winter Olympics, which had finished on 23 February – a direct link between the soft power of staging an international sporting event and the hard power of supporting a seizure of territory. Those Ukrainian troops who were stationed in Crimea did not attempt to prevent the invasion. They 'did not get any orders'.[14]

Crimea was taken from Ukraine. The identity of those who had captured it was hardly in doubt, of course. A lack of military insignia was not sufficient to disguise Russian uniforms and weapons – and the fact that the new arrivals also spoke Russian. They were variously referred to at the time as 'little green men' and 'polite people', or simply ordinary Crimeans who had formed volunteer forces to demand independence. Even Putin himself abandoned these pretences in April that year, during his 'Direct Line with Vladimir Putin' – an annual live phone-in carried by all major state TV and radio channels. 'Of course, the Russian servicemen did back the Crimean self-defence forces. They acted in a civil but a decisive and professional manner, as I've already said.'[15]

By the time Putin held his annual marathon conversation with the Russian Federation, it had acquired new territory: illegally, by force of arms, in the eyes of the West; in the eyes of the Kremlin, legally, as a consequence of a military operation and a referendum. The referendum was staged a little over two weeks after the 'little green men' had made their appearance. Voting took place on Sunday 16 March. The result given by election officials in the territory was 96.77 per cent in favour of Crimea becoming part of Russia.[16] Western reactions were predictable, with both the EU and the US quick to dismiss the vote. A statement from the White House rejected 'the "referendum" that took place today in the Crimean region of Ukraine' – the punctuation designed to show disdain; the word order designed to restate Ukrainian sovereignty. Western refusals to recognise the result were given weight by the rapidity with which the vote had been organised and held. The number of votes cast for union with Russia – just shy of 97 per cent – also put the result in the company of the kind of figures usually achieved by autocrats seeking to extend their terms in office without the inconvenience of offering the electorate a genuine choice. The White House statement also declared the vote to have been 'administered under threats of violence and intimidation from a Russian military intervention that violates international law'.[17]

None of this made the slightest difference to Putin. The annexation complete and – whatever protests might follow – irreversible for the foreseeable future, the executive order recognising Russia's new reality was signed the following day.[18] The day after that, 17 March 2014, Putin addressed members of the Russian parliament and heads of the Russian regions in the Kremlin. The detail, length and depth of Putin's speech suggested that it had been long in the making – as, perhaps, had the plan to annex Crimea. When the anti-government protesters had prevailed in Kyiv, or, in Putin's words, 'Nationalists, neo-Nazis, Russophobes and anti-Semites executed this coup',[19] Putin swiftly reacted, according to the authoritative political analyst and former Soviet army officer Dmitry Trenin, 'putting in motion contingency plans that Moscow had drafted for the eventuality' of Kyiv seeking NATO membership'.[20] In that sense, Crimea had been a newer, more ambitious, version of the war with Georgia in 2008. The Russian leadership had waited until the conditions were right to strike, and done so. On both occasions, Moscow's actions had successfully thwarted the NATO ambitions of those countries given promised membership in Bucharest in 2008. In the case of Crimea, Russia had gone a step beyond recognising the breakaway territory as independent. Crimea had actually been absorbed into Russia.

In his speech, Putin showed his skill at understanding his domestic political audience. He emphasised Russia's historical connection with Crimea. He set out themes to which he would enthusiastically return in the coming years as his interpretation of history increasingly served to justify Russia's actions in international affairs, especially where going to war was concerned. Referring to the medieval monarch of Kyivan Rus who first adopted Christianity, Putin recalled that Crimea was where 'Prince Vladimir was baptised. His spiritual feat of adopting Orthodoxy predetermined the overall basis of the culture, civilisation and human values that unite the peoples of Russia, Ukraine and Belarus.' The key word here is 'unite'. While it might seem to be an expression of cooperation and friendship between peoples, it was at the same time a reflection of Putin's view that such unity, in which Orthodox Christianity was the binding force, was stronger than any separate, modern, political identity. Putin continued, 'The graves of Russian soldiers whose bravery brought Crimea into the Russian empire are also in Crimea', later reassuring his audience, 'Crimea is historically Russian land and Sevastopol is a Russian city'. That the land could be both historically Russian and brought by soldiers into the Russian empire was not seen as contradictory. In a sense, as Richard Sakwa noted in *Frontline Ukraine*, this was a revival of the idea of Novorossiya, which between 1764 and 1917 was 'a distinct administrative unit of the Russian Empire along the entire Black Sea coast from Transnistria in the west to Mariupol in the east, and to this day remains predominantly Russian-speaking'.[21] The idea chimed well with the intellectual movement that supported this reborn Russian nationalism. As Charles Clover pointed out, it was Alexander Dugin, the nationalist writer and thinker, who first used the term in reference to eastern Ukraine – before the occupation of territory, and before Putin himself used the word.[22]

Putin did not limit his historical analysis to the distant past. He brought his analysis up to date. 'Now, many years later, I heard residents of Crimea say that back in 1991 they were handed over like a sack of potatoes.' The reference was to the inclusion of Crimea within Ukraine when the USSR broke up. Since imperial conquest, the region had been part of Russia until the then Soviet leader, Nikita Khrushchev, handed it to Ukraine in 1954. At the time, it was a largely symbolic gesture. Both

Russia and Ukraine were part of the USSR, so the territory remained under Moscow's overall control – until 1991. 'What about Russia?' Putin went on. 'It humbly accepted the situation. This country was going through such hard times then that realistically it was incapable of protecting its interests. However, the people could not reconcile them-selves to this outrageous historical injustice.'[23] With military subterfuge while a neighbour was caught up in political chaos, and a few strokes of a presidential pen, that 'outrageous historical injustice had been reversed'. Putin not only gained territory. His popularity – already high enough to make many Western politicians deeply envious – skyrocketed. In June 2013, it had been 63 per cent. By June the following year, after the annexation of Crimea, it stood at 86 per cent – and would remain at a similar level for years to come.[24] Samuel Greene and Graeme Robertson, who conducted their own surveys in Russia during this era, found that the number of people in their group expressing anger at Russia's leaders fell by half, to 18 per cent. The annexation of Crimea, they persuasively argued in their 2019 book, *Putin v. the People*, 'was evidence of Russia's turnaround that was hard for Russian patriots to ignore'.[25]

The world had changed. The statement from the White House responding to the result of the Crimea referendum included the words: 'In this century, we are long past the days when the international community will stand quietly by while one country forcibly seizes the territory of another.' Putin simply ignored such cautions, and did so without suffering serious consequences. The annexation of Crimea complete, other regions in eastern Ukraine became battlegrounds as the central government struggled to retain control. One of the Maidan protesters' main demands was met in 2014, however. Ukraine did sign the Association Agreement with the EU. In May, Ukraine held presiden-tial elections. Petro Poroshenko, a wealthy businessman who also had a long political pedigree including working with Victor Yushchenko, who had come to the presidency following the 2004 Orange Revolution, was the winner. Poroshenko took up office as separatist forces in the regions of Donetsk and Luhansk (Lugansk in its Russian spelling) prepared to challenge the authority of the government in Kyiv. War in Ukraine had not ended with the annexation of Crimea: it had begun. In the summer of 2014, the fighting would cause a tragedy that became a major international incident.

As Putin had made clear in his moment of triumph announcing the annexation of Crimea, the ideology behind Russia's actions was based on a notion that Russia, Ukraine and Belarus were united; they were one. That being so, Russia saw itself as having a right to a say in what happened in Ukraine. One of the points that Russian officials frequently emphasised during this period of the start of the war in Ukraine was that of language. In late March, the Russian foreign minister, Sergei Lavrov, met the US secretary of state, John Kerry, in Paris. In the aftermath of the annexation of Crimea, there was still an understanding on both sides that the diplomatic process needed to continue even if Russia's action, as the White House suggested, was not something that could be accepted in the twenty-first century. There was almost no common ground. The statements that Kerry and Lavrov made afterwards, however, demonstrated the differences between the US and Russia on Ukraine – ones that would persist through the changing nature of the conflict, and changing administrations in the US. There was no similar change in Russia, of course. Ten years later, the Russian foreign minister and Russian president were the same as they had been during the start of the war in Ukraine in 2014.

Both Kerry and Lavrov spoke to journalists after their meeting, although they did not do so together. In a media age when many more people would see pictures than read either man's remarks, images were of supreme importance. In a political moment where Russia had broken the post-Second World War consensus that European borders were not changed by invasion, Kerry probably did not wish to be photographed or filmed with his Russian counterpart. Both emphasised the importance of Ukraine being left to decide its own future. Lavrov said, however, 'We are convinced that federalisation is a vital component', on the grounds that 'the West, the East and the South advocate fairly contradictory values. For this country to function as a single state, a compromise between each and all the regions, which are now part of Ukraine, should be found.' Kerry noted that Lavrov had 'indicated that Russia wants to respect the right of Ukrainians' to make the choice over their country's future. He continued, 'It's not up to us to make any decision or any agreement regarding federalization'.[26] For Russia at that time, this was the solution, that which was proposed in public at least. But Moscow's willingness to annex territory as it had just done undermined its credibility. Lavrov also mentioned language. In his opening remarks, he referred to 'such priority tasks like ensuring the rights of national minorities, language rights'. He later returned to the subject. 'Ukrainian national identity still has to be strengthened. I do not think that this process can be sustainable, if the fact that Russian is the second main language in Ukraine is ignored.' Despite saying, as Kerry did, that Ukrainians must themselves decide the future of their country, much that Lavrov said undermined this. He argued that 'the history of modern Ukraine is before your eyes, when each presidential and parliamentary election is accompanied by a change of the constitution. This is another confirmation that the model of a unitary state is not working there.'

Lavrov made these remarks less than two weeks after the annexation of Crimea. If the unitary state was not working, annexing part of that state was Russia's solution. His words reflected the enduring belief, among changing Russian political elites, that Ukraine could not really exist as a country without Russia. If it did so, Russia had at least to be involved. Lavrov concluded, 'only an agreement about respect for each region with its traditions, customs, culture and language, will ensure the unity and sustainability of the Ukrainian state'.[27] Yet Russia had just acted, with military force, directly against the unity and stability of Ukraine. Lavrov's references to language are significant. For most people in southern and eastern Ukraine, Russian, not Ukrainian, is the first language. Frequent mention of language was an important part of establishing Russia's right to act as it did. Lavrov's comments in Paris echoed the ideas set out by Putin, albeit in a drier tone, more suited to public diplomacy, than the epoch-making historical rhetoric that Putin permitted himself in the gilded halls of the Kremlin. Putin's words – on Orthodox Christian 'culture, civilisation and human values' – echoed the concept of 'Russky Mir'.

The most obvious literal, but not the only, translation of 'Russky Mir' is 'Russian World'. It is the name given to a foundation established by presidential decree in 2007, according to the English-language version of its website, for the purpose of 'promoting the Russian language, as Russia's national heritage and a significant aspect of Russian and world culture, and supporting Russian language teaching programs abroad'.[28] In that sense, it is similar to cultural institutes operated by many countries in many other countries around the world. In the political climate of the time, Russky Mir was more than that. Along with the Russia Today TV channel, it was part of a wider ideological, propaganda and media support network for Russian foreign policy. The word 'mir' has other meanings in Russian, one of which is community. The third, as one of the most senior figures involved in setting up the organisation reminded me when I, then correspondent in Moscow, discussed it with them in 2007, is 'peace'.

Even with Crimea secured for Moscow, there would not be peace. The most serious confrontation between Russia and the West since the end of the Cold War had begun, and now continued. In the days before the referendum held in Crimea, Russia had assembled thousands of troops in regions neighbouring Ukraine. The German chancellor, Angela Merkel, in a speech in the Bundestag, also evoked history. Hers, though, was not a story of imperial glory, but of a bloodier era of Europe's past: 'It is in this context, fellow members of this House, first in Georgia back in 2008 and now in the heart of Europe, in Ukraine, that we are witnessing a conflict about spheres of influence and territorial claims, such as those we know from the 19th and 20th century but thought we had put behind us.' Merkel was also clear Russia's actions in Ukraine should not lead to wider war. 'The conflict cannot be resolved by military means. I say to everyone who is worried and concerned: military action is not an option for us.'[29]

158

It was an option for Russia, though not directly. Before his talks with Kerry in Paris at the end of March, Lavrov had been quoted as telling Russian TV that his country had no intention of sending troops into Ukraine.[30] Years later Russia would do that in massive numbers – but for now they continued the war by other means: targeting their efforts in regions bordering Russia and where they thought they could undermine the Kyiv government politically and militarily. The focus was the Donbas, an area in the east of the country, its name derived from the Donets which flows through the region. It is best known for its heavy industry, especially coal mining. The main city, Donetsk, has previously been called Yuzovka (Yuzivka in Ukrainian), after John Hughes, a Welsh businessman who in the nineteenth century founded coal mines and a steel plant there. It was later named for the twentieth-century Soviet dictator, Josef Stalin. From 1961, it became Donetsk. As with many places on former Soviet territory, the history of the city's name reflected the political changes it had lived through. Now, though, Russia sought to make the Donbas – formed of the regions of Donetsk and Luhansk – a centre of opposition to the Kyiv government. Geographically, this made sense. Politically, even if this was a region Putin saw as part of historically Russian territory, less so. As the Ukraine scholar, Andrew Wilson, has pointed out, 'According to a massive opinion poll conducted throughout eastern and southern Ukraine in April 2014, a mere 15.4 per cent as a whole supported separatism and union with Russia (7.1 per cent definitely; 8.3 per cent more or less). The figure was higher but still only 27.5 per cent in Donetsk and 30.3 per cent in Luhansk 11.9 per cent and 13.2 per cent definitely.'[31]

The Donbas was where the war continued to spread. As Wilson put it, 'The Donbas leaders copied the Crimean scenario by announcing their own "referendum" for 11 May'.[32] The result, according to a leaked phone call, was fixed at 89 per cent in favour of separatism – and, given it was arranged in advance, this proved easy to achieve.[33] Military action followed, with units crossing the borders – although these were always claimed to be irregulars, and Russian officialdom persistently denied any formal involvement of the Russian army. Any serving Russian personnel who might be there were said to have gone there while on leave. Such claims were undermined by media reports, including one by the BBC's Steve Rosenberg and colleagues, which told the story of a woman whose soldier brother had been killed 'in military exercises on the border with Ukraine'. The woman, named in the report as Oksana, said the official who gave her the news admitted that he himself did not believe that version of events.[34] The Ukrainian government sent troops to crush the rebellion. Donetsk airport, rebuilt to gleaming contemporary standards as part of the infrastructure improvements that came with Ukraine's joint hosting with Poland of the 2012 European football championships, was reduced to rubble by early 2015. Thousands of people were killed – 'At least 6,417' between mid-April 2014 and the end of May 2015, according to a UN report published in June 2015. The report itself said that these figures were 'a conservative estimate' and that the actual numbers could be 'considerably higher'.[35] It is customary, and usually superfluous, for media reports to describe wars as brutal. The brutality of this conflict merited some emphasis. The UN recorded accounts of torture and summary execution committed by both the separatist fighters and Ukrainian government forces. Diplomatic considerations – though not, apparently, lack of evidence – meant that the report did not positively conclude that the Russian army was directly involved. It did note, though, that 'reports of sophisticated heavy weaponry and fighters being supplied from the Russian Federation persisted'.

Heavy weaponry caused the tragedy that became a major international incident. On 17 July 2014, Malaysian airlines flight MH17 from Amsterdam, bound for Kuala Lumpur, was shot down over eastern Ukraine. All 283 passengers and 15 crew on board were killed. The separatist forces denied any involvement. The investigative website Bellingcat, working from social media posts and other open-source material, concluded that the fatal missile had been fired from a Buk launcher (a system originally developed during the Soviet period, and later still manufactured in Russia) situated in separatist-held territory. Their investigation tracked the mobile launcher's movement on the day the flight was shot down.[36] Their conclusions were largely confirmed by a Dutch court case which ended in November 2022. The trial found three members of the command of the 'Donetsk People's Republic' (the name the separatists gave to their region following their 'referendum') armed groups guilty of murder. The three, Leonid Kharchenko, Sergei Dubinskiy, and Igor Girkin, a former FSB colonel, were found guilty in absentia of 298 murders. They were sentenced to life imprisonment. A fourth defendant, Oleg Pulatov, was acquitted.[37] Girkin was later sentenced to four years' gaol in Russia – but not for his involvement in the shooting down of MH17. He was found guilty of 'inciting extremism'.[38] This is a consequence of his criticism of the conduct of the conflict in Ukraine. He was one of those prominent, pro-war voices who felt that Russia was not being sufficiently forceful in the way it prosecuted the war.

While Western opinion was united in outrage at the mass killing of civilians, the Russian propaganda machine went to work. Various different versions of what might have happened to MH17 (including suggestions such as that the Ukrainian armed forces had shot down the flight believing it was Putin's own plane, or that the bodies, seen in media footage, strewn across the crash site were not actually of people killed in the disaster[39]) were spread across Russian legacy and social media platforms. The aim was to undermine versions of the crash that had been reported in the international media and accepted by Western governments. It seemed to work. A Levada Center poll conducted in Russia's major cities from 18 to 24 July suggested that 82 per cent believed that the Ukrainian armed forces had shot down MH17, either from a missile launcher or from a warplane. Only 3 per cent thought 'Donbas volunteers' were responsible.[40]

If Russia had had no direct involvement in the conflict in Donbas, then there would have been no need to promote narratives that deflected blame from the separatists. Bellingcat concluded that 'there was a very high probability' that the missile launcher their research traced had arrived in the area in a military convoy from the Russian city of Kursk the previous month.[41] Whether or not that was so, the Dutch investigation agreed with their conclusion that the missile had been fired by separatists. Russia's support for the separatists – covert or overt – would be much harder to justify if it were accepted that the separatists were to blame for almost 300 civilian deaths. So the confusion had to be spread. It was a logical continuation of the disinformation about the 'little green men'. During his phone-in, Putin had owned up to that lie. Now, as the war in Ukraine continued, the Russian leadership promoted false or confusing narratives to deflect blame from their proxies over the shooting down of MH17. At the end of July, Lavrov gave a news conference in Moscow. He held it, he said at the beginning, in response to multiple requests for interviews. After lengthy complaints about sanctions that had been imposed on Russia following the disaster, he turned to the subject of the 'Malaysian Boeing': 'It seems that now, ten days later, some pictures are published. What did they do to them during all this time – did they cut them into pieces or not – we do not know. We would prefer honest work rather than the aspiration to search of a reason to punish Russia or even return to the deterrence policy.'[42]

Lavrov was speaking a week after Obama had accused Russia of failing to use its influence to stop separatist fighters obstructing the work of crash investigators. Obama asked, referring to the rebels, 'What exactly are they trying to hide?' Obama accused Putin of having 'direct responsibility' for the fighters on the ground, on the basis that 'Russia has extraordinary influence over these separatists'. Obama warned that unless Russia compelled the rebel groups to cooperate with investigators, it faced greater isolation.[43]

Moscow had already been isolated in some senses. At the end of March, the other seven members of the G8 group had suspended Russia in response to the annexation of Crimea. The timing of the suspension was made more diplomatically embarrassing by the fact that the group's next summit had been due to take place in Sochi in the summer after the annexation. It was held in Brussels instead, without Russia. In 2017, the Kremlin spokesman, Dmitry Peskov, said the idea that Russia might return was 'not being discussed in Moscow in any way'.[44] Russia did not return. It was only eight years since Putin had welcomed his fellow G8 leaders to his home city of Saint Petersburg. That kind of international prestige had been supplanted by another: the glory of conquest. Putin's approval ratings showed that he had understood what was more likely to please his compatriots.

Yet there was greater isolation, too. Both the US and the EU imposed sanctions on named individuals, including close advisers to Putin. Among them was his adviser, Vladislav Surkov – although, according to Zygar, in the case of Surkov censure from the West 'dramatically rescued'[45] his Kremlin career, which was on the slide. In his news conference, Lavrov tried his best to be dismissive, suggesting in his 28 July news conference that Russia's 'western partners' must have 'had a wish to adopt as many sanctions as possible before the August period of vacations, so that they can have a rest then. This all looks artificial.'[46] It was not so artificial that Russia did not respond. In retaliation for the EU sanctions, Russia imposed an embargo on food imports from the bloc, a move that the EU calculated affected €5.1 billion worth of goods. The bloc was able to find other markets for some, but not all, of the affected produce.[47]

Alongside embargoes and sanctions, there was a political process. As the UN noted, thousands of people were dying in the war in eastern Ukraine. The first concerted attempt to stem the bloodshed took the form of talks, held in Geneva on 17 April 2014, involving diplomats from Ukraine, Russia, the EU and the US. The meeting succeeded to the extent that it 'agreed on initial concrete steps to de-escalate tensions and restore security for all citizens', the first of these being, 'All sides must refrain from any violence, intimidation or provocative actions'. The agreement foresaw a special role for the OSCE. 'It was agreed that the OSCE Special Monitoring Mission should play a leading role in assisting Ukrainian authorities and local communities in the immediate implementation of these de-escalation measures wherever they are needed most.'[48] As the political scientist Paul D'Anieri later pointed out, this 'intervened in Ukraine's constitutional process, where Russia strongly supported decentralization'.[49] This was a provision in tune with Lavrov's remarks earlier in the year about federalisation. Despite the commitment to end the violence, the fighting continued and, with the downing of MH17, brought the conflict to international attention in the bloodiest of ways.

More talks followed after leaders had gathered on 6 June to commemorate the seventieth anniversary of the Normandy landings. This was the start of the 'Normandy Process', between Ukraine, Russia, Germany and France. The US was not involved. Nor, perhaps more surprisingly, was the UK. The UK was still then a member of the EU, but was not to be a member of the group that tried to find a solution to what would become the biggest security threat to Europe since the war in which the Normandy landings had been such a decisive moment.

This was followed in September by the Minsk protocol, named for the capital of Belarus in which it was signed, and later referred to as 'Minsk-1' to distinguish it from its successor, signed the following year. 'Minsk-1' did, as D'Anieri has written, 'achieve its immediate aim, which was to consolidate a decrease in the violence'.[50] Longer term, the Minsk protocols were less successful. As Duncan Allen pointed out in a paper for the London-based international affairs research institute, Chatham House, in 2020, 'The Minsk agreements rest on two irreconcilable interpretations of Ukraine's sovereignty: is Ukraine sovereign, as Ukrainians insist, or should its sovereignty be limited, as Russia demands?'[51] This contradiction, which Allan named 'The Minsk Conundrum', proved beyond diplomatic resolution.

Short-term success could not hide longer-term threat. As the annexation of Crimea was underway in March, the secretary general of NATO, Anders Fogh Rasmussen, called a meeting of the North Atlantic Council, the alliance's main political decision-making body. 'What Russia is doing now in Ukraine violates the principles of the United

Nations Charter. It threatens peace and security in Europe. Russia must stop its military activities and its threats', Rasmussen said.[52] At the end of the meeting, on 5 March, Rasmussen announced a series of measures that the alliance would take in response to Russian actions in Crimea. These included putting 'the entire range of NATO–Russia cooperation under review'. Rasmussen did add, 'we do want to keep the door open for political dialogue. So we are ready to maintain meetings of ambassadors in the NATO–Russia Council, as we have done today.'[53]

Rasmussen's term as NATO secretary general was coming to an end. His successor was going to have an even more difficult time with Russia, but he had been proposed for the role precisely because of his long-term experience of dealing with the country. Jens Stoltenberg took up his post in the autumn of 2014. He remained in office until October 2024. As he recalled in a 2023 interview, he had first met Putin in 2000: the year Stoltenberg became prime minister of his native Norway and Putin became president of Russia. Stoltenberg recalled meeting a leader who spoke in a way that 'was to the point. It was rational. It was logical while some of the former Russian leaders I met, spoke in a totally different way.' He added, 'And then of course, it reflected also the kind of optimism we had at that time.'[54] Stoltenberg's long-term understanding of Russia had included, during his political career in his native Norway, meetings with a KGB agent stationed in the Soviet embassy in Oslo.[55] Being leader of a smaller country that shared a border with Russia, as well as having this long-term understanding of the country, helped Stoltenberg's candidacy. 'Chancellor Merkel, but also President Obama, one of the reasons that they told me that they picked me was my relationship with Russia over a long period of time.' The leaders of the big NATO member states, who wielded the greatest influence over the appointment of the secretary general, chose Stoltenberg anticipating a time when NATO and Russia would continue to work more closely together. Of his appointment, Stoltenberg said, 'Of course, my experience working with Russians fitted very well into the idea that we should expand, continue our cooperation. So early [20]14, NATO leaders didn't foresee the illegal annexation of Crimea. So I was appointed under very different circumstances than I met when I took my job in October, the same year.'

What followed was not an expansion of cooperation, but an expansion of defences, and a boosting of NATO defence budgets: 'After years of cutting defence budgets all NATO allies started to increase the defence budgets. For the first time in our history, we decided to deploy combat troops in the eastern part of the line – so the battle groups in the Baltic countries; we developed new defence plans.' Of the year he came to office, he said, 'So 2014 triggered this big change of NATO.'

It had triggered a big change in Europe, too: a change the full consequences of which would be more widely understood only years later. The borders of a European country had been changed by military force rather than by referendum and consequent legislation. The Russian foreign ministry would dispute that. The Russian foreign ministry would argue that there was a legitimate referendum followed by a legal process. But 'little green men' have no place in such a process. Their presence negated its validity.

The Western response to the annexation of Crimea did not reverse the conquest. It did not stop further military action. War followed in Donbas. 'At the seizure of Crimea time, our reaction, in retrospect, was insufficient', Brenton, the former British ambassador to Moscow later concluded. Stoltenberg said in the 2023 interview, 'Maybe we should have sent a clearer message back in 2008', when Russia went to war against Georgia. Manning later argued that, 'because Ukraine was in a grey zone, it's very hard to see what the West would have done differently'. Of Ukraine, he said: 'Ukraine has no fixed place in the European Security System. One of the things that disappeared at the end of the Cold War was the accepted, if often tacit, "rules of the road" that applied to relations between Moscow and Washington. In my view, Ukraine will only have an assured future, and a stable and settled relationship with Russia and its neighbours, when it is in the EU and NATO.'

The Ukrainian leadership during the Crimea crisis, and every Ukrainian leadership since, would agree. Reflecting later on the period she remembered as 'having a real sense of impending chaos', Ashton wondered if the EU had lost sight of the true significance of what unfolded in Ukraine that winter and spring:

> I think the criticism I would lay at our door was that we had turned something that was deeply political into a technical process, suddenly a negotiation about things or institutions or money or whatever. So the right people to do that were working on it. All the technical people were working on it and doing a brilliant job. It was done. It was initialled all of it was done. And somehow the politics of what this all meant, didn't surface.

Hill pointed out that – for all Putin's warning's about NATO's enlargement menacing Russia – it was Ukraine's desire eventually to join the EU that ignited this crisis, citing: 'his belief that Ukraine belongs to Russia, and whether it's NATO, or whether it's the European Union, it's a problem for him – because remember the annexation of Crimea comes in 2014, right after Ukraine is close to an agreement with the EU, and that's got nothing to do with the role of the United States.' Membership of any Western-led international organisation was seen as a threat to Russia. Hill also emphasised the importance of the influence Putin's view of history had on his actions: 'Putin thinks about this in all of these terms, and that's all embedded in his speeches. And our problem is we keep losing *his* plot. And he keeps seeing the same kind of plot ongoing in the U.S. and we never recognize how he's interpreting everything.'

In the case of the annexation of Crimea, Putin saw an opportunity and rapidly executed a plan possibly long prepared for the time when such an opportunity would come along. Western responses, in the form of criticism and sanctions, did nothing to deter Russia from continuing the conflict in Ukraine. The Donbas now became like a pot full of water just below boiling point: Putin could turn up or turn down the heat under the pot at will, threatening the government in Kyiv with a situation that could boil over if he so decided. Ukraine had got its association agreement. Putin had got part of Ukraine and, along with new territory he had called 'historically Russian land', a boost to his popularity at home that would encourage him to go even further.

Russia Marches Back onto the World Stage

The Russian nationalist politician Vladimir Zhirinovsky's many bizarre and publicity-seeking pronouncements included the fact that he dreamt of the day 'when Russian soldiers can wash their boots in the warm waters of the Indian Ocean'.[1] His vision was of a revived Russian Empire: respected; feared; a peer or superior of devious Western powers; a source of patriotic pride at home. Zhirinovsky died in 2022. His Indian Ocean dream did not come true, but he did live to see Russian soldiers on the shores of the Mediterranean, part of a military intervention in the Middle East to change the course of the biggest armed conflict that followed the Arab uprisings in early 2011.

In annexing Crimea, Putin had shown his strength, and his skill in understanding his constituency. While the West raged at the changing of a European border by military force, Putin's approval ratings soared to heights many Western leaders would not even dare to dream of. Emboldened by his success, and sensing a Western policy vacuum in Syria, Putin's next move was to intervene decisively in the Syrian civil war. Military and media resources were marshalled to show that Russia was a reliable ally that would not let down a friend such as Syrian president Bashar al-Assad – that Russia would prosecute a successful war in the Middle East after the US had failed in Iraq.

When mass demonstrations demanding reform or even revolution spread across the Middle East and North Africa in early 2011, President Assad was among the leaders facing demands for change. A generation earlier, the Syrian state had shown unflinching ruthlessness in putting down a rebellion by the Muslim Brotherhood in the city of Hama. Syria's president then was Assad's father, Hafez al-Assad. When the 2011 demonstrations did not die down but continued to grow, and were eventually accompanied by an armed insurgency, Assad the younger showed that he had inherited some of his father's ruthlessness. Attempts at a negotiated peace all failed. Syria was soon at war with itself.

The US had long made its view on the conflict clear. As early as August 2011, Obama had said, 'Assad must go'.[2] There was also a view at the time, widely held, including, as McFaul later wrote, within the US government, that Assad could not last. 'But then Assad did not fall. Our judgments about his weakness were incorrect.'[3] If US attempts to remake Iraq by military force influenced Russia's view of what should happen in Syria, then the fiasco that military campaign became also cast a shadow over Western policy. Despite concerns over the growing numbers of civilian dead, those Western countries who had gone to war in Iraq showed no desire to do the same in Syria. 'We must now explore all options to support the opposition to enable greater support for the protection of civilians,' the British prime minister, David Cameron, said in December 2012.[4] The options being considered did not include major military intervention.

Four months earlier, the White House press secretary, Jay Carney, had said to reporters during a West Wing briefing room, 'Looks like there's a surprise guest here.' According to the official transcript, Obama's opening comment, 'Jay tells me that you guys have been missing me', prompted laughter. Obama began with some remarks on Medicare, the US federal health insurance programme. But it was his response to a question about policy on Syria for which the meeting with the news media was remembered rather than the meeting's light-hearted beginning. The journalist Chuck Todd asked Obama whether he was confident that the chemical weapons that Syria was known to possess were safe. In his reply, Obama said, 'I have, at this point, not ordered military engagement in the situation.' He then added: 'We have been very clear to the Assad regime, but also to other players on the ground, that a red line for us is we start seeing a whole bunch of chemical weapons moving around or being utilized. That would change my calculus. That would change my equation.'[5]

A year later, there was a chemical weapons attack in the Ghouta region, east of Damascus. More than 1,000 people were reported killed. The US and the EU, which then included the UK, believed that government forces were responsible. The UN confirmed that chemical weapons had been used. Their investigation, based on evidence collected later in August, found evidence of the use of sarin.[6] Syria and Russia suggested opposition forces had staged the attack.

The US was convinced that the 'red line' that Obama had set out the year before had been crossed. Speaking on 30 August, Kerry claimed that the US knew that the missiles carrying the deadly chemicals had only been launched from regime-held areas. Not all the information that the US had, he said, was made public, 'in order to protect sources and methods'. Kerry continued, 'And our choice today has great consequences [. . .] It matters because a lot of other countries, whose policy has challenged these international norms, are watching. They are watching. They want to see whether the United States and our friends mean what we say.'[7] He seemed to be preparing the US, and the rest of the world, for military action in response to the Assad regime's use of chemical weapons.

It did not happen. McFaul later wrote that Obama 'did not want to take this step alone', but the US also knew that Russia would veto any UN Security Council resolution to authorise the use of force. According to McFaul, 'Some proposed that Obama ask NATO, as President Clinton had before the bombing campaign against Serbia in 1999, but that idea fizzled out when the British parliament stunned us all by voting against the use of force.'[8] Instead, the crisis led to an agreement, on which the US and Russia, together with others, cooperated on the removal and destruction of Syria's chemical weapons. There was one sour note struck in the aftermath of the annexation of Crimea, when Russia was excluded from a naval escort for the US ship *Cape Ray*, which was to 'neutralise' the weapons.[9] The process was declared complete in August 2014.[10] In that sense, the agreement was a success. McFaul later conceded, however, that 'Obama paid a reputational price, in both the United States and the world. He had drawn a red line, but then did not act when Assad crossed it.'[11] Bristow, at that time the British Foreign and Commonwealth's Director for National Security, and future ambassador to Moscow, expressed in a 2023 interview the view that Syria had been very important for 'the West setting its red lines over use of chemical weapons, and other atrocities, and then not enforcing them – which is understood in the Kremlin as a signal weakness, a signal of lack of resolve, just inability to stand up for your own interests'. For Russia, on the other hand, success was judged to have gone beyond that inherent in reducing Assad's chemical arsenal. In Dmitry Trenin's view, in his article of July 2014, the agreement meant Russia was being treated as the diplomatic heavyweight equal of the US, as the USSR had been. This was a moment that redefined Moscow and Washington's relationship: 'The need to come up with a joint U.S.-Russian plan to rid Syria of chemical weapons led to arguably the first eye-to-eye discussions between U.S. and Russian representatives since the downfall of the Soviet Union. In discussions in Geneva, Switzerland, Russia essentially won back the diplomatic parity with the United States that it had lost in the early 1990s.'[12]

Moscow's role in the Syrian war was shaped by the place it had had in the world since its loss of superpower status. In that sense, there were echoes of older, Soviet policies in the region. The historian Sergei Radchenko has described the Soviets rebuilding 'the militaries of their Arab clients, battered in the 1967 war against Israel, while fearing all the same that another showdown could yet lead to a new defeat, with all that meant for Soviet prestige and credibility as a superpower'.[13] Now in his third term as Russian president, Putin sensed an opportunity to regain some of that 'credibility as a superpower', to make Russia a major force on the world stage again, as the USSR had been in the second half of the previous century. During the Cold War, Moscow and Damascus had been close. As the Russia and Eurasia expert Roy Allison pointed out in 2013, 'this Cold War relationship was based on strategic interdependence rather than ideology', and yet, in the mid-1970s, Soviet military advisers were 'more numerous in Syria than anywhere else in the world'. As late as 2006, up to 2,000 Russian military advisers were still thought to be serving in Syria.[14] So there was a certain symbolism to Russia's decision to intervene: an echo of Moscow's history as the Soviet superpower. But there was also a strong sense of the present, and of an opportunity to build a role in international affairs for the future.

For if Iraq and the so-called colour revolutions had filled Putin and his administration with horror – not only in the chaotic downfall of friendly regimes, but also because of the implication it might happen one day in the Kremlin – here was a chance to bring about a different outcome. In its foreign policy concept published in 2013, Russia had made clear its opposition to military intervention without a UN mandate (knowing, of course, that as a permanent member of the Security Council it would always have the opportunity to veto any such intervention). The foreign policy concept stated, 'Another risk to world peace and stability is presented by attempts to manage crises through unilateral sanctions and other coercive measures, including armed aggression, outside the framework of the UN Security Council.' The document mentioned, in particular, that 'some concepts that are being implemented are aimed at overthrowing legitimate authorities in sovereign states under the pretext of protecting civilian population'.[15] This document pre-dated Euromaidan but followed the Arab uprisings of 2011, and it was published as Assad struggled to gain the upper hand against his opponents in Syria – and also struggled against the expectation among the US political elite that he would not prevail. Two years after the publication of the 2013 foreign policy concept, and with Assad's fate still in the balance, Putin spoke at the UN General Assembly.

The UN was marking its seventieth anniversary, and Putin opened his speech with a historical reference to when the USSR had enjoyed its moment of supreme military triumph as one of the victors in the war against Hitler's Germany. 'In 1945, the countries that defeated Nazism joined their efforts to lay a solid foundation for the postwar world order.' Putin's words grew bolder as he focused on one issue in particular that had defined and inspired the foreign policy of his time in power: NATO. Having noted that the Warsaw Pact 'had ceased to exist', he continued:

Nevertheless, NATO has kept on expanding, together with its military infrastructure. Next, the post-Soviet states were forced to face a false choice between joining the West and carrying on with the East. Sooner or later, this logic of confrontation was bound to spark off a major geopolitical crisis. And that is exactly what happened in Ukraine, where the people's widespread frustration with the government was used for instigating a coup d'état from abroad. This has triggered a civil war.

Putin's analysis would not countenance the possibility that popular discontent had itself been the principal factor behind the fall of Yanukovych's presidency. Rather, in his view, this discontent had itself been exploited by external powers bent on exploiting the situation for their own undefined ends.

Before turning on NATO, Putin had discussed the situation in the Middle East. The terms in which he did so drew parallels between what he saw as the causes of war in Ukraine, and the deadly lawlessness that had plagued Iraq in the aftermath of the 2003 invasion, when, he argued, 'aggressive intervention rashly destroyed government institutions and the local way of life. Instead of democracy and progress, there

1. President Boris Yeltsin (left) of Russia and President Bill Clinton of the United States pictured in 1995. The two leaders' good personal relationship was often obvious when they appeared in public together – though behind the scenes many in the Russian elite remained suspicious of their former Cold War foe.

2. Muscovites buy bread at a state-owned bakery in downtown Moscow, 12 January 1993. The massive inflation that followed the end of the Soviet Communist Party's planned economy caused great hardship for many Russians. Older people, whose pensions lost most of their purchasing power, were especially badly affected.

3. On Monday 4 October 1993, Muscovites watch the smoke billowing from the parliament building in Moscow during the assault by the Russian army. President Yeltsin ordered the attack against parliamentarians and their supporters after a political confrontation escalated into armed conflict.

4. Unburied bodies in a field on the outskirts of Grozny, the main city in Chechnya, April 1995. Tens of thousands of civilians were among those killed after the Russian army went to war against the separatist rebels in the Chechen Republic in late 1994.

5. Conscript soldiers pose for a photograph in Grozny, March 2000. As Russian prime minister from the summer of 1999, Vladimir Putin built his political reputation on his tough line against Chechen rebels when the second Chechen war broke out in the autumn of that year.

6. With Boris Yeltsin looking on, Vladimir Putin takes the oath of office as president of the Russian Federation for the first time, in May 2000. Putin came to the presidency as a relative unknown, but his decades at the summit of Russian power defined the country's politics, and its relations with the West.

7. Putin at the state funeral of Boris Yeltsin, with his wife Lyudmila and former US presidents Bill Clinton and George H.W. Bush, Moscow, April 2007. Putin was by now in the final year of his second term as president, though he would return in 2012.

8. The Cathedral of Christ the Saviour in Moscow. Demolished in the 1930s as the Soviet state sought to stamp out religious worship, it was rebuilt in the 1990s as Russia embraced Orthodox Christianity as part of its post-Soviet identity.

9 *(top left)*. A column of Russian armoured vehicles, headed towards the breakaway republic of South Ossetia's capital Tskhinvali, is seen in North Ossetia, Russia, Friday 8 August 2008. The Georgian government's hopes of taking back control of South Ossetia were crushed when Russia launched an invasion in support of the separatists.

10 *(top right)*. The Millionaire Fair in Moscow, 2009. All kinds of luxury goods were on display, from fur coats and jewellery to sports cars and helicopters. The Millionaire Fairs were popular gatherings for Russia's emerging class of new rich, people who had amassed their fortunes during the 1990s and early 2000s.

11 *(above)*. Putin on the ship *Solitaire* in the Gulf of Finland, 200 kilometres west of Saint Petersburg, 20 September 2010. Putin was visiting part of the Nord Stream gas pipeline, then under construction. Nord Stream was built to supply gas from Russia to Germany under the Baltic Sea, bypassing transit countries.

12. US President Barack Obama and Putin at the G8 summit in Enniskillen, Northern Ireland, June 2013. The following March, Russia invaded Crimea and later annexed the territory from Ukraine. In consequence, Russia was expelled from the G8.

13. The Mamayev Kurgan war memorial, Volgograd, March 2019. The site honours Soviet forces killed during the Battle of Stalingrad, as Volgograd was known during the Second World War.

14. An aerial view of Volgograd, showing the *Motherland Calls* monument. The statue of Mother Russia imagines her urging Soviet forces onto the offensive against Nazi invaders.

15. The Volgograd Arena, one of the football stadiums built for the World Cup in 2018, when the tournament was hosted by Russia.

16. Flowers and placards placed in tribute to the murdered Russian politician, Boris Nemtsov. This photograph, from 2019, was taken shortly after the fourth anniversary of his assassination, at the site, close to the Kremlin, where he was shot dead on 27 February 2015.

17. Stonework in the centre of Saint Petersburg, showing damage from German shelling of the city, then called Leningrad, during the Second World War. Putin, who was born in Leningrad, has made remembrance and celebration of Soviet victory a key part of twenty-first-century Russian politics.

is now violence, poverty, social disasters and total disregard for human rights, including even the right to life.' In particular, he highlighted the rise of militant groups as a consequence: 'The so-called Islamic State has tens of thousands of militants fighting for it, including former Iraqi soldiers who were left on the street after the 2003 invasion.' Putin's section on the Middle East came right up to the present time: 'And now radical groups are joined by members of the so-called "moderate" Syrian opposition backed by the West. They get weapons and training, and then they defect and join the so-called Islamic State.' The single theme was clear: the West was to blame both for the war in Ukraine, and for the wars in the Middle East. Russia, respecting international law, advocated a new approach: one that did not involve the removal of Assad. Putin framed it in a way that recalled previous Western interventions that had removed leaders but failed in the longer term. 'Above all,' he said, 'I believe it is of utmost importance to help restore government institutions in Libya, support the new government of Iraq, and provide comprehensive assistance to the legitimate government of Syria.'[16]

Two days later, the defence ministry in Moscow published a short statement entitled 'Russian aviation performed high-accuracy strikes against international terrorist organization ISIS'. The statement claimed, 'All targets have been successfully engaged.' Russia had intervened in the Syrian civil war on the side of the government, a military intervention that would prove as decisive for the future of Assad, at least for the coming decade, as the US and its allies' wars on Iraq and Libya had proved for the leaders of those countries. The difference in this case was that the intervention was aimed at keeping the leader in power. There were echoes – presumably deliberate in a media-saturated age – of the way the US and other Western powers had presented their own interventions. The Russian defence ministry web page that carried the statement also had an embedded YouTube video showing the strikes hitting their targets.[17] Not only could Russia also intervene in the Middle East, it could borrow the propaganda techniques previously used by the US, too. The video went on to be viewed more than

5 million times.[18] Russia was adapting Western media techniques in order to emphasise that it could do the same – as well, if not better. While this competition was largely contested in propaganda and diplomacy, there was at least one occasion when it became an exchange of fire. In 2018, American forces sent to Syria to fight so-called Islamic State became involved in a battle with pro-regime forces, later reported to include Russian mercenaries.[19] The Russian fighters were with Wagner, the 'private military company' later to become infamous for its activities in Africa, and especially in Ukraine.

Even if Putin had spoken at the UN in terms of 'assistance to the legitimate government of Syria', Russia was keen to stress a different message once its military campaign was underway. The emphasis was placed on the fact that this was an attack on the 'international terrorist organization ISIS'. While the US and its Western allies disagreed on the future of Assad, none of the major international powers wanted the so-called Islamic State to prosper. This enabled Russia to try to portray itself as a leader in an international coalition against international terrorism: a new kind of 'war on terror', as George W. Bush had characterised the US's response to 9/11, but one where Russia was a global leader, and where chaos did not ensue. As Jade McGlynn concluded on the basis of her extensive analysis of the Russian media coverage of the intervention in Syria, 'Russian media were more interested in the geopolitical angle than events on the ground. Put simply, they cared more about how Syria made them look than how Syria itself looked.'[20] It did not always make Russia look good. As Russian assistance, together with that of another Syrian ally, Iran, led Assad's government increasingly to gain the upper hand in the civil war, their superior firepower was misused to hit civilian targets in areas that had dared to challenge the regime. A UN report published in 2021 concluded that 'both the Syrian military and the Russian air force attacked civilian neighbourhoods, including crowded markets during the day, with explosive bombs with wide-area effects, killing and injuring civilians in attacks that amounted to war crimes'.[21] Anyone who had survived the furious and indiscriminate bombing of Chechnya in the two wars fought there would have recognised this description. Having won those wars in the Russian Federation, the Russian armed forces were expanding and exporting the same tactics with murderous effect beyond Russian borders. International censure made little difference.

From the Russian point of view, this had been a success. Russia had launched a military campaign to protect an ally and achieved its objective. It had dealt with the US as an equal in the Middle East. It had been treated as the USSR might have been in the days of superpower rivalry. Putin had followed popular success with the annexation of Crimea with military success in the international arena. That last point was especially significant. For the US had sought to take the shine off the annexation of Crimea not only by sanctions and public condemnation but also with stinging rhetoric aimed at belittling Russia itself. In a news conference in March 2014, the month Russia annexed Crimea, Obama had described Russia as a 'regional power' that was threatening its neighbours, 'not out of strength but out of weakness'. In the same news conference, Obama also suggested that the annexation itself was 'not a done deal', an assertion that has been undermined by the passage of time.[22]

Obama's dismissive remarks notwithstanding, the intervention in Syria was useful to the Kremlin in that it came at a time when success abroad was useful domestically. Putin's foreign policy in this era was motivated, as we have seen, by ideas of Russia's being an equal of the US, enjoying the same level of influence in international affairs. To do this, Russia needed to show that it was a reliable ally, as in Syria. There, the policy was to keep those Russia judged to be 'legitimate authorities in sovereign states' in power, rather than seeing them overthrown. Any human rights abuses they may have committed were a secondary consideration, rendered irrelevant by the given regime's 'legitimacy'. These international policies had their domestic counterpart. In the late 1990s, when he rose to power, Putin had understood that what most people in Russia craved, rather than the chaotic liberty that had come with the end of communism, was stability and a degree of prosperity. In the early 2000s, thanks in part to rising oil prices, he was able to deliver this. The implicit contract with the people stipulated that, in return, they would accept curbs on freedom of expression and political freedom. When standards of living ceased to rise, Putin was in danger of not keeping his side of the bargain. His fear of sharing the fate of Saddam Hussein, Muammar Qaddafi or even Viktor Yanukovych meant that any kind of protest might be seen as the beginnings of an existential threat.

If the years 2014 and 2015 brought success on the battlefield, the same was not true for the Russian economy. In the second half of 2014, the year that Russia annexed Crimea, oil prices fell dramatically. The Organization of the Petroleum Exporting Countries (OPEC), the oil producers' cartel, described the effect as the 'longest losing streak since the 2008 financial crisis'. Russia was not in OPEC, but it did count on oil exports all the same, and it was in no way immune. In December 2013, OPEC's 'reference basket' – the average price for its producer countries – was $107.67.[23] Twelve months later, that had fallen to $59.46.[24] Sanctions, and the counter-sanctions in the form of the ban on food imports from the EU, also had an effect on the Russian economy. Economists were not convinced by the Russian Central Bank's handling of new realities. 'The Russian Central Bank's mistakes led to powerful turbulence in the foreign currency market and to a drop of exchange rate of [the] ruble from 33–35 rubles per dollar to 50–60 rubles per dollar', concluded a paper from the Russian Academy of Sciences' Institute of Economic Forecasting published in early 2015.[25] That weaker exchange rate meant higher prices on imported goods for those Russian consumers who had come to be used to them in the decade and a half since the end of the scarcities of the Soviet era. Later that year, the Russian economy went into recession, only returning to growth in 2016, by 0.2 per cent.[26] Such is the importance of the oil price to the Russian economy that the annual budget is based on the expected value of a barrel of oil. In December 2015, Putin said that the budget had been prepared on the basis of oil at $50. At the time, it was trading at $30.[27] As recession loomed in late 2014, Putin had showed his populist touch. Russia had become used to enjoying a long New Year holiday, beginning on 1 January and taking in Orthodox Christmas on 7 January, with the next official working day being 10 January. That year, Putin told government officials that they should be working, rather than taking a long break, because of the economic crisis.[28] It was not enough. Recession did follow in the New Year.

So too did a shocking political murder. The killing in 2006 of the journalist Anna Politkovskaya had shown that words were enough to get you shot in Russia. The shooting of Boris Nemtsov in February 2015 took Russia's post-Soviet political violence to a new extreme. Nemtsov had once been a deputy prime minister during Yeltsin's presidency, one of a number of young liberals dedicated to taking Russia in a new direction, and given a government portfolio. When Nemtsov was still only in his early thirties, Yeltsin appointed him governor of the Nizhny Novgorod Oblast. His youth, and lack of history in the Soviet political system, meant he was a representative of a new kind of political elite in a new kind of political system. He was also a representative of a different kind of political system than the one that was eventually established in Russia. His career in government did not last into the Putin era. Out of favour, Nemtsov had become an implacable critic of the political direction his country had taken. He was a prominent participant in opposition demonstrations. He focused his protests on the pillars of the Putin presidency: in particular, the Sochi Olympics and the war in Ukraine (although he was murdered a full seven years before the huge escalation of that war in February 2022).

As noted previously, the Sochi Olympics were the most expensive ever. In May 2013, the year before the games, Nemtsov and his fellow opposition leader, Leonid Martynyuk, had declared the games 'a monstrous scam'.[29] Nemtsov and Martynyuk said that they had initially been among the millions of Russians who 'rejoiced' on learning in 2007 that their country had been awarded the right to host the 2014 Winter

Olympics – but their report was a tale of disappointment and alarm, not celebration. They alleged that as much as $30 billion had been stolen during the preparations for the games. 'In effect,' said a translation of their report, 'the Sochi Olympics have highlighted the main flaws of Putin's system in a nutshell: Lawlessness, corruption, high-handedness, cronyism, incompetence, and irresponsibility.'[30] Such views were hardly welcome in the patriotic and internationally powerful atmosphere that Putin was trying to create, and of which hosting an international sporting event was such an important part.

Nemtsov also distinguished himself with his high profile, and principled, opposition to the war in Ukraine. On the day that he was shot, he had been appealing for support for a demonstration, that was due to take place the following Sunday, against the war.[31] His murder was planned as a terrifying and bloody spectacle, designed by those who orchestrated and executed it to have maximum effect on the public imagination. Nemtsov was shot late on a Friday evening on a bridge across the Moskva River right in the city centre. The place where he was killed affords such a good view of the Kremlin, and St Basil's Cathedral, that it is quite common to see Muscovites and tourists alike taking pictures there. The last time I was able to visit, in March 2019, was shortly after the fourth anniversary of Nemtsov's death. The flowers placed there then looked relatively new, presumably having been laid there on the anniversary, and kept fresh by the chill damp of the end of the Moscow winter. Placards bore Nemtsov's name and image – and noted the nature of his death. 'On this spot, 27.02.2015, with shots in the back, was murdered Boris Nemtsov.' Nemtsov was indeed shot in the back by an attacker firing from a car, according to police quoted in media reports at the time.

To the sorrow and shock of Nemtsov's supporters and admirers were added official condolences from the Kremlin. The text of a telegram that Putin had sent to Nemtsov's mother, Dina, was published on the Kremlin website. Putin expressed his 'deepest condolences' and said he shared Nemtsov's mother's grief. He noted that Nemtsov had worked in 'significant posts during the difficult transition period for our country'. The message concluded with a pledge that everything would be done to make sure that those responsible received the punishment they deserved.[32] Five men of Chechen origin were later convicted of killing Nemtsov and jailed. Yet an investigation by the BBC, Bellingcat and The Insider, published in 2022, found that, in the run-up to his death, Nemtsov 'was being followed across Russia by a government agent linked to a secret assassination squad'. The investigation, based on data that the Russian authorities hold on train and air passengers, named an agent of the FSB, who had tracked Nemtsov's movements. The last time this had happened was just ten days before Nemtsov was shot.[33]

Nemtsov had said, in an interview earlier in February, that he feared Putin might have him killed, 'but not that much'.[34] The Kremlin has always denied having anything to do with Nemtsov's murder, but the investigation cited above strongly hinted at some level of official involvement. At the time of his death, Nemtsov was not only campaigning against the war in Ukraine but also, with allies in the Russian opposition movement such as Ilya Yashin, investigating and recording the deaths of Russian servicemen in Ukraine – this at a time when any such Russian military presence, at least beyond recently annexed Crimea, was denied. In May 2015, three months after Nemtsov's murder, a report that he had participated in preparing was published. It claimed that 220 Russian soldiers had been killed in Ukraine. Presenting the findings, Yashin said, 'We cannot say that Nemtsov was killed over the preparation of this report, but we cannot rule that out.'[35] Boris Nemtsov had been a leading member of a new generation of Russian politicians that grew out of communism's chaotic collapse, but never finally flourished. His last political act was campaigning against a war that would eventually mark the end of any remaining good relations between Russia and the West.

There were still at this time important areas of cooperation, though: especially on Iran's nuclear programme. That had been growing for years until, in the autumn of 2013, the country appeared, in the view of the arms control expert Mark Fitzpatrick, 'to be on the brink of becoming a nuclear-armed state'.[36] As the EU's senior foreign policy official from 2009 to 2014, it fell to Catherine Ashton to chair and lead the international negotiations on Iran's nuclear programme. These talks had begun in 2003, the year after Iran's nuclear programme had first come to light, and had been followed by extensive sanctions aimed at stopping Iran from acquiring a nuclear weapon. The negotiations had involved France, Germany and the UK, sometimes collectively referred to as the E3, where 'E' stood for European. Russia, China and the US joined in 2006.[37] Thereafter, the group was more often referred to as the P5+1, where P5 stood for the five permanent members of the UN Security Council, with Germany being the '+1'.

Little progress was made, and so the sanctions continued, as did Iran's programme of enrichment of nuclear material. In the summer of 2013, Iran held presidential elections. The winner, Hassan Rouhani, 'had campaigned on a pledge to improve Iran's stagnant economy by getting sanctions lifted'.[38] This proved to be the starting point for more productive negotiations, to the extent that by November that year, an interim agreement had been reached for Iran to continue its nuclear programme for peaceful purposes only in return for the lifting of sanctions. This led eventually to the Joint Comprehensive Plan of Action (JCPOA), which was agreed in Vienna in July 2015. Ashton, as chair of the negotiations, remembered this as a time when the Russians 'were pretty helpful'. She recalled in a 2024 interview, 'They always took the brief I gave them. They always made the statements we asked them to make, they always stuck to the agreed position, even though it was much more than they needed.' Had subsequent events been different, Ashton even hoped this format might prove a model for cooperation on other global issues, 'And I think had we not had the Ukraine crisis, I had hoped that the example of the Iran talks would lead to the P five, together with Europe, working on other things.'[39]

The international cooperation that the Iran nuclear deal represented was a rare achievement of cooperation between Russia, leading Western powers and, of course, China. But the Ukraine crisis, and war, that was eventually to place such a deep divide between Russia and the West was already looming when the provisional deal was done in Geneva in November 2013. Ashton's memoir described finishing the negotiations on the interim agreement – on 24 November – and then being in Vilnius for the start of the EU meeting at which Yanukovych was due to sign the association agreement. That was 28 November. The Iran deal went ahead, and when it did meet an obstacle, it was because of the US, not Russia. At the same time, though, confrontation was simmering over Ukraine: its place in the European political landscape still undecided more than twenty years after the end of the USSR.

Much as former Cold War foes had tried to put the conflict of the twentieth century behind them, some aspects of it inevitably remained, including espionage. It is not within the scope of this book to give a detailed account of intelligence-gathering during the period, but as some incidents had important political consequences both within Russia and for Russia's relations with the West, it is important to list a few. In early 2006, Russian television claimed that British spies in Moscow were communicating with their contacts by using a fake rock, apparently left in an ordinary street in the capital, and used to pass messages. The report showed one man slowing down as he passed the rock, and another picking it up. It also showed a fake rock which opened to reveal what appeared to be some kind of video or computer equipment. 'I am afraid you are going to get the old stock in trade of never commenting on security matters', the then British prime minister, Tony Blair, said in January 2006 when asked about the case during a news conference. The Russian TV footage was later included in a BBC documentary series, *Putin, Russia and the West*, broadcast in 2012. The documentary also claimed that Jonathan Powell, Blair's chief of staff, had admitted that the spy rock was what the Russian authorities claimed it was.[40] In a 2023 interview, however, Powell said that the case had 'burst on us as a complete surprise'. For Powell, the real significance of the incident was the way it played out in the media: 'I have no idea whether it was true or not true, but we were left with a big media problem which Tony had to deal with. So I don't think actually the spy rock was a big political event. It was a media thing. That was the problem with it. The Russians had something to beat us with and they used it.'[41]

Aside from this being an embarrassment from a public relations perspective, the timing played into Putin's hands. The same month, Russia introduced legislation allowing the state to monitor more closely the activities and finances of non-governmental organisations (NGOs).[42] This did not prompt much alarm or response among Western leaders, in public at least. It was six months later that the G8 met in Saint Petersburg, Putin proud to host world leaders in his home city. NGOs themselves, however, were worried about where this might lead. Carroll Bogert, then associate director of Human Rights Watch, warned in an opinion she contributed to the *International Herald Tribune* that Putin's 'crackdown on Russian nongovernmental organizations is only the latest stroke in an ongoing battle to emasculate the opposition and silence criticism of the Russian state'.[43]

It was not just Western spies who were caught and exposed. In June 2010, the US Department of Justice announced that it had charged ten people 'with conspiring to act as unlawful agents of the Russian Federation within the United States'.[44] The ten were 'illegals' – that is, they were operating in the US without diplomatic cover. The case was 'the result of a multi-year investigation conducted by the FBI'. The FBI was proud of its success, even later putting on its website a picture of a laptop it said had been used by one of the spies, Anna Chapman (her British surname had come from a marriage, that ended in divorce, to an Englishman). The FBI said that the spies 'targeted colleagues and friends, seeking to develop sources in U.S. policymaking circles. They also conducted support activities on behalf of Russian intelligence'.[45] The FBI named their surveillance 'Operation Ghost Stories' because 'many of the Russian spies assumed the stolen identities of dead Americans'.[46] In court, the accused all pleaded guilty. In an interview with ABC News published the following year, the FBI's Counterintelligence Assistant

Director Frank Figliuzzi described Chapman as 'a new breed of illegal operative', who was 'capable of spying in plain sight'.[47] In New York, she had posed as a realtor. Chapman returned to Moscow, where she used her fame, or notoriety, to launch a career as a television presenter. Her show was called *Secrets of the World* and included such edifying items as 'This woman returned from Egypt a cripple. A shark ripped off her arm.'[48] Shortly after they pleaded guilty, she and her fellow spies were exchanged at Vienna airport for four prisoners from Russian jails who had been convicted of helping Western powers. It was the biggest such exchange since the Cold War.[49] Among those released from Russia was Sergei Skripal. He was a former colonel in Russian military intelligence who had been convicted of spying for the UK.[50] His name would become much more widely known for a shocking attempt on his life years later, after he had settled in England.

The spy rock, and the realtor who was really a Russian agent, might seem to belong more to the world of twentieth-century Cold War fiction or film. But both were reminders that this part of Russia and the West's Cold War rivalry had not ended with the collapse of communism. Other elements of human life had been transformed beyond all recognition or even imagination since 1991, and these lay at the heart of some of the biggest incidents dividing Russia and the West as the relationship that had been defined by hope at the close of the Cold War was cursed by deepening suspicion and fear.

In the summer of 2013, the *Guardian* revealed an extraordinary source who had given them evidence of extraordinary surveillance that the US National Security Agency (NSA) was carrying out on US citizens. It was on a scale few outside the system could have suspected. Edward Snowden, a former technical assistant for the CIA and contractor for firms carrying out work for the NSA, gave a series of explosive interviews in Hong Kong, where he had fled before making his revelations. He had brought with him extensive evidence of what he now made public: 'the communication records of millions of US citizens are being collected indiscriminately and in bulk – regardless of whether they are suspected of any wrongdoing'.[51] Unable to return to the US for fear of arrest, Snowden went to Moscow. At first permitted to stay there temporarily, he was eventually allowed residence, and, in 2022, Russian citizenship.[52] In a 2017 interview, Putin told the US film director Oliver Stone that he did not consider Snowden a traitor, adding that the former US contractor did things 'publicly'.[53]

Less public – at least to begin with – was Russia's next major international intervention. This was not a military campaign like that in Syria. It was an attempt to influence who would secure political power in another country: the US. This time, however, the purpose was not to protect the incumbent so much as advance a political insurgent.

Barack Obama's second and final presidential term was due to end in January 2017. The election for his successor, the previous November, put the democratic challenger, Hillary Clinton, against the businessman and television personality Donald Trump. From the Kremlin's point of view, Clinton was a known quantity. She had served as secretary of state under Obama, during his first term from 2009 to 2013. Trump had secured the Republican nomination despite never having held elected office. While he claimed extensive commercial experience, he had little experience of international affairs or diplomacy. As such, he was an unknown quantity to a Kremlin administration that strongly favoured predictability. Even if they had not liked many of Clinton's policies, they knew what to expect. Nevertheless, Trump seems to have been the Kremlin's preferred candidate – one whom they actively tried to help to win.

As Fiona Hill wrote in her book *There is Nothing for You Here*, 'The Kremlin anticipated that Hillary Clinton would win the election and seek to constrain Russia's room for maneuver.'[54] Seeking to prevent a Clinton victory, Russia mounted an operation that was, in Hill's view, 'straight out of a Cold War "active measures" textbook'. In its twenty-first-century incarnation, this meant using 'a sophisticated combination of new cybertools, alongside the state-backed media, to hack the email messages of prominent American political figures, disseminate leaked documents, and amplify inflammatory news items'. Naturally, this was not done 'publicly', as Putin said Snowden had acted. Companies were set up to do the work and give the Kremlin the possibility of distancing itself from the illicit work done to further its cause. One such entity was the Internet Research Agency, headed by Yevgeny Prigozhin – later infamous as the leader of the Wagner mercenary company.[55]

In October 2016, shortly before the election, Wikileaks released emails hacked from the Democratic National Committee. They caused embarrassment to Clinton as candidate and to her campaign. They detailed financial dealings of her husband, the former president Bill Clinton, since leaving office. They included members of her team discussing her perceived shortcomings, including that 'her instincts can be terrible'.[56]

A US government enquiry noted that these emails 'were reported to have been hacked by Russia',[57] though Hill was clearer, writing in her later memoir that 'Russian operatives from the military intelligence services, the GRU' were behind the hack.[58] The US Department of Justice Report, published during the Trump presidency, recorded that Trump 'expressed skepticism' about this but also made reference to the fact that 'the President expressed concerns to advisors that reports of Russia's election interference might lead the public to question the legitimacy of his election'. Such a perception might have been strengthened by the fact that Trump had business interests in Russia, including a plan to build a Trump tower in Moscow.[59] There were also meetings in the run-up to the election between members of Trump's team and 'politically-connected Russians who promised potentially damaging information on Hillary Clinton' – though the investigation, led by Special Counsel Robert Mueller, found no conclusive evidence of actual collusion between Russia and the Trump campaign.[60]

Trump actually came second in the popular vote, but his majority of votes in the electoral college won him the White House. His victory was a great shock to the US's political establishment, and political elites around the world. His candidacy had not been taken particularly seriously at the outset, but various scandals along the way failed to derail his campaign, and he pulled off what at the outset had seemed a most unlikely win. There had been a similar shock to the wider Western political establishment earlier in 2016, when the UK voted to leave the EU (and did in 2020). Speaking at a public event in London in the autumn of 2024, Ciaran Martin, the former chief executive of Britain's National Cyber Security Centre, said that during the campaign for the referendum on Britain's EU membership 'there were low quality attempts at social media interference, but no cut through'. In short, he said, 'There was no evidence of successful digital interference'.[61] That does not mean there were no other Russian attempts to influence the referendum result. The UK's eventual departure from the bloc was no source of regret for Russia, weakening as it did a union that Russia had come to see as a rival in Ukraine.

The Brexit referendum was not the only occasion on which Russia was suspected of trying to influence the course of British politics. Two years earlier, Scotland had voted in an independence referendum, on whether the country should leave the UK. Fifty-five per cent of votes were against independence, and Scotland remained part of the UK. As with the UK's departure from the EU, the departure of Scotland from the UK would have led to political and economic unpredictability, and possible instability. The UK security services detected attempts by Russian social media users to influence the result. In a 2024 interview, Martin dismissed these as showing no understanding of local politics. 'The intent and activity is there, the impact, I would argue, isn't', he said. 'The quality of it was risible, and the impact of it absolutely must be assessed as zero.'

Martin said that – as a serving government official at the time – he gave evidence to the British parliament's Intelligence and Security Committee for its 2020 report on Russia. The report sought to answer a number of questions relating to UK–Russia relations, including 'What does Russia want?'[62] The report itself had an impact on UK politics. It was completed eighteen months before it was eventually made public: publication was delayed until after the 2019 general election.

There was a procedural reason for this. When an election is called, parliamentary committees are disbanded and reformed once members of the new parliament take their seats. The delay in this case had possible advantages for the governing Conservative Party. The report noted: 'Several members of the Russian elite who are closely linked to Putin are identified as being involved with charitable and/or political organisations in the UK, having donated to political parties, with a public profile which positions them to assist Russian influence operations.'[63]

Since the fall of the USSR, London had been a welcoming destination for the vast wealth of the minority of Russians who got rich. So much money flowed into Britain – benefiting in particular estate agents, private schools, public relations and 'reputation management' executives (and lawyers, when wealthy Russians decided to take each other to court) that little was done about this kind of influence until it was very well established. As Catherine Belton put it in her book *Putin's People*, 'Instead of bringing Russia into line with its rules-based system, slowly the West was being corrupted. It was as if a virus was being injected into it.'[64]

Trump's relationship with Russia in general and with Putin in particular has continued to be a source of speculation throughout his political career. Suggestions that Russia might hold some compromising material – *kompromat*, as it is called in Russian – have never been proved. Nor have they gone away. In the election campaign of 2024, future US policy on Ukraine, and how policy on Russia might affect that, was, along with the war in the Middle East, one of the most frequently discussed foreign policy issues. Hill, from her vantage point on the US National Security Council, has persuasively argued that Trump 'admired the way Putin ran Russia like his own private company. People like Putin, who was simultaneously an autocrat and reputedly super-rich, were an elite of their own. This was the group Trump wanted to see himself in – the internationally very rich, very powerful, and very famous.'[65]

Some six months of the Trump presidency passed before he met Putin, the two presidents' first encounter being at a G20 summit in Hamburg in July 2017. That occasion was remarkable for Trump's act of pocketing the US interpreter's notes. Hill, briefed on what had been discussed, wrote later that 'nothing that had emerged about the first Trump-Putin meeting implied that Trump was the "Russian candidate" receiving secret instructions from Putin'.[66] The idea that Putin could somehow influence his American counterpart did not die, though – and was given a huge boost a year later.

By then, another serious – and deadly – incident involving the Russian intelligence services had greatly damaged Russia's relations with the West and led to a huge round of diplomatic expulsions. On 4 March 2018, Sergei Skripal, the former colonel in Russian military intelligence who had been released as part of the 2010 exchange that saw Anna Chapman and her fellow Russian spies freed in the US, was found, severely ill, on a bench in the English town of Salisbury. With him was his daughter, Yulia, who was also dangerously unwell. Paramedics who were called to the scene took them to hospital. It was later announced that they had been poisoned with a Novichok nerve agent, a type of chemical weapon first created in the USSR. Both survived. Three months later, on 30 June, Dawn Sturgess, who lived locally, sprayed herself with the contents of a perfume bottle that her partner, Charley Rowley, had found. She died in hospital on 8 July – from Novichok poisoning. It appeared that the bottle had been discarded by whoever had administered the poison – reportedly by smearing it on the handle of the door of the property where the Skripals were staying – and later found by the unsuspecting Rowley.

The British authorities later named two suspects, Alexander Petrov and Ruslan Boshirov, both Russian nationals. The announcement from the British counterterrorism police noted that 'it is likely that they were travelling under aliases and that these are not their real names'.[67] Bellingcat, working with the Russian investigative news organisation The Insider, later named the two as Anatoly Chepiga and Alexander Mishkin: both men, according to the investigation, GRU officers.[68] Before the publication of the Bellingcat/Insider investigation, the two had done some media work of their own. Back in Russia, they gave an interview to RT, as Russia Today had rebranded itself. In it, they claimed that the names they had used were their real names, and they also claimed – however implausibly – that they had visited Salisbury in order to see the spire of the cathedral and one of the world's oldest working clocks.[69]

Some of the more credulous members of the RT audience may have believed this version of events. Certainly, it seems to have been widely accepted in Russia. A Levada Center poll conducted in Russia in October 2018 found that only 3 per cent of respondents believed that the Russian 'special (i.e. intelligence) services' were behind the poisoning. Rather more, 28 per cent, believed that the 'English special services' were to blame. Perhaps gratifyingly for the architects of the bizarre media campaign about the cathedral, whoever they were, 56 per cent said 'it could have been anyone'.[70] Britain and its allies had no such doubts. By the end of March, twenty-six countries had announced they were expelling Russian diplomats in response to the Salisbury poisoning. These included twenty-three, 'believed to be intelligence officers', from the Russian embassy in London.[71] The US expelled sixty. Earlier that month, Trump had called Putin to congratulate him on his victory in the 2018 Russian presidential election.[72] Putin had been returned for a fourth term as Russian president, with 76 per cent of the vote.[73] According to the *Washington Post*, Trump had been told not to congratulate Putin.[74] This was apparently written in capital letters in briefing notes. The Skripal case was not the only reason why congratulations might not have been appropriate. The election had been carried out in conditions that hardly justified the idea of 'choice'. Putin's most high-profile and outspoken opponent, Alexei Navalny, had been prevented from standing. The media, as will be discussed in the next chapter, were by now far from free. In his message to Putin, Trump mentioned that he hoped they would meet 'in the not too distant future', when they could 'discuss the arms race'.

According to Hill, 'When it came to nuclear weapons, Trump always had a pattern break with the norm, which showed he really cared about the topic'.[75] This had not stopped him from taking the US out of the JCPOA, an agreement he declared to be 'defective at its core', in May

2018.[76] A meeting arranged for Helsinki in July 2018 'was supposed to be Trump's big arms-control summit' that would be like the grand meetings of the late Cold War.[77] That is not how it turned out. It was remarkable mostly for a news conference at which Trump accepted at face value Putin's denial of any interference in the 2016 presidential election, and also appeared to have agreed to Russian investigators questioning Bill Browder, an American-born businessman who had worked in Russia in the 1990s and had subsequently acquired British citizenship. Browder had been the driving force behind the Magnitsky Act, legislation aimed at imposing sanctions on Russian officials involved in the death in custody of Sergei Magnitsky, a lawyer who had worked with Browder. Hill, who was in the audience, called the episode 'Agony in Helsinki' in her memoir.[78]

Hill's 'Agony in Helsinki' was justified. For what happened there was a symbol of the way that Russia's relations with the West were changing as Putin continued to grow stronger at home and more confident abroad. The whole idea in the 1990s had been that the West would help Russia to become more like the West: with similar political and economic systems. Now the opposite was happening. In Trump, the US had a president who wanted the US to become more like the autocracy into which Russia was rapidly evolving. As Hill said in a 2024 interview, Trump's presidency 'basically confirmed everything that Putin ever thought: that we were just transactional, cynical, and full of it, that we don't believe any more in democracy than anybody else does. And his view it was just who shouted the loudest, who had the most money. We were just as corrupt. We were an oligarchy.'[79]

Hill, a fluent Russian speaker, used the word 'oligarchy' with full knowledge of its resonance in post-Soviet Russia: a reference to the hugely wealthy businessmen (almost all of them were men) who first made fortunes and then acquired huge influence over the course the country took in the years following the collapse of communism. Trump may have ignored his advisers when he congratulated Putin. Putin's advisers may have congratulated him when Trump became president. Indeed, Putin said, when discussing the 2016 election at the Helsinki news conference, 'While a candidate, Mr Trump spoke of the necessity to restore Russia–US relations. Naturally, the Russian public developed a liking for this candidate.'[80] Kremlin propagandists had been gleeful when Trump won. Margarita Simonyan, editor-in-chief of RT, had tweeted, 'People are tired of war. People are tired of the media. People are tired of aggressive liberalism. People are tired of immigrants. Good or bad, but it's a fact.'[81] Simonyan's words demonstrated the double-think rapidly becoming necessary for continuing career success in the Russian political elite in the Putin era. As an editor-in-chief, she was undoubtedly part of the media of which people were apparently so fed up; with an Armenian family name, she presumably had immigrant heritage. This was just the start of a triumphant message that would soon be amplified. In a 2019 interview with the *Financial Times*, Putin declared – perhaps a deliberately ironic echo of the triumphant claims made for liberal democracy at the end of the Cold War – that 'the liberal idea' had 'outlived its purpose'.[82]

The election of Trump and the UK's exit from the EU could both be presented as evidence to support Putin's case. Nevertheless, as Alex Younger, the outgoing head of MI6, pointed out in a 2020 interview, 'The Russians did not create the things that divide us – we did that. They are adept, albeit in a rather crass manner, at exacerbating those things and I believe that we should prevent that.'[83] Still, the spectre of interference continued to haunt the Western political system at election times for years to come. Speaking in the autumn of 2024, just a little over a week before the presidential election in the US, Ciaran Martin noted that Russia could see interference in the 2016 election as 'a win' in any case, 'Because two electoral cycles later Americans are still arguing about it.' Vladimir Zhirinovsky did not live to see Russian soldiers washing their boots in the waters of the Indian Ocean, but he did see them on the shores of the Mediterranean. He would also no doubt have been satisfied that the footprints – real or imagined – of their fellows in the Russia intelligence agencies were reported from the Atlantic to the Pacific, as well as both sides of the English Channel.

10

Protest, Propaganda and Press Freedom

At the Helsinki news conference, Putin had performed like a master tactician, one who understood performing on the global stage much better than his newly arrived opposite number. When a football (soccer) team outwits and outplays another, sports reporters might say the losers were 'taught a footballing lesson'. Putin did not miss a trick here, either. Russia had just finished hosting the World Cup, a tournament generally agreed to have been a great success both on and off the field. With the world's media watching, Putin took the opportunity to remind them how well it had gone. Standing at the podium in the news conference, he was passed a football, which he then passed on to Trump, noting that the US was due to host the tournament in 2026.[1] Putin's gesture also implied a challenge for the US to stage as successful a World Cup as Russia had done.

Sporting success and the staging of international events had become a pillar of the propaganda of the Putin era. The hosting of the Champions League final in 2008 had been followed one month later by the Russian national team's strong showing in the European Championships. Russia reached the semi-finals, the country's greatest footballing achievement since the end of the USSR. The fact that on the way they beat the Netherlands, who had defeated the USSR in the 1988 final, was not lost on the Russian TV commentator. He recalled having been at the 1988 match, where there were only about twenty Soviet supporters.[2] Now not only was Russia back in the elite of European football, but the fans from this newly wealthy and confident country could afford to travel abroad in far greater numbers to watch their team.

Ten years later it was Russia's turn to play host. Since that 2008 European tournament, held in Austria and Switzerland, much had changed politically. Just weeks after Russia's footballers claimed third place on the pitch, Russia's soldiers were marching to the battlefield in South Ossetia. When Russia hosted the 2018 World Cup, the annexation of Crimea was already four years old. The decision to award the tournament to Russia had been taken before the seizure of the territory. The governing body of international football, FIFA, had very quickly made it clear that there was no prospect of the World Cup being taken away from Russia because of its conquest of Crimea. Just days after Putin signed the legislation formalising the annexation, the then president of FIFA, Sepp Blatter, said, 'The World Cup has been given and voted to Russia and we are going forward with our work.'[3] There were also persistent allegations of corruption having influenced the bidding process, but neither those allegations, nor the war in Ukraine, stopped Russia from playing host.[4] Instead, Moscow and the other Russian cities whose stadia were used for the tournament were allowed to shine on world football's biggest stage.

Those venues chosen reflected well on Russia: in soft power, if not in sporting terms. Neither Russia nor the USSR had ever won the trophy. Russia did enjoy some success on the pitch, eliminating Spain, before being knocked out themselves by Croatia in the quarter finals. Off the pitch, the success was more marked. While the Russian political elite would have liked nothing more than to see their team conquer the world, that was never seriously expected. Hosting the tournament was always more about projecting an image of Russia as one of the world's leading countries, one to which visitors from all over the world would flock in admiration, and leave impressed. This is a long-established idea in the way Russia wants to be seen by the rest of the world. Alexander Pushkin, in his 1833 poem 'The Bronze Horseman', imagines Peter the Great's thoughts as he prepares to build Saint Petersburg. 'All flags will visit us,' the tsar muses. Certainly, the Russian state had committed resources not only during the bidding process, but to pay for the tournament itself. Media reports from the time suggested that hosting the World Cup had cost Russia more than $14 billion.[5] That made it at the time the most expensive World Cup ever, though that was soon surpassed by the next World Cup, held in Qatar in 2022. The rehearsals – with the relaxation of visa requirements and unusually polite police officers – for the UEFA Champions League final in Moscow a decade earlier paid off. Fans who came seemed largely to enjoy themselves, and Russian media were happy to celebrate the patriotic public relations success. One tweet from an England fan talking about what a great time he had had suggested that 'the British media should be ashamed of themselves for their clear propaganda against the Russian people. Absolutely class country.'[6] It was gleefully amplified by Kremlin-friendly news outlets.

For this was really the point of hosting the tournament. As relations had soured the previous spring in the wake of the poisoning of the Skripals, the foreign ministry spokeswoman, Maria Zakharova, had accused the West of 'trying to take the World Cup out of Russia'.[7] Her remarks followed the announcement from the British prime minister, Theresa May, that no British officials or members of the royal family would travel to Russia for the World Cup. Prince William, the grandson of Queen Elizabeth, and at that time second in line to the throne, held the post of president of the English football association. As the association's president, he would normally have been expected to go to the tournament. Theresa May had been speaking in March when she announced the expulsion of Russian diplomats after the attack on the Skripals.[8] A suggestion from the then British foreign secretary, later prime minister, Boris Johnson that attending the World Cup bore comparison with attending the 1936 Berlin Olympics prompted particular outrage and even a trip to the Moscow archives. At a briefing on 29 March, Zakharova claimed to be holding a brochure published in Berlin in 1936 that listed the names of British dignitaries who had attended the now infamous games. 'What were all those respectable British sporting functionaries and lords doing as Hitler's guests? Tell your countrymen about this,' Zakharova demanded.[9] Her comments reflected fury that Russia's hosting of the tournament might in any way be tarnished – and also drew on a longstanding Russian public diplomacy technique of 'whataboutism', where Russian officials deflect criticism of their country not by denial but by comparison with something equally bad, or even worse.

There were domestic problems, though. Demonstrations had been banned during the tournament, but there was growing discontent over proposed reforms to pensions. Measures to increase the retirement age had been announced on the opening day of the World Cup. It was the day Russia played the first match, in which they beat Saudi Arabia 5-0. The authorities presumably hoped that the start of the football would mean it was a good day to announce unpopular plans. On 14 June, the government of Prime Minister Dmitry Medvedev outlined measures that would see the retirement age for men rise, over a number of years, from sixty to sixty-five, with that for women going up from fifty-five to sixty-three.[10] As *The Economist* pointed out in an article later that month, the retirement ages that would now rise had first been set during the Stalin era, when the USSR first started paying pensions.[11] More pertinent was the fact that in post-Soviet Russia male life expectancy had fallen alarmingly, then risen. Having been sixty-five in 1986, by 1994 it was just fifty-eight, before rising then falling again to fifty-nine in 2003. Since then, it had continued to rise again. Research published in 2019 by the World Health Organization (WHO) found that alcohol consumption in Russia had fallen by 43 per cent between 2003 and 2016. The WHO report said: 'This trend mirrored a drop in all-cause mortality by 39% in men and 36% in women between 2003 and 2018.'[12] In 2018, the year the reforms were announced, male life expectancy was sixty-eight: 'a historic high', in the words of the WHO.[13] Russia was getting stronger and more sober at the same time.

The statistic that truly troubled men not yet old enough to draw their pension was the fact that a significant number of them still could not expect to live that long. In 2016, just 61 per cent of Russian males survived to age sixty-five; in 2018, it was 63 per cent.[14] For women, the corresponding figures were 85 and 86 per cent.[15] So while a greater proportion of women than men could expect to live to draw their pensions, they were still being asked to work significantly longer. The reforms were not popular with demographic groups who could generally be relied upon to form part of Putin's core constituency.

The World Cup and the summer over, the protests began. In late August, Putin announced a softening of the measures, with the retirement age for women to rise only to sixty, not sixty-three. He perhaps expected his personal involvement to make it more palatable. It was not enough. When often he proved himself adept at deflecting blame for unpopular measures onto ministers, this was not one of those occasions. In consequence, his personal popularity suffered, with the polling organisation VTsIOM recording a fall in support for the Russian president from 80 to 64 per cent.[16]

In September, more than 800 people were detained during protests against the pension reforms. Alexei Navalny, who had tried unsuccessfully to run for president against Putin earlier in the year, was not among those who took to the streets. He was in gaol – as he frequently was during these years. On this occasion, he had been locked up for breaking protest laws. The authorities continued to find reasons to charge him on grounds that his supporters always insisted – with good reason, given his eventual fate – were politically motivated. Navalny's absence did not silence him. In a post on the eve of the demonstrations, his blog listed the times that protesters were due to assemble in Moscow and Saint Petersburg, with a link to information about other cities. Directly above, the post warned: 'If you stay at home, it means that with your silent agreement the authorities will continue to rob our country.'[17] On the day of the demonstrations, Navalny's blog celebrated the numbers that had turned out to join the protests, showing pictures of the crowds in Moscow, Saint Petersburg and elsewhere. Demonstrators carried signs with slogans including, 'Putin when will you take your pension?'[18] A post the following day described what it called the Kremlin's trial of a new tactic: 'detain all well-known opponents preventatively'. The post went on to remind readers that Navalny himself had been detained two weeks earlier, apparently for actions during a march on 28 January. The police had supposedly been unable to find Navalny in Moscow for half a year, the blog sarcastically noted, but then, 'what a success!', found him before the next demonstration. The post was headlined, 'Don't allow yourself to be frightened.'[19]

The words on this occasion were published by Navalny's team, but the cutting tone was typical of Navalny himself. Since he had first come to prominence as a protester in the demonstrations in the wake of the 2011 elections to the Duma, Navalny's campaigning had become more sophisticated and effective – and part of that effectiveness lay in his trademark wit. In the same way that he was in effect banned from running for elective office (with predictable regularity, as with the anti-pension reform protests, he would be charged with an offence at a key moment), Navalny was kept away from the mass media. In Russia – historically, given the size of the country – this meant principally television. In their research on Russian journalists, censorship and self-censorship, the researchers Elisabeth Schimpfossl and Ilya Yablokov characterise Russian TV networks as 'critical elements of the political system in Putin's Russia'.[20] On the one occasion Navalny did make his electoral mark, in the Moscow mayoral election of 2013, where he came second with 27 per cent of the vote – he did so without access to media channels owned by the state or by wealthy businesspeople loyal to the state.[21] By 2013, as will be discussed below, that described every mainstream TV channel in Russia. Denied normal media access, Navalny and his supporters used their understanding of digital technology to bypass the restrictions as best they could. For this was a period in Russian history when the authorities wanted to be able to claim that Russia had free media. They did not want to be seen to be imposing the same kind of restrictions that characterised, for example, the Chinese authorities' approach to the internet. This gave Navalny and his supporters an opportunity to talk directly to a constituency who were equally at home with internet media. The imaginative, and highly effective, use they were able to make of YouTube actually succeeded in making the authorities attempt to keep them out of the public eye look clumsy and flat-footed. Perhaps the most effective example of this came when in 2017 Navalny turned his anti-corruption lens on Dmitry Medvedev, former president, and by then prime minister.

As his political star had risen as Putin's anointed successor, Medvedev had made much of his legal background. 'Russia is a country where people don't like to observe the law. It is, as they say, a country of legal nihilism,' he told the *Financial Times* in an interview in late 2008.[22] In making statements such as these, Medvedev showed an understanding of the situation one might expect from a well-informed leader. Post-Soviet Russia invariably scored poorly in surveys conducted by Transparency International, a global movement against corruption in public life. Their 2016 report, in which citizens had been asked to assess levels of corruption in their homelands, placed Russia third from bottom among more than forty countries. Only Serbia and Ukraine were ranked lower.[23] So Medvedev's comments were well founded in both public perception and available evidence. The problem for Medvedev was that he himself was alleged to be corrupt – at least, according to an investigation carried out by Navalny's Anti-Corruption Foundation, often known by its Russian initials, FBK.

In March 2017, on a YouTube channel whose numbers of viewers and subscribers continued to soar, Navalny presented a fifty-minute video, 'Don't Call Him "Dimon"'. The title came from an admonishment that Medvedev's press secretary, Natalya Timakova, had issued to internet users, whom, she felt, by referring to him using a diminutive form of his first name, were not showing the prime minster (as Medvedev then was; this was 2013) sufficient respect.[24] The video began with dramatic title music and captions promising that luxury premises such as 'palaces', 'vineyards' and 'yachts' would feature. The opening to the video included a short clip of Medvedev enjoying what might best be called 'dad dancing' at what the viewer later learns is a class reunion.

'You would never take this man for some kind of a villain or an underground billionaire,' Navalny began. Navalny was on camera, in a shirt and tie, though his shirt sleeves were rolled up, a visual symbol of unstinting hard work to get at the truth. The only background was a set of bookshelves – but the video was enlivened by further animations and video inserts (including Timakova delivering her rebuke, just after Navalny has used the offending version of Medvedev's name). Most of all, it was distinguished by Navalny's considerable televisual presence and the rigour of his organisation's research. Its central allegation was that Medvedev was the true owner of a huge number of luxury properties that, according to official documents, belonged to 'non-commercial and charity foundations controlled by his close friends'. Medvedev dismissed the allegations as 'false statements of political adventurers'.[25] In the years that followed, the video got more than 47 million views and prompted almost 130,000 comments.[26]

Even these figures were far surpassed by the video 'Putin's palace. History of world's largest bribe'. Navalny began that video in Dresden, where Putin had once been stationed as a KGB officer. He wanted to find out, he said, 'how an ordinary Soviet officer turned into a madman'. The video alleged that a huge palace on the Russian Black Sea coast belonged to Putin. Putin denied this. A close associate of his, Arkady Rotenberg, claimed it belonged to him.[27] Posted in January 2021, by the autumn of 2024 the video had 133 million views. It first appeared on YouTube just after Navalny had been imprisoned for what would prove to be the last time – a gesture of defiance from behind bars.[28]

Navalny was not a journalist or broadcaster. His professional background was in law and business. Yet in his blog and on YouTube he showed great skill in making use of the journalistic tools of the twenty-first century. In this sense, he identified himself with a number of Russian traditions: his false incredulity with social satire in a country where political elites had rarely tolerated it; his position outside the journalistic mainstream with a long tradition of Russian political dissent that had often only found its outlet in exile. Beginning the Putin film in Germany, while there was a clear editorial point, was an example of this. Navalny's subsequent return to Russia from a place of relative safety, which will be discussed in the next chapter, was a departure from the exile tradition as well as a departure from his host country. There were other, less savoury, aspects of Russian political thought with which Navalny identified himself, too. Anti-immigrant remarks from earlier in his campaigning career resurfaced in 2021, leading the human rights organisation Amnesty International to stop considering him a 'prisoner of conscience'. At the time, the BBC reported that the complaints that prompted Amnesty International to act were an 'apparently co-ordinated move'. The editor-in-chief of RT, Margarita Simonyan, welcomed the outcome on social media.[29] His views on the annexation of Crimea were not those that placed him in the same camp as the overwhelming majority of Putin's international critics. While he did condemn the seizure of the peninsula, he also criticised its transfer to the Soviet republic of Ukraine in 1954. His refusal entirely to distance himself from the Russian nationalist view of the annexation may have reflected his own views. It also reflected the views of a politician seeking broader support in a country where a huge majority were, on this occasion, in favour of its government's conquest of part of a neighbour's territory.

If Navalny was the inheritor of an older tradition of Russian dissent against the authorities, he was also part of a more contemporary kind of protest. His use of digital media was just part of this. He was also an extremely effective street campaigner. The 2011 protests against the Duma elections, and Putin's planned return to power, were not the beginning of challenges to his power, even if they were the beginning of Putin starting to see such protests as a potential threat. As noted in Chapter 4, the former world chess champion, Garry Kasparov, had organised marches 'of the Dissenters', under the banner 'Another Russia'. They held rallies that attracted a few thousand people. They chanted for 'A Russia without Putin'. The protesters were sometimes outnumbered by the riot police, some specially brought in from outside Moscow, deployed to keep an eye on them. Kasparov claimed to be unconcerned by the numbers. 'At a time when the government controls mass media, and the election process is turned into a mockery, I think to talk about public support is probably useless,' he told me in a 2007 interview when I was a correspondent in Moscow. The Russian political establishment was untroubled. Vyacheslav Nikonov, who was named as the head of the Russky Mir cultural organisation (see Chapter 8) the same year, and who, as the grandson of Stalin's foreign minister, Vyacheslav Molotov, was a scion of the Soviet political establishment, dismissed it as 'a coalition of the losers'.[30] The large number of riot police showed that the 'losers' did not go unnoticed.

Kasparov announced at a news conference in Geneva in 2013 that he did not plan to go back to Russia. Having seen that Navalny, and his fellow activist Sergei Udaltsov, were then on trial, Kasparov said, 'I have serious doubts that if I return to Moscow I may be able to travel back. So for the time being I refrain from returning to Russia.'[31] By then, his assessment of the nature of Russian society, and the ability of the political opposition to act, had been proved prescient. In that sense, the movement that Kasparov had worked to bring together had played an important role. Those politically different dissenters he had assembled for rallies during Putin's second term had seen something that their compatriots – perhaps in the shops nearby, enjoying the benefits of the economic boom – had not. It would take the election of 2011 to make more of them set aside their shopping and question whether the Putin consensus – economic stability and financial comfort in exchange for fewer press and political rights – was still working. By then, it was already harder to change. Having survived the public challenge to his authority in the election season of 2011–12, Putin had also learnt from experience. The next time the political opposition encouraged their supporters onto the streets in large numbers, in the summer of 2019, the action focused not on national elections but on voting for the Moscow city Duma. Before then, and after it, new legislation that would restrict protesters' ability to organise and act had already been presented to, and then passed by, the national parliament.

That legislation, couched in terms of national security, concerned access to the internet. In April 2019, the Duma adopted the 'Stable Runet Law'. The purpose of the legislation, as the Russian news agency TASS reported, was to provide for 'the sustainable operation of the Russian Internet segment in case it is disconnected from the global infrastructure of the World Wide Web'. One of the sponsors of the legislation was Andrei Lugovoi, the former KGB agent accused of the murder of Alexander Litvinenko, and by now a Russian MP.[32] Those lawmakers who supported the new law cited what they termed an 'aggressive' cyber security strategy drawn up by the US and published the previous year.[33] This was a reference to the document's noting that 'Russia, Iran, and North Korea conducted reckless cyber attacks that harmed American and international businesses and our allies and partners without paying costs likely to deter future cyber aggression'.[34]

This had led to fears among Russian parliamentarians that if relations with the West were to continue to worsen, the US might even cut off Russian IP addresses. The Russian political elite were very keen to present the plans as a defensive measure against such a situation. Medvedev himself, then prime minister, even specifically denied that Russia was seeking to emulate the internet controls imposed by the Chinese authorities. 'Certainly, we won't have Chinese-style regulations', he said. 'Moreover, we are not even seeking regulation. No firewall will emerge here.'[35] Many Russians simply did not believe him, nor did they believe that this was only about national security. In March, thousands of protesters had demonstrated against what they saw as an attempt by the authorities to prepare not for the US cutting Russia off from the internet, but for Russia to cut itself off from the internet.[36] I was in Moscow then, visiting for meetings with Russian academic colleagues and for research for a previous book. I considered going to witness the demonstrations but then hesitated. Should the police ask me what I was doing, I no longer had what protection a Russian foreign ministry press accreditation might once have afforded me. I stayed away. I realised Russia had changed from the country I had known as a young journalist a quarter of a century earlier.

The legislation came into effect on 1 November that year, although the technology that had so concerned activists – 'deep packet inspection', which offered the opportunity to filter content – was not yet operational.[37] Nevertheless, the following month, Russia claimed successfully to have tested its 'sovereign' internet.[38] Medvedev's protest that Russia was not creating a firewall was harder to take at face value once the construction of the foundations of such a firewall were underway. The legislators themselves who had backed the new law gave as justification their fear that the US might one day act to restrict Russian internet access. The creation of the sovereign Runet was a preparation for any such isolation. It might also serve as a preparation for a future war.

It was also the latest milestone on post-Soviet Russia's road away from a society in which, however chaotic, press and political freedoms had flourished. This was the reversal of a process that had begun before the fall of the USSR. Greater media freedom had been an indispensable part of the reform programme that the last Soviet leadership had intended should save the system, but ended up speeding its collapse. When Mikhail Gorbachev had launched his *perestroika* (reconstruction) programme in the 1980s, he had made *glasnost* a pillar of his plans. Knowing that he would face strong opposition to some of his plans from more conservative elements in the Soviet Communist Party which he led, Gorbachev sought to rally the news media to his cause. He offered them greater freedom than the Soviet system, certainly at a national level, had previously permitted. In return, the idea was that their reporting would draw attention to the system's shortcomings in an honest and frank way that might serve as the start of a process of addressing them. This openness continued under Yeltsin: partly because his administration believed in press freedom; partly because in that era the state had far fewer means to control the media even had they wished to. The lawlessness that plagued that era of Russian history also meant that the media could do largely as they pleased: until they displeased the wrong person.

Now, where once Russian journalism had thrived in an atmosphere where journalists were largely free, though subject to the whims of wealthy owners, it no longer did. For by Putin's fourth term as president, the mass media were largely under the control of the Kremlin, or of owners close to the Kremlin – and thus dependent on its goodwill to keep their wealth. 'With regard to censorship one must not report negatively about Vladimir Putin', Schimpfössl and Yablokov wrote of their survey of Russian reporters in the 2010s.[39] Oligarchic control of the media had been transformed into direct and indirect state control. As Arkady Ostrovsky wrote of the main TV news programme *Vremya* ('Time') in the Putin era, 'Every programme followed the same repeated pattern – like a lullaby – starting with Putin travelling round the country or receiving ministers in his office [. . .] Its aim was to assure viewers that they could sleep peacefully in the knowledge that the country was being governed and guarded by a wise and caring president.'[40] It was very different television from the sensationalism and violence that had often been seen during the 1990s.

On the way, Russian journalism had itself made compromises some would later come to regret: in particular, widespread unquestioning support for Yeltsin in the election of 1996 for fear of what a victory for the Communist candidate Zyuganov might mean. That is not to say that there was no good journalism in Russia in this period. The opposite is true. Russian journalism at its best took hold of all the freedom that came with the end of communism and made the most of it, with courage, determination and resourcefulness. These qualities were best exemplified in the work of Politkovskaya, but she was not alone. Her colleagues at her own newspaper, *Novaya Gazeta*, TV Rain and other independent outlets did admirable work in increasingly difficult circumstances. *Novaya Gazeta*'s editor-in-chief, Dmitry Muratov, would later be recognised as joint recipient of the 2021 Nobel Peace Prize. Nor was it just these small outlets. While some Russian journalists were increasingly content to work as propagandists for the Kremlin, others strove to honour their professional commitments even as the organisations for which they worked made it harder for them to do. From 2014 onwards, following the annexation of Crimea, however, a steady number of Russian journalists looked to the future in despair. Some decided even then to leave Russia, fearing not only for their professional freedom, but for their liberty, and perhaps their lives, if they stayed. Their numbers greatly increased after the escalation of the war in Ukraine in February 2022.

Before then, legislation was making journalistic life harder and harder. As the Kremlin's establishment of RT had shown in 2005, media was a field which Putin wanted to use to control the message at home, and as a resource in international competition. Throughout the Putin era, this has been enshrined in official policy. The foreign policy of the Russian Federation, in the version published in 2023, included a section on 'information support for the foreign policy of the Russian Federation'. This section defines its purpose as 'forming an objective perception of Russia abroad, strengthening its position in the global information space'.[41] In practice, this blending of foreign policy objectives with expectations of the role of journalism had a detrimental effect on journalism in Russia: not least because, as the Putin era continued, media deemed insufficiently pro-Kremlin or patriotic increasingly found themselves branded 'foreign agents'. The label was designed to undermine the credibility of criticism of the Kremlin.

Russia's foreign agent legislation in the Putin era had its origins in laws first introduced to restrict the activities of NGOs, especially those linked to bigger international organisations and receiving funding from outside Russia. The measures became law in 2012. They required NGOs to register with the justice ministry, and to file a report on their activities every quarter.[42] The laws were passed the year after the protests that had greeted the announcement that Putin would return to the presidency. They were part of a broader policy drive to consolidate control over political activity in Russia. Now back in the Kremlin, Putin wanted to stay there. He therefore minimised the risk that any colour revolution, or other popular uprising, might drive him from his place at the summit of Russian power. NGOs were not the only target. McFaul, appointed ambassador to Moscow in 2012, later described it as the year when 'Putin stopped playing defense and went on the offensive regarding our competition over values.'[43] In McFaul's case, that meant responding to a Russian demand that the USAID cease its activities in Russia. USAID had been working in Russia since the 1990s, its work then, in McFaul's words, 'focused primarily on fostering economic reform and economic development'. By 2012, McFaul later wrote, 'roughly half of its programs in Russia focused on civil society, rule of law, or other programs aimed at fostering democracy and human rights. And that's why Lavrov wanted them to end.'[44] The US acceded to the demand. For NGOs, the reality of dealing with the new laws was as they had feared. In 2016, reflecting on four years of working under the legislation, Sergei Nikitin, director of Amnesty International Russia, wrote, 'The foreign agents law was designed to shackle, stigmatise, and ultimately silence critical NGOs. It has caught a wide range of NGOs in its net and come at considerable cost to individual rights and the quality of civic discussion in Russia.'[45]

The targeting of NGOs and representatives of foreign governments alike suggested a belief among the Russian political elite that opposition to the political system that Putin had built could not possibly be home grown. It must have its roots, and its resources, in forces outside the country that sought to weaken Russia. There was an echo here of early Soviet thinking, of Stalinist suspicion of foreigners, even those foreign communists who were genuine believers in the Soviet project. Stalin himself had warned, 'All bourgeois foreign specialists are or could be spies.'[46]

Journalists had come under particular suspicion in the early Soviet era, sometimes with good reason, as in the case of Marguerite Harrison, an American correspondent in the era following the First World War who had also been a spy. Yet she was clearly in the minority and, in her case, had been pushed towards taking this option because of her gender. Newspapers then would not readily employ a female foreign correspondent, and Harrison wanted to report from Russia.[47] As relations between Russia and the West once again soured, journalism was again a casualty.

It was not a one-sided affair. The US too had foreign agent legislation, and had done since the Foreign Agents Registration Act of 1938.[48] In 2017, RT was required to register, following a report from intelligence agencies in the US that the channel was 'Russia's state-run propaganda machine', and that it had been involved in Russia's attempts to influence the outcome of the 2016 presidential election. Russia soon responded, widening its own foreign agent legislation to provide for the possible prosecution of media organisations.[49] When, in 2021, Dmitry Muratov of *Novaya Gazeta* was named the co-recipient of the Nobel Peace Prize, the Russian justice ministry's response was to add nine journalists and three media companies to the foreign agents list.[50] The overall effect of the law was to make life harder for outlets affected by it to build trust with their audiences. In order not to break the law, outlets such as TV Rain had to attach to their social media posts a notice – much larger than the post itself – stating that it was material from a foreign media organisation fulfilling the function of a foreign agent, or a Russian legal entity doing the same.

In Putin's third and fourth terms as president, worsening relations between Russia and the West were increasingly codified in law. The foreign agent legislation restricted political and press activity in Russia, even in cases where there was no genuine foreign connection. The logic increasingly was that opposition, criticism or even questioning of government policy was somehow unpatriotic, and must therefore be the work of foreign hands, however carefully hidden.

Suspicion clouded even spiritual matters. As discussed in Chapter 5, Putin's public observance of Orthodox Christian rites was increasingly part of his political identity. The church was also a means of strengthening Russian cultural identity, and not only within Russia. Orthodox Christianity was one of the forces that, in Putin's view, bound together the people of Russia, Belarus and Ukraine. The 2018 decision of Ukraine's major Orthodox churches to institutionalise one independent Orthodox Church of Ukraine, outside the authority of the Moscow patriarch, was therefore seen as an act of defiance. The US's support for such a move was seen almost as a hostile act.

On 5 January 2019, ahead of Orthodox Christmas, which falls on 7 January, the spiritual head of Orthodox Christianity, Ecumenical Patriarch Bartholomew, formally granted the Ukrainian Church independence from Moscow. The Ukrainian president, Petro Poroshenko, attended the ceremony in Istanbul.[51] A spiritual change, in one sense, independence for the Ukrainian Church was in its wider significance deeply political. The previous month, Putin had reacted angrily to a report that the US secretary of state, Mike Pompeo, had spoken to Kyiv to express support for the Ukrainian Church's plans. Putin had also warned against property disputes that he said were already happening between that part of the Ukrainian Church that wished to be independent, and others that preferred to remain with Moscow. 'It's already going on and it can be grave – if not bloody.'[52]

Weeks later, in March, Putin travelled to Crimea for ceremonies marking the fifth anniversary of Russia's annexation of the peninsula. Putin referred to the events of five years earlier as 'reunification', not missing an opportunity to refer to the Second World War. At an evening concert, he addressed the crowd: 'The actions of the people of Crimea and Sevastopol remind me of the actions of Red Army soldiers during the first tragic months after the breakout of the Great Patriotic War, when they tried to battle through to join their comrades and carried their field flags close to their hearts.'[53] Putin wanted his audience to believe, as he apparently did, that the 'reunification' was a continuation of the Red Army's heroic struggle against Nazi Germany. I was visiting Russia at the time and watched the extensive coverage of the events on state television. For this predominantly domestic audience, much was made of the presence of a delegation of French politicians. They did not represent the government. One member of the delegation, Thierry Mariani, spoke in a meeting with Putin of his regret that the French government, under the then president François Hollande, had blocked attempts to lift sanctions imposed on Russia. Mariani had himself been one of those seeking the change.[54] He continued to defend his actions after Russia's full-scale invasion of Ukraine in 2022. Quoted by *The Economist* in November of that year, he rejected any allegations of wrongdoing in relation to his links to Russia.[55] That Putin met the delegation at all showed the importance he placed on any kind of international, especially Western, approval or even acceptance of the new reality. Other reports broadcast that week as part of the coverage marking the fifth anniversary of the 'reunification' included an item on the bridge between Russia and Crimea, and how it would make it easier for viewers to travel to the peninsula, by road or rail, for holidays on the Black Sea. The bridge had been completed in 2014 and was lauded as just one of the many benefits Russian annexation had brought to both Russia and Crimea. The same bridge would become a target following the escalation of the war in Ukraine in 2022, suffering damage in attacks both later that year and in 2023 and 2025.[56]

At the end of 2019, NATO leaders met in London to mark the seventieth anniversary of the founding of the alliance. The actual anniversary had fallen earlier in the year, in April. The Russian foreign ministry marked the anniversary by publishing a statement saying that the 'alliance is not going to stop building up its military and political confrontation with Russia. The bloc's key goal – to rally its allies for containing "the threat from the East" – has not changed since its establishment in 1949.'[57] Invited then to speak to the US Congress, Stoltenberg did begin by recalling the formation of NATO from countries 'determined to stand up to the expansion of the Soviet Union. Which was taking control of its neighbours. Crushing democracies. And oppressing their people.'[58] There was a common starting point in history, and a complete divergence of celebration. The Russian foreign ministry brought international political communication right up to date on Twitter, sarcastically wishing NATO 'inner peace and less nervousness'.[59]

In fact, the celebrations in London later that year were not all inner peace and less nervousness. There were blunt words about money. Stoltenberg met Trump ahead of the main summit. Photographs released later, and published on the NATO website, showed Trump looking rather unimpressed, but he did say that he was 'a big fan' of Stoltenberg. Trump announced an agreement under which NATO member states other than the US would increase their contributions to the alliance. 'Through some work and some negotiation, we've increased the budget of countries other than the USA, because we're paying far more than anybody else, and far more even as a percentage of GDP.'[60] The increase was worth another $130 billion. Only the year before, at a NATO summit in Brussels, Trump had threatened that the US would leave the alliance if others did not contribute more.[61] His apparent satisfaction at the pledge of an increase in funds, and his expressed admiration for Stoltenberg, made that seem a more distant prospect. Any such divisions among Western institutions would not go unnoticed in Moscow. Even at the time the UK was hosting the summit, it had been involved in a political crisis over its departure from the EU. The week after the NATO meeting, the Conservative Party, by then under the leadership of Boris Johnson, won a general election. The majority they now enjoyed was such that they passed the legislation for the UK finally to leave the EU, which it did on 31 January 2020.[62]

Protests in Ukraine against Yanukovych's refusal to sign the association agreement with the EU had precipitated his downfall. That led in turn to Russia's taking advantage of political uncertainty in Kyiv to seize Crimea. Now, nearly six years later, the EU experienced the loss of one of its larger member states, following a referendum in which ideas of national identity and sovereignty had trumped arguments of potential economic disadvantage. The departure was, like Trump's threat to leave

NATO, a sign of dissatisfaction and disunity at the heart of one of the West's major institutions. Russia's official response to Brexit was diplomatic and muted, with Lavrov insisting that Russia was not 'rubbing its hands and gloating'.[63] Given that – after Maidan – Moscow increasingly saw the EU as a geopolitical rival, this was hard to take at face value.

While protests in Ukraine had altered that country's history by leading to a change of leadership, such a prospect had become ever more distant in Russia. Repression within Russia, in the form of increasing restrictions on media and political freedoms, was final confirmation that the country's post-Soviet political system had settled, settled as something very different from that which many in the West – and many in Russia, too – had hoped for when the USSR fell. The Communist Party elite who had tried to put a stop to reform in 1991 had failed. Nearly three decades on, however, there was a former KGB officer very firmly established in the Kremlin. The kind of Russia that was emerging was a kind of Russia with which the coup plotters might have been content. Re-establishing control over all the territory that Moscow had lost in 1991 was out of the question, although Putin had proved that 'reunification' with some of it was achievable by using force, and choosing the moment carefully.

11

Tales of Bygone Years, and Future Wars

As 2020 dawned, the Russian government declared that the coming twelvemonth would be 'The Year of Memory and Glory'.[1] The centrepiece was to be the military parade on Red Square on 9 May, marking the seventy-fifth anniversary of the defeat of Nazi Germany by the USSR and its allies. Ever since military parades had resumed in 2008, official propaganda had sought to amplify and exploit the patriotic pride that many Russians already felt. For this major anniversary – certainly the last for some of the dwindling band of surviving veterans – plans were made to expand the celebrations to something truly spectacular. In February, the defence minister, Sergei Shoigu, announced that twenty countries had been invited to send troops to take part in the parade. Some Russian soldiers would wear period uniforms. T-34 tanks, the mechanical workhorses of the Soviet victory, would be among the host of military hardware that would draw up to clatter across the cobblestones in front of Lenin's mausoleum. 'A total of 15,000 troops and 375 items of ground-based and aircraft hardware are set to take part in the parade,' Shoigu said. The parade itself would be larger, and last longer – an hour and a half – than those in previous years.[2]

This was a different world, and a different Russia, compared to that which had celebrated the fiftieth anniversary of the end of the conflict a quarter of a century earlier. Culture, as well as politics, was becoming more militarised. The T-34 tanks that were to feature in the victory parade had already been honoured the previous year with a film, simply called *T-34*. The movie told the story of a group of Soviet soldiers and their T-34 fighting the Nazi invaders. Released for the 2019 New Year holiday, it took more than $10 million at the box office in its opening weekend – a record for a Russian-made film in Russia.[3] When President Clinton had given his speech regretting that the Cold War had intervened to stop the West fully acknowledging the Soviet role in the defeat of Nazi Germany, he had done so in a Moscow that was the capital of a former foe destined to be an enemy no more. The student audience to whom he spoke at Moscow State University was a new generation who would benefit from, and build on, the opportunities offered by the end of the Cold War. The celebrations were remarkable for the large number of countries represented: a total of fifty-six.[4]

Such international concord between Russia and its Western partners – as Putin often referred to them (the word is the same in Russian, and he would sometimes roll the first 'r' as if to suggest disdain) – was now in the past. Even before Western countries considered whether they should send delegations after the annexation of Crimea, a diplomatic disagreement over the causes and history of the conflict itself broke out: a diplomatic disagreement that prompted some very undiplomatic language.

The dispute started over whether the USSR should take part of the blame for the start of the war. At issue was the Molotov–Ribbentrop Pact, secret agreements between Stalin's USSR and Hitler's Germany that in effect agreed spheres of influence over the countries that lay between their borders. The previous autumn, the European parliament had angered Russia by passing a resolution that described the pact as 'dividing Europe and the territories of independent states between the two totalitarian regimes and grouping them into spheres of interest, which paved the way for the outbreak of the Second World War'.[5] During one of his lengthy annual news conferences, Putin described this view of history as 'totally unacceptable and inaccurate'.[6] The US ambassador to Poland joined in, tweeting, 'Dear President Putin, Hitler and Stalin colluded to start WWII. That is a fact. Poland was a victim of this horrible conflict.'[7] The row also included Putin's reference to a wartime Polish diplomat as an 'antisemitic pig'.[8] Such a confrontation would have been unthinkable among the harmonious tone of the commemorations of 1995. It was not that such different interpretations of history did not exist then. It was that the diplomatic priority was not to emphasise them. That had changed in the intervening twenty-five years. History was now drawn up to the front line as an extra weapon in a diplomatic conflict.

It was a conflict to which there were many willing parties. Putin was happy to let the disagreements over the past echo in the present, for the past which was in dispute was an era in which Russia had exercised its military muscle to change the course of European, and world, history. Then, Russia had been respected as an ally by both Washington and London, a respect that had endured into the Cold War even as that alliance perished.

As the twentieth anniversary of his first victory in the Russian presidential election approached, in March 2020, Putin gave a lengthy interview to the Russian news agency TASS. Military matters naturally came up. 'We are not going to fight against anyone,' Putin told the interviewer, Andrey Vandenko, before continuing, 'We are going to create conditions so that nobody wants to fight against us.' The interview also included an account of a conversation Putin said he had had with Trump about the relative sizes of their military budgets. The impression given was of two commanders-in-chief of massive military forces comparing notes to see how the other responded.[9]

As 9 May approached, Western powers found themselves with a diplomatic dilemma. They wished to honour the Soviet war dead, and the surviving veterans, and to pay tribute to the role that they had played in saving Europe from Hitler. The prospect of looking approvingly on a parade that might well include troops involved in the annexation of Crimea was less appealing. By January, while President Emmanuel Macron of France had accepted the Kremlin's invitation, the Russian ambassador to Washington, Anatoly Antonov, admitted, 'There are still several heads of states who have not yet responded to our invitation.'[10] The worst global pandemic for a century meant that they did not have to make a decision. Having first become widespread in China in the later part of 2019, the coronavirus Covid-19 soon gripped many other parts of the world.

In Russia, the first major move in response to the virus was the closure of the border with China at the end of January 2020. As in many other parts of the world – those areas of Asia which had had to contend with outbreaks of Severe Acute Respiratory Syndrome (SARS), or bird flu, being exceptions – the government in Russia was dealing with a situation it had not faced in living memory. To begin with, the virus did not affect Russia as badly as some other countries. By 20 March, there were just 199 reported cases, and Putin's spokesman, Dmitry Peskov, said that the president was not going to be taking a test because, 'Thank God, he always feels brilliant.'[11] As the pandemic continued, the situation became graver. On 28 March, TASS reported that the number of cases in Russia had risen to 1,264. Four people had died of the virus.[12] Peskov's relaxed optimism no longer seemed so reassuring. The authorities declared a 'non-working week' – in effect, a week of public holidays. People were expected to stay at home to help to stop the spread of the virus. Many Russians seemed to take advantage of the unscheduled layoff to fall back on a traditional source of solace in times of trouble. After years of falling alcohol consumption, sales of vodka were 31 per cent higher in the last week of March than they had been in the same period the previous year. Sales of whisky were up 47 per cent; beer by 25. 'People are grabbing everything they can – vodka, cognac and beer,' an employee of a supermarket in the Moscow region told the Reuters news agency.[13]

This was not the springtime that Putin had foreseen when he gave his in-depth interview to TASS in early March. In addition to the grand plans for the celebration of the seventy-fifth anniversary of victory in the Great Patriotic War, 2020 was set to be a major political year for Russia. On 22 April, the country was due to take part in an 'all-Russian vote', which would introduce changes to the constitution. Most importantly, it would change the law on presidential terms. Putin was then in his fourth term as president. The planned changes would permit him to run twice more: standing for election in 2024, and even in 2030. He could in theory stay in power until 2036, by which time he would be in his eighty-fourth year. Among a large number of other proposed amendments was one which would legally define marriage as the union between a man and a woman. The formal outlawing of same-sex marriage was a strong sign of the social conservatism that Putin saw as defining the Russia he led, in comparison to those – from a conservative Russian perspective – decadent Western legal systems that included marriage equality.

The pandemic led to the postponement of both the parade and the vote. For Putin, the delay to the national vote had some benefits. By this stage in his presidency, the result of any kind of election was not in doubt. Things were not looking rosy for Russia, however. Living standards had been declining for some years.[14] In 2020 overall, the Russian economy shrank 3 per cent – though Germany and the UK fared worse.[15] Economic stability and rising prosperity had been cornerstones of Putin's entire presidency. In return, he expected respect and obedience – as the steady erosion of political and press freedom during his time in the Kremlin, and particularly since his return to the presidency in 2012, had demonstrated. Now damage to the economy as a result of the pandemic, sanctions and falling oil prices were making it harder for him to keep his side of the bargain. A Levada Center poll conducted in February 2020, two months before the national vote was originally due to take place, found that 46 per cent of respondents thought that Putin should 'probably' or 'definitely' step down as president when his term ended in 2024. Forty-five per cent of respondents thought he 'probably' or 'definitely' should not give up leadership of the country.[16] Even with the Kremlin's confident control of Russia's electoral machinery, these were still the kind of numbers that Putin and his administration did not want to see.

Another data set provoked threats against international news organisations. In May 2020, both the *New York Times* and the *Financial Times* published stories suggesting that official data for Covid deaths in Russia were inaccurate, and that the real figures were much higher. The Russian authorities' response demonstrated that intolerance of dissent from official versions of events would now be extended to international media. As the *Financial Times* report noted on 11 May, 'Russia has made it illegal to publish or discuss "fake news" about the pandemic in the country'.[17] The problem for the Russian authorities on this occasion was that both the *Financial Times* and the *New York Times* were working from official data. Their journalists had compared the number of deaths recorded in Moscow and Saint Petersburg in April 2020 with the same month in previous years. Even allowing for the official number of deaths of which Covid was given as a cause, there was a large number of other excess deaths. The *Financial Times* report concluded that if these were added to official figures, it 'would mean a 72 per cent increase in Russia's national death toll'. The *New York Times* quoted Tatiana N. Mikhailova, a senior researcher at the Presidential Academy of National Economy and Public Administration in Moscow, saying that 'the number of Covid-19 victims is possibly almost three times higher than the official toll'.[18]

Although both newspapers based their reporting on official data from official sources, the Russian authorities accused them of spreading 'disinformation' – a criminal offence that carried a potential prison sentence of up to five years. One member of the Duma even demanded that the two news organisations be stripped of their accreditation, a move that would make their continuing to report from Russia illegal.[19] In the event, the Russian foreign ministry contented itself with its angry condemnation of the reporting – but the response was a warning. It was a warning to international journalists that their foreign passports would not protect them from serious reprisals if their work was seen to challenge or contradict too blatantly the official line. For a government's response to the pandemic had become a matter not only of public health but of national pride. Alongside stability and prosperity, security had always been a pillar of the Putin presidency: witness the way that his tough line with Chechen separatists had helped to propel him to power at the start of his rise. A president who could not protect his people against the pandemic could not be said to be providing security.

There was another reason why this was such a sensitive matter. As the disease spread, the race to find a vaccine sped up. In August, Russia would be the first country to announce that it had licensed one: Sputnik V, its name a reference to a Soviet victory in the space race of the previous century. While there were questions over the fact that Sputnik V had been approved even before clinical trials were complete, Russia saw the cost (less than $10 per dose) as another win in the international soft power (and commercial) contest that the vaccine race represented. As an article in the *British Medical Journal* in March 2021 pointed out, however, 'The early approval, and Russia's bombast around the vaccine, provoked scepticism among scientists.'[20]

Large parts of the Russian population seemed to be sceptical, too. Despite the scientific victory that the release of Sputnik V supposedly represented, Russians were reticent. When, in March 2021, Putin's spokesman announced that the president had had a vaccination, he would not say which one. At the time, 6.3 million Russians had reportedly been vaccinated – a mere 5 per cent of the adult population.[21] Their scepticism may have been strengthened by a more sinister turn in the competition to be first. In October 2020, two months after the announcement that Sputnik V was ready, *The Times* of London reported on what it called 'a Russian disinformation campaign to undermine and spread fear' about a vaccine that was being developed at the University of Oxford. The absurd suggestion was that the vaccine could turn people who had it into monkeys.[22] Nor were these the only dirty tricks alleged to have been used as world powers competed for the prize of being first with a vaccine. In July 2020, the British government accused Russia of being behind a cyber attack on the Oxford laboratories where the vaccine research was underway.[23]

Whichever of the vaccines Putin had, wherever the research was done, and however it was obtained, he took no chances with the virus. When lockdown measures in Russia were relaxed in the summer of 2020, Putin did not change his personal precautions. Having retreated to one of his residences outside Moscow, from where he conducted most of his meetings remotely, the Russian leader continued to insist on the strictest conditions for contact with anyone else. Journalists and others seeking to come into the president's presence were required to quarantine for lengthy periods before doing so. The coronavirus pandemic was a time of isolation for many people. For Putin, as he entered his third decade at the peak of Russian power, it seems also to have been a time when he reassessed his political philosophy, and made plans for the future.

Even if Putin remained distant and cautious, in the summer of 2020 general restrictions in Russia had been eased to the extent that both the commemoration of victory in the Great Patriotic War and the vote on the constitution went ahead. June was a key month in modern Russian history as the country celebrated its past military glory in a way that also emphasised state and presidential power in the present. The previous month, on the anniversary of the end of the war, a social media spat served as a reminder not only of the increasingly antagonistic nature of relations with the West, but also of the decline of conventional public diplomacy in the Twitter era.

On 8 May, the White House tweeted, 'On May 8, 1945, America and Great Britain had victory over the Nazis!'[24] RT responded with a story that pointed out that the tweet was guilty of 'leaving out the nation that sacrificed the most – the Soviet Union'.[25] The following month, with the parade having been rescheduled for 24 June (the date chosen as it was the anniversary of the first victory parade, in 1945), Putin added his own lesson in the form of a long historical essay published on the website of *The National Interest*, and also that of the Kremlin. The commemoration of the anniversary having been long in the planning, the essay which Putin published apparently had been, too. '75th Anniversary of the Great Victory: Shared Responsibility to History and our Future' ran to more than eighty pages, including additional supporting documents added at the end for reference. Putin began on a personal note, recalling his own family experience of the conflict, including the death of his brother, aged only two, during the siege of Leningrad. In an apparent response to the European parliament's condemnation of totalitarianism, and the spheres of influence it had created on the continent in the twentieth century, Putin then went on the rhetorical offensive: 'Historical revisionism, the manifestations of which we now observe in the West, primarily with regard to the subject of World War II and its outcome, is dangerous.'

Putin understandably placed great emphasis on Soviet losses during the conflict, taking care to compare them with those of allies: 'Almost 27 million Soviet citizens lost their lives on the fronts, in German prisons, starved to death and were bombed, died in ghettos and furnaces of the Nazi death camps. The USSR lost one in seven of its citizens, the UK lost one in 127, and the United States lost one in 320.'[26] As a barbed reminder to the USSR's wartime allies, Putin also quoted Churchill's 1944 letter to Stalin in which the wartime British prime minister wrote: 'It is the Russian Army that tore the guts out of the German military machine.'[27]

Clinton's admission that, because of the Cold War, Western powers had not recognised the scale of Soviet loss and sacrifice already belonged to a different diplomatic era. Putin had played a major part in the return to a more confrontational relationship. He was not willing to let the West forget again something that it had taken so long to recognise. Of course, this was not simply about remembering history. It was about the domestic politics and international relations of the moment, too. At home, Putin was facing declining popularity among an electorate whose standard of living was stagnating – just as he was due to ask them to grant him greater power than he had ever enjoyed in his twenty years as Russia's most powerful politician. Victory Day of 9 May had passed with no parade at all: grand plans reduced to nothing by a pandemic, and celebrations ignored by wartime allies unwilling to overlook the annexation of Crimea. The parade went ahead on 24 June, with some 14,000 soldiers, and intercontinental ballistic missiles on show beneath the towers of the Kremlin. Putin's tone was more conciliatory. 'We will never forget our allies' contribution to the common victory, the significance of the second front that opened in June 1944,' he said in a speech to mark the occasion.[28]

From commemoration of the past, to the reality of the pandemic present, and on to plans for the future: Putin had been speaking on 24 June, the day before voting started on the planned changes to the constitution. Putin's essay, in common with his earlier evocations of the history of ancient Rus' as part of his justification for the annexation of Crimea, was an attempt to put his presidency on a plane with glorious eras of Russian power during the country's past. Putin may have given some thought to the way the future counterparts of the authors of ancient chronicles would remember him. Yet his big ideas of Russian history were also about reinforcing a strong sense of national identity as a means to the consolidation of power in the present, and securing it for the future.

As expected, the national vote delivered Putin the result that he wanted. The changes to the constitution became law on 4 July. They had passed by a very comfortable majority: almost 78 per cent of those who voted had supported them; a little over 21 per cent had expressed opposition.[29] As the final day of voting approached – it had been spread out over a week because of concerns for public health that still persisted at that time during the pandemic – Putin had encouraged people to come to cast their ballots, appealing to 'our respect for our history, culture, mother tongue, traditions, our memory of achievements and feats of our ancestors, that ensure the sovereignty of Russia'.[30] Only in the aftermath of the overwhelming approval of the plans was this declared to be about Putin's popularity, rather than the more noble and abstract idea of patriotism. 'It's definitely considered a triumph. What took place was in effect a de facto triumphant referendum on trust in Putin,' said the presidential spokesman, Peskov.[31] Already in power for twenty years, Putin could now legally remain in the Kremlin for a further sixteen. He had no serious opposition. The entire post-Soviet political system had evolved such that it was now based around one man: him. In that sense, his position was secure.

Looked at another way, serious challenges lay ahead. His first decade in power had been built on two things: understanding the stability and material comfort his constituency craved above all else and – aided by rising oil prices – delivering them. In his second decade, he had grown bolder, and more adventurous: building on the military success in Georgia in 2008, Putin had won an easy victory in Crimea and flexed martial muscle in the Middle East with intervention in Syria. On both occasions, he had chosen his moment, and his target, in a way that had wrongfooted the West. At the end of the decade, Assad remained in power and Crimea remained in Russian hands. Whether or not Western powers were willing formally to recognise that mattered little when it had given such a terrific boost to his popularity at home. Yet at the dawn of Putin's third decade in power it was not obvious that those previous formulas for success could be repeated. Oil prices were rising as Covid restrictions eased, though at $39.20 for the OPEC average at the end of June, the highs that had been reached in the months before the 2008 financial crisis were simply a memory of times not expected to return. Instead of booming as it had previously under Putin, the economy – in common with Covid-affected global trends – was forecast to contract by 6.6 per cent.[32]

Even if the opinion polls conducted before the national vote had suggested that the electorate included a significant number who thought Putin should step down in 2024, the result of the vote itself suggested no serious threat to his authority. Yet a leader worried by any prospect – however remote – of a colour revolution or other regime change must work to eliminate risk. Although the obstacles that the Kremlin had placed in his way ensured that Alexei Navalny was not a serious challenger to Putin's authority in electoral politics (and there was no certainty he would have prevailed in completely fair elections, either), he continued to challenge, provoke and, almost certainly, annoy. His blog post in June 2020 questioning the cost of the military parade to mark victory in the Second World War cannot have been well received in the Kremlin. The post also included a section on regional elections scheduled for the following September. Navalny called on his supporters 'to strike at' Putin and United Russia, using the 'smart voting' system his movement had devised. The system allowed people to use their votes to minimise support for pro-Putin candidates.[33]

In August 2020, Alexei Navalny was poisoned. He had been in the Siberian city of Tomsk and was on a flight back to Moscow when he was suddenly taken ill. The plane made an emergency landing in Omsk. Navalny was taken to hospital. His team said that the toxin must have been administered in a cup of tea, as that was the only food or drink he had taken that morning. On behalf of the Kremlin, Peskov wished Navalny a speedy recovery. He also said that any request for Navalny to receive treatment abroad would be considered.[34] After three days' treatment in Omsk, Navalny was flown to Germany. On 2 September, the German government made public results of tests carried out in a military laboratory. They concluded that Navalny had been poisoned with a Novichok nerve agent – one of the same kind used to attack Sergei Skripal and his daughter Yulia in Salisbury two years earlier. Angela Merkel said that the result of the toxicology report meant that there were 'serious questions that only the Russian government can and must answer'.[35]

Predictably, the Russian government's answer was that it had had nothing to do with the incident. The foreign ministry spokeswoman, Maria Zakharova, asked, 'Where are the facts, where are the formulas, at least some kind of information?'[36] Navalny's team remained convinced that he had been poisoned on the orders of the Kremlin. He had been lucky to survive. In December, sufficiently recovered to resume his investigative and campaigning activities, Navalny even seemed to trick one of those responsible for his poisoning into giving more details of what had happened. An investigation by Bellingcat and CNN succeeded in identifying a team of FSB agents who, the investigation concluded on the basis of mobile phone and flight records, had been following Navalny for years before the attack in Omsk in September 2020. Four months after the attempt on his life, Navalny telephoned one of the agents, named as Konstantin Kudryavtsev. Navalny pretended to be one of the agent's superior officers, seeking information about what had happened. The ruse seemingly worked, and Navalny learnt that the poison had been smeared into his underpants. The person on the other end of the phone also suggested that the stopover in Omsk had saved Navalny's life. 'If you don't land the plane the effect would've been different and the result would've been different.' The flight from Tomsk to Moscow is around three hours, after which time, apparently, Navalny would have died. The FSB dismissed the recording of the conversation – which was later shared online – as a fabrication by Western intelligence.[37] The previous week, during his annual news conference, Putin had been asked for his response to the Bellingcat/CNN findings. He suggested that if the FSB had indeed been responsible, 'they would've probably finished it'.[38]

The entire episode showed a combination of paranoia, cruelty and arrogance on the part of the Kremlin and its agents. During his news conference, and subsequently, Putin refused to refer to Navalny by name. He also sought to undermine Navalny's significance, asking during his news conference, 'Who needs him anyway?' An opinion poll conducted in September had suggested that large numbers of Russians – 50 per cent – did not approve of Navalny's activities (with only 20 per cent saying they did). The same poll did find, however, that by September a majority of people had heard of him, something that had apparently not been the case in May.[39] Putin's refusal to say Navalny's name may have been a response to his adversary's growing public profile.

The apparent willingness of state agents to use a chemical weapon to poison an opponent suggests a callous mercilessness that needs no extra explanation. Navalny's eventual fate – death in prison in 2024 – only serves to make Kremlin attempts to deflect blame for the August 2020 attack all the more implausible. The agents seem to have been identified – as were the suspects behind the Salisbury poisonings – by examination of public or easily obtainable sources. Phone and flight records, along with other official data such as vehicle licensing details, are quite easy to purchase illicitly in Russia. This suggests that caution was not seen as necessary. Being caught might have been embarrassing, but the impunity with which agents of the Russian state were apparently able to commit crimes also served as a warning to anyone else thinking of challenging the system.

Navalny now found himself facing a dilemma he had in common with many leading political figures in Russian history: whether to return to Russia with all the risk that might involve (of all political exiles in Russian history, Navalny certainly needed no convincing how hazardous that might be), or whether to remain in relative safety outside the country. For Germany was only relatively safe. In 2019, a Chechen militant had been gunned down in Berlin by Vadim Krasikov, a Russian. The trial judge had described the killing as 'state terrorism'. The fact that Krasikov was exchanged in 2024 as part of a swap for Westerners held in Russia seemed to confirm that he was indeed an agent of the Russian state.[40] The fate of the Skripals had similarly shown that being abroad did not mean being beyond the reach of would-be killers.

During the autumn of 2020, Navalny made clear his determination to return to Russia once he was sufficiently recovered. 'It's maybe a good thing for a politician facing death once,' he had said during an interview with CBS in October.[41] A previous criminal conviction – for embezzlement, one of many Navalny had always insisted were politically motivated – meant that he had to attend court before the end of December or risk breaking parole conditions. In the event, Navalny returned to Russia in January 2021 and was immediately taken into custody at the airport. He was initially sentenced to thirty days in jail for breach of parole conditions. In a characteristically impudent challenge to Putin, the video about the palace that the Russian leader was alleged to own on the Black Sea coast was posted just after Navalny had been in court. Navalny's detention prompted protests that brought thousands of Russians onto the streets to demand his release. More than 3,000 people were detained, for the demonstrations were deemed unlawful.[42] Navalny's return had inspired his supporters to act, but their options were limited against a powerful state apparatus, to which the security forces showed unfailing loyalty. Navalny's movement would continue to campaign, and he would continue to inspire his supporters. But his flight back from Germany to Russia in January 2021 was the last time his charismatic wit would be expressed in public, albeit behind the mask that Covid restrictions then demanded. He would remain in custody until his death on 16 February 2024 in a penal colony in the Russian far north.

Navalny's final incarceration was not the only step that the Kremlin took to protect Putin's power and that of the political forces, especially the United Russia party, that supported him. Duma elections were held in September 2021. Navalny himself was behind bars. His supporters were kept from standing by new legislation, passed in June, that outlawed their movement as extremist. The election, which took place over three days because of Covid precautions that still remained in force, produced no surprises. United Russia took nearly half the vote, leaving the party's supermajority (more than two-thirds of the seats in the Duma, sufficient to pass legislation without the support of other parties) intact. Smart voting failed to have any significant effect. Both Navalny's supporters and the communists alleged fraud, but there were no significant street protests in response to the result. The authorities had apparently succeeded in laying to rest the spectre of 2011. The US, EU and UK all criticised the conduct of the election, with London describing it as 'a setback for democratic freedom'.[43] None of this, of course, was sufficient to trouble Putin and his supporters. There was only one cloud on the Kremlin's horizon: the official turnout, at just under 52 per cent, suggested a lack of enthusiasm for more of the same.[44] Given the extent of Kremlin control over the political process, there was perhaps a belief that the result of the election would not be greatly altered by ordinary voters going to the polls. The faltering economy had failed to prove sufficient cause for a serious challenge to Putinism, but the genuine enthusiasm of earlier years was seemingly starting to drain away.

The same was not true in neighbouring Ukraine. A presidential election in 2019 had produced a political earthquake: the shock second-round result of a defeat for Petro Poroshenko by an opponent who was a political novice. Volodymyr Zelensky had built his presidential campaign profile on his previous role in a popular television series, *Servant of the People*. In the series, Zelensky had played a history teacher whose obscenity-laden monologue expressing bitter dissatisfaction with politics in Ukraine is filmed by a student, who then shares it on YouTube. It goes viral. Zelensky's character is eventually elected president.[45] In April 2019, Zelensky completed his own career change, victorious in the second round of a presidential election in which he won almost three quarters (73.22 per cent) of the votes cast.[46]

He came to office in a country that was still suffering from the war that Russia had launched with the annexation of Crimea five years earlier. The conflict did not command the international attention it once had, but the lack of attention did not mean it had gone away. In January 2022, the UN Human Rights Monitoring Mission in Ukraine put the number of casualties in the war in eastern Ukraine at between 51,000 and 54,000 in the period from 14 April 2014 to 31 December 2021. Between 14,200 and 14,400 people were estimated to have died, as many as 9,000 of those reckoned to be civilians.[47] As might be expected of a president coming newly to office, even one with no previous experience of elected office, and no clear agenda except a promise to be different, Zelensky could not ignore the situation in the east of the country – even if much of the rest of the world was trying to do exactly that. Russian annexation of Crimea had led to sanctions and suspension from the G8, but, as the World Cup in 2018 had showed, Russia had not been ostracised. 'Our first task is ceasefire in the Donbas,' Zelensky said in his inaugural address in May 2019. 'Our next challenge is returning the lost territories. In all honesty, this wording does not seem entirely correct to me because it is impossible to return what has always been ours. Both Crimea and Donbas have been our Ukrainian land.'[48]

Zelensky's first meeting with Putin, in December 2019, took place in Paris. There was no progress. There could not be. There was no common ground. Earlier in the year, Putin had spoken triumphantly at a concert in Crimea to mark the fifth anniversary of the annexation, or reunification, as his official propaganda prefers to describe it. As Mikhail Zygar summarised it, writing later, in 2023, 'Putin is generally satisfied by the lack of agreement: the frozen conflict is a huge stumbling block for Ukraine on the road to new alliances'.[49]

Zelensky's first experience of international politics was not the easiest introduction. Not only was there a war with a bigger and much more powerful neighbour, he was also drawn into controversies in the presidential politics of the US. In July 2019, in a telephone call, President Trump asked President Zelensky to 'look into' the then vice president Joe Biden and his son, Hunter. Hunter Biden had had business dealings in Ukraine. There was also a suggestion that Ukrainians might have had something to do with the theft of emails from the Democratic National Committee, an allegation that had already been levelled at Russia.

It was an issue that would return the following year, when the US held presidential elections once more. That would put Trump, as incumbent, against Joe Biden, as Democratic challenger. In a report, 'Foreign Threats to the 2020 US Federal Elections', published in March 2021, the US National Intelligence Council concluded, 'We assess that President Putin and the Russian state authorized and conducted influence operations against the 2020 US presidential election aimed at denigrating President Biden and the Democratic Party, supporting former President Trump, undermining public confidence in the electoral process, and exacerbating sociopolitical divisions in the US.' The report did add, however, 'Unlike in 2016, we did not see persistent Russian cyber efforts to gain access to election infrastructure.'[50]

If Putin and the Russian state did indeed seek to denigrate Biden and the Democrats, then they did not stop Biden being elected president. Biden was inaugurated as president of the US on 20 January 2021. Relations with Russia were at their worst since the end of the Cold War. Biden's agreement with the suggestion, during an ABC News interview in March, that Putin was 'a killer' reflected the state of the two presidents' personal relationship.[51] A month later, Russian troops were massing on the border with Ukraine in numbers that suggested they might be planning a huge escalation of the war. On 13 April, Shoigu said that the troops were taking part in exercises in response to 'threatening' actions by NATO. This may have been a response to a US decision to send two warships to the Black Sea, but Shoigu further accused Washington of moving troops towards regions bordering Russia.[52] By the following week, the EU said that there were 100,000 Russian soldiers on the Ukrainian border.[53] On 22 April, the tension diffused as Shoigu announced that the exercises were over and the troops had been ordered back to their bases.[54]

In less than a year, they would be back – and this time it would not be over quickly, or simply an exercise. The massive troop movement of the spring of 2021 may have satisfied the Russian defence ministry, and the Kremlin, that the Russian army could mount a major military operation against Ukraine. The ability to mobilise was not enough in itself – for the start, or escalation, of any war relies also upon the mobilisation of public opinion. The civilian population will also experience hardship and privation in time of war: everything from shortage of food and other goods to death and bereavement as family members of service personnel, or as new recruits drafted themselves into the armed forces. In Zelensky, Putin faced an adversary who had played a history teacher on TV. Putin now took his turn to give the world – and Russia and

Ukraine in particular – a history lesson based on his own reading of the region's past.

In July 2021, Putin published on the Kremlin website a lengthy article, 'On the Historical Unity of Russians and Ukrainians'.[55] To make his point, Putin went all the way back to the time, in 988, when his namesake, Vladimir (Volodymyr in Ukrainian), converted to Christianity – and even further, to the *Tale of Bygone Years*. Also known as the *Primary Chronicle*, the text is a collection that includes diplomatic documents and treaties, as well as longer stories about adventures and military campaigns in and around ancient Rus'.[56] By citing it, Putin was presenting himself as the modern counterpart of the heroes whose deeds appeared there. His long account of Russian and Ukrainian history included a warning of the time when – after Russia's revolutionary year of 1917 – Ukraine had briefly enjoyed independence from Moscow. Suggesting that this independence had actually put Ukraine at the mercy of other forces, Putin drew a comparison with the present. 'For those who have today given up the full control of Ukraine to external forces, it would be instructive to remember that, back in 1918, such a decision proved fatal for the ruling regime in Kiev,' he said. His words demonstrated his inability to comprehend, or strong desire to ignore, the fact that any people who might share some linguistic or historical roots with modern Russia might not wish to be part of a modern Russia – especially a Russia where his authority was unchallenged. Putin also made several references to the Second World War, especially to those Ukrainians who had fought on the side of German invaders in the hope of breaking free from Soviet domination. The fact that this had happened in the past was associated with the Ukraine Putin saw then, in July 2021. 'This is what is actually happening. First of all, we are facing the creation of a climate of fear in Ukrainian society, aggressive rhetoric, indulging neo-Nazis and militarising the country.'

Alongside Putin's essay, the environment for the news media became even more restrictive than it had previously been. While some courageous Russian journalists continued to report as they saw fit, most of the main news outlets were reliably loyal. There was a warning shot to the international media when, in late August 2021, the BBC correspondent Sarah Rainsford was expelled from Russia.[57]

By the end of the year, to military muscle, presidential propaganda and repression of the press was added diplomatic ultimatum. On 17 December, the foreign ministry in Moscow announced that the US had been given what it termed 'a draft treaty' on security guarantees. The text of this treaty, along with that of an 'Agreement on measures to ensure the security of The Russian Federation and member States of the North Atlantic Treaty Organization', were published on the ministry's website.[58] The text of the draft treaty included the following:

> The United States of America shall undertake to prevent further eastward expansion of the North Atlantic Treaty Organization and deny accession to the Alliance to the States of the former Union of Soviet Socialist Republics.
>
> The United States of America shall not establish military bases in the territory of the States of the former Union of Soviet Socialist Republics that are not members of the North Atlantic Treaty Organization, use their infrastructure for any military activities or develop bilateral military cooperation with them.[59]

Russia was seeking a return to an age in international relations when Moscow and Washington divided Europe in two, and each had the final say on what happened militarily in their part of the continent. The 'treaty' did include an implicit recognition that those members who had joined NATO since the end of the Cold War could not be forced to leave it. But the reference to the USSR betrayed a bitter nostalgia for a bygone era, and spoke of a desire to reverse the perceived injustice and humiliation that had followed the end of that era.

12

Losing Putin's Plot

Moscow's summoning of the spectre of the USSR haunted the first weeks of 2022. Western intelligence suggested that Russia was preparing for war – and went so far as to share some of what they knew. In January, the British foreign secretary, Liz Truss, even claimed that there were plans to replace Zelensky with a post-invasion puppet government led by a Ukrainian former MP, Yevhen Murayev. In reporting Truss's claims, the *Sunday Times* suggested that this making public of classified material was 'understood to be the first time the British government has published secret intelligence to justify a policy decision since the Iraq War'. The historical reference resonated for the damage that war had done to Russia's relations with the West. The paper also reminded its readers that, on that occasion, the intelligence 'later turned out to be false'.[1]

That history did not repeat itself, though the reference to Iraq reflected the enduring scepticism engendered by the Blair government's decision to go to war on the basis of unreliable information. This time there was more to come. On 18 February, Biden said, 'We have reason to believe the Russian forces are planning to, intend to, attack Ukraine in the coming week, in the coming days.' Biden said he was 'convinced' that Putin had made the decision to launch the invasion, his statement based on US intelligence.[2] The Russian defence ministry, Reuters reported, insisted that, in fact, troops were pulling back from regions near Ukraine, having completed exercises. The US secretary of state, Anthony Blinken, was not convinced. 'There's what Russia says. And then there's what Russia does. And we haven't seen any pullback of its forces,' he said.[3]

The British and American decisions to reveal information based on intelligence material demonstrated to the Kremlin that Washington and London knew what was afoot. If the purpose of putting it in the public domain was to prevent the invasion, it failed. The UK and US leaderships did not necessarily expect that they could stop the war by this late stage, but they could make it clear to their countries' people that Russia had planned the war and was about to put the plan into effect.

The point of no return was reached the following week, in the Kremlin on 21 February. Even if the Russian military was ready for war, Russian public opinion had not yet been fully prepared. Though it may be that Putin expected little resistance in Ukraine, and that Kyiv might easily be captured, still the population needed to believe that the war was just – and that the Russian political elite held that view as one.

The chosen method of delivering the propaganda point was a televised meeting of the Russian Security Council. Putin began by hearing from ministers and other senior officials reports on the situation in Donbas. Lavrov was called upon first. He referred to the 'draft treaty' that the foreign ministry had made public in December, noting that a response had been received in January. A minister of Lavrov's experience, especially in dealing with the West, can hardly have been surprised by the response. The requirements of the TV show in which he was appearing meant he had at least to feign disappointment. 'The assessment of this response shows that our Western colleagues are not prepared to take up our major proposals, primarily those on NATO's eastward non-expansion.' His later remarks suggested a certain satisfaction, also reflected in the nostalgia for the time of the 'Union of Soviet

Socialist Republics' implicit in the 'draft treaty' itself, that Moscow was back dealing, as an equal, with its great geopolitical rival. Lavrov emphasised this when he said, 'We have sent our response only to the United States for now, partly, primarily because we see NATO's role as ancillary since they would determine their steps mainly, maybe even exclusively based on Washington's policies.' For his part, Putin was keen not to miss an opportunity to recap historical wrongs done to Russia. He made reference to the 2008 NATO meeting in Bucharest, at which it was agreed that Georgia and Ukraine would eventually join the alliance. 'We have been told that some NATO countries are against Ukraine becoming a member,' Putin said. 'But if they took one step under pressure from the United States, who can guarantee that they will not take another step under pressure? There is no guarantee.' Lavrov said that he had arranged a meeting with Blinken in Geneva on 24 February – but that would not be the reason why that date would come to be remembered.

In addition to persuading the domestic – and to a lesser extent, international – audience watching the drama unfold that the cause was just, Putin needed to demonstrate unity among the Security Council itself. The meeting heard from the director of the FSB, Alexander Bortnikov, that Ukrainian shelling had forced tens of thousands of refugees to cross from Donbas into the Russian Federation (the figures an important part of creating the impression, for domestic propaganda purposes, that the coming invasion would be a war of self-defence). Medvedev, president when in 2008 Russia recognised the independence of the separatist Georgian regions of South Ossetia and Abkhazia following that short summer war, made a plea on behalf of 'about 800,000 citizens of the Russian Federation [who] are currently residing within the borders of these two unrecognised entities', the two entities in question being the Donetsk and Luhansk regions of Ukraine. Together they make up the Donbas. Like Lavrov, he made reference to the US to reinforce his point. 'Everyone is aware that, for example, when US citizens run into any problem at all, when just one is abducted somewhere, the Americans conduct special operations. I think that we, as the Security Council members, cannot ignore this fact.' Medvedev was exhorting his fellow members of the Security Council to rise to the challenge of proving that once again Russia was a worthy rival to the US; a worthy heir to the USSR.

Each person present was then called upon to give their opinion on whether Russia should recognise the independence of Donetsk and Luhansk (Lugansk in Russian). Perhaps for the benefit of the more credulous members of the audience, Putin added, 'each of you knows that I did not discuss anything with anyone in advance. I want to emphasise this. I did not ask for your opinion in advance. What is happening now is happening, so to say, unrehearsed.' Perhaps that was literally true – but anyone who had survived in the Security Council had enough sense not to need a rehearsal. It was clear that Russia was heading to war in Ukraine, and to disagree with Putin's decision would have been career suicide at the very least. Every member of the Security Council agreed that Russia should recognise the independence of the separatist regions. The power that Putin had over Russia's most powerful, and its intimidatory nature, was clear when Sergei Naryshkin, director of Russia's foreign intelligence service, seemed to go on a little too long. Putin said, 'Do you propose starting a negotiating process or recognising the sovereignty of the republics? Speak plainly.' Naryshkin, like a nervous nineteenth-century schoolboy who had not learnt his Latin grammar and so feared a thrashing, eventually said what was expected, and he was told to sit down. This was a Russia in which no form of dissent was any longer possible, save at great risk to the dissenter: media, politics and public protest were all closed areas.[4] Even a seasoned spymaster might get nervous.

Three days later, on 24 February, Russia attacked Ukraine: an invasion of a scale unseen in Europe since the Second World War. The US and its NATO allies sided with Ukraine, supplying weapons as the Ukrainians struggled to save their sovereignty. As during the Cold War, Europe was once again divided.

❊❊❊

How did this happen? There is no question that the end of the Cold War provided an opportunity to break a cycle of confrontation between Russia and the West. In the Napoleonic wars, and the Second World War, Russia had intervened decisively in European conflict and politics, and changed their course. Its interventions on those occasions came with some European powers as allies, some as enemies. At the end of the Cold War, there was a European-wide willingness to make a lasting peace that would benefit all. The US, guarantor of European security since the Second World War, was only too keen to see this come to pass. Yet the opportunity was squandered, with the result that Europe is now far less secure than it was in the latter part of the 1980s, when, in Gorbachev, Russia had a leader well disposed towards the West and seeking to end the Cold War, or in the 1990s, under Yeltsin.

Andrei Kozyrev, Yeltsin's disaffected and dismissed foreign minister, in his 2019 memoir accused the US in the 1990s of 'self-congratulatory remarks on having won the Cold War'.[5] This triumphalism was followed by a belief that because the US had won the Cold War, Russia would fit into a new world order built by the West. The problem was that this new, post-Cold War order was not only built by the West but, from a Russian perspective, for the West. The West's mistake was to believe that Russia would always share its vision of a post-Cold War world and, if it did not, there would be little that Russia could do about it. That the West was self-congratulatory at the end of the Cold War is under-standable. For decades, Washington and Moscow and their allies had faced off across a divided Europe (and beyond, in proxy conflicts). The last, most dangerous phase of the Cold War (in the sense that it was an extended period of rearmament; the Cuban missile crisis of 1962 was the closest the US and the USSR came to nuclear conflict), in the early 1980s, was characterised by a new surge of deployment of nuclear weapons. My generation, then in our teens, recall it as a time of genuine terror that nuclear war might break out at any moment, either by accident or design. To go from that to a united Germany and an increasingly united Europe, in which Russia was no longer seen as a major threat, in less than a decade naturally led to a huge sense of relief. Because it was liberal democratic capitalism that survived as a system, not Soviet socialism, naturally there was a feeling of victory. As President George H.W. Bush put it in his State of the Union address in January 1992, 'the biggest thing that has happened in the world in my life, in our lives, is this: By the grace of God, America won the Cold War'.[6] Such triumphalism may have been understandable – but it tended too towards hubris, and complacency.

It was also short-sighted. Russia's history in the nineteenth and twentieth centuries had shown its willingness not only to resist invaders, but to chase them back whence they came. Whether those invaders came in armies or in the shape of expanding military alliances, Russia's understanding of its own history has led it to be deeply distrustful of any threat, real or potential, from the West. As Gregory Carleton has written, 'Hitler, in sum, is not a lone wolf in the nightmares haunting Russia's historic imagination'.[7] These threats are seen as especially menacing when Russia knows that it is weak in military and geopolitical terms. The breakup of the USSR in 1991 came just seventy-four years after the fall of the Russian Empire. It is hard to imagine a lower point in national self-esteem than a second crumbling of a strong state in the space of less than a century. There is a fascinating note on this subject in the British National Archives in Kew, West London. On his retirement in 1997, Tony Bishop, who had been a Russian translator for the British Foreign Office since the time of Harold Macmillan (prime minister from 1957 to 1963), offered 'a few parting thoughts and suggestions about handling the present-day Russian administration'. Russians, Bishop wrote, 'enjoy and (having suffered so much humiliation in recent times) psychologically <u>need</u> to show off things of which they are proud & to indulge their fabled hospitality'. Bishop further counselled that to 'spare them only half a day' risked 'offending them'.[8] Yet time is something that diplomats increasingly had less and less of during this period. Even in 1993, travelling with John Major and having to respond to Yeltsin's assault on the Moscow White House, Roderic Lyne remembered having to deal with multiple challenges at once. Their host in Malaysia, Mahathir Mohamad, had made a speech critical of British foreign policy; there was an internal political crisis in Downing Street. Lyne recalled, 'So we had the lines buzzing on that. We had the lines buzzing on Mahatir's onslaught. And then we had a major issue to decide in Moscow and you have to do this all at once in the middle of the night when you're completely exhausted after flying from Japan. And with the benefit of more time, for reflection, I suppose our response would have been rather more nuancé.'

The threat that the West posed to Russia at the end of the Cold War was of course nothing like that posed by Hitler or Napoleon. Militarily, it posed no threat at all because diplomatic relations were such that any military confrontation was inconceivable. Russians did not see it in those terms. It was something different – but it was also something that came from the West and was seen as weakening Russia to the West's advantage. For the consequences of the coming of capitalism to Russia in the late twentieth century – the vast majority much worse off, a tiny minority enjoying untold riches – were sufficient to turn many Russians against the version of democracy and the 'market economy' they were being so enthusiastically sold by their new friends from the West, with the help of Russian evangelists for the new Western ways. Much was made in the 2010s of the growing gap in opportunity and outlook between big cities and smaller, former industrial towns, and rural areas in developed economies. The first, unexpected, presidential election win for Trump in November 2016, hard on the heels of the UK's decision to leave the EU in June of the same year, were cited as evidence of the existence of a liberal elite out of touch with ordinary people. Be that as it may, in Russia it was certainly the case. Those who had benefited from greater economic opportunity in the post-Soviet era, and who then sought to consolidate that in greater political freedom (those originally gained in the 1990s having been gradually taken away under

Putin) did not understand that there were a very large number, a majority, of their compatriots who were happy with the stability that Putin had brought after the chaotic 'democracy' of the 1990s. Mikhail Zygar's belief, recorded in his 2023 book, that 'in the winter of 2012 I am absolutely certain that Putin has only a few months left in power' was sorely mistaken.[9] It was not how many Russians imagined their country's political future, nor was it what came to pass.

If Russian liberals were mistaken, so were Western policymakers. The West – as Bush's 1992 State of the Union address demonstrated – thought it had won the Cold War, but actually the resulting complacency, combined with the vulnerabilities in the Western system – short-termism, lack of capacity (this affects all leaders, of course, as Lyne's experience in 1993 showed) and lack of understanding of culture and history, contributed to the renewed crisis.

The 'treaty' published in December 2021, and Lavrov's remarks about dealing directly with the US, speak of a yearning on the part of the Russian political elite to be treated as an equal by the US, as the USSR was. Dmitry Trenin, in his 2014 essay also cited in Chapter 9, declared that – already then – the 'Ukraine Crisis' had 'brought an end to the post–Cold War status quo in Europe'. He defined this yearning to be seen as an equal in the following terms: 'Russia, despite the loss of its superpower status, was also too independent-minded, with a huge nuclear-weapons arsenal and an elite that still reasoned in great-power terms and craved equality with the United States'.[10]

This craving began in the 1990s, the time of humiliation, and never went away. Western policy continually misunderstood, underestimated, or simply ignored the possibility that this humiliation might eventually have political consequences. Yet it did: firstly, in Russia, with the election of a former KGB officer as president, and, secondly, internationally, with consequences that began in Georgia in 2008, before escalating to the annexation of Crimea, and eventually all-out war on Ukraine. Russia's rage smouldered slowly for many years before bursting into flame. While it did, much of Western policy was focused on an idea that Russia would someday adopt Western norms – perhaps with more Russian characteristics, but recognisably Western norms all the same – because they were the best and everyone else in the world would surely aspire to them. More than thirty years after the end of the Cold War, what Kozyrev called the 'self-congratulatory remarks on having won' now echo as idle boasts that may have seemed true in the moment. They have proven wrongheaded in the longer term. The arrogance of the era of the end of history was a grave error, for Russia, given its history and geography, was always likely to seek to return as a global superpower, at least on its own terms, if not recognised as such by others. Obama's description of the 'regional power' may have been accurate from his point of view. As a piece of political communication, it may have been designed to wound. It did – but also provoked a desire to change the perception, by force of arms if necessary. So it turned out, with military campaigns in the former USSR, and the West's indecisive response, creating the courage to intervene in Syria to come to the aid of a dictator. Putin's apparent victory in Syria was not to last. In December 2024, President Assad was driven from power, and from Syria. He fled to Moscow, where his presence was a reminder of a military campaign that had raised Russia's standing in the Middle East for so long. When Assad was faced by yet another insurgency, Putin, by then fighting a large-scale war in Ukraine, could not save him a second time.

Reading the findings of the opinion polls that the USIA conducted in Russia in the 1990s (see Chapter 2) leads to the bleak conclusion that the post-Cold War relationship was irrevocably damaged by the end of that decade. By the end of the 1990s, renewed confrontation between Russia and the West was inevitable. The nature and scale of that confrontation was not yet determined. It could perhaps have been limited to the occasional diplomatic spat, round of sanctions or trade war. Military confrontation was not inevitable: not yet, at least – but that was the way it was to turn out from February 2022 onwards. While Russia and the West stopped short of direct armed conflict, Russia inflicted huge loss of life and property on Ukraine, while Western military supplies sought to limit the damage.

Putin's frequently articulated suspicion and fear of NATO, and its intentions for Russia served as the basis of his justification for starting, and then escalating, the war. In a much discussed, and much dismissed, 2014 essay in *Foreign Affairs*, John Mearsheimer argued of the situation in Ukraine: 'The United States and its European allies share most of the responsibility for the crisis. The taproot of the trouble is NATO enlargement, the central element of a larger strategy to move Ukraine out of Russia's orbit and integrate it into the West.'[11]

Mearsheimer also identified the EU's 'eastward expansion' as a critical element. One can agree or disagree with the wisdom or otherwise of NATO enlargement after the end of the Cold War. Mearsheimer's argument that Putin was provoked has been frequently challenged.[12] What is beyond dispute is that Putin used NATO enlargement very effectively to seek domestic support for his view that the West was out to complete a military encirclement of Russia. NATO officials quoted in this book point to Putin's apparent willingness to accept enlargement early in his presidency. Another interpretation is that Putin was then in no position to do anything about it, so did not openly oppose it until such time as he felt strong enough to do so. In any case, the desire of some Ukrainian governments to join NATO, combined with the alliance's inept response, can hardly be justified as a cause for war. The responsibility for the escalation of the conflict in 2022 lies with Vladimir Putin. Renewed confrontation between Russia and the West was inevitable by the end of the 1990s. Putin decided that confrontation would be military.

The war in Ukraine raises two important questions with huge implications for the West's future relations with Russia, for the outcome of that conflict will define to a large extent what those relations look like. The first is the question of what NATO should do. At the end of the Cold War, NATO officials and enthusiasts argued that there was no case for disbanding NATO, as the Warsaw Pact had been dissolved, because the alliance was a guarantor of European security. As M.E. Sarotte has pointed out, 'a cynical view would be that after its essential function was put into question by the end of the Cold War, NATO expanded itself into necessity again'.[13] Sarotte was writing before the 2022 escalation of the war in Ukraine, but that larger Russian invasion of Ukraine only tended to reinforce her point. NATO found renewed purpose and justification in its opposition to the escalation of the war. With Russia at war in Eastern Europe, there is a clearer reason now for NATO's existence than at any time since the fall of the USSR.

It is a matter of speculation whether different behaviour by NATO might have led to a different kind of confrontation. Enlargement definitely falls into the category of one of those issues in which Russia's views were largely ignored, and which contributed to renewed confrontation with the West. With NATO enlargement having been such a fundamental part of Putin's public justification for war in Ukraine, Lyne's view that the Bucharest summit declaration (promising Georgia and Ukraine NATO membership, but not saying how or when) was 'the biggest mistake that's been made on the western side, in the whole of the Putin period' is highly persuasive. It is true that those countries of the former USSR, and of the wider twentieth-century socialist bloc in Europe, who have joined NATO have not been attacked. We can never know whether NATO membership would have spared Georgia and Ukraine from Russia's warlike wrath. We can be certain that vaguely worded promises of eventual membership had precisely the opposite effect, and arguably provided Putin with what he would see as a perfectly legitimate casus belli. There is little to be gained, however, in discussing whether NATO expansion/enlargement was a good idea. Opinions on the matter are so hardened as to be impossible to change: none of the NATO sources I spoke to for this book would concede that NATO should have ended with the Cold War; none of the Russian sources I consulted suggested that Russia had ever seen NATO's post-Cold War activity as anything other than aggressive in varying degrees.

Yet the nature of the alliance's future existence and operation was thrown into question as never before with President Trump's return to the White House in January 2025. Even before his election victory in November 2024, he returned to his frustration with NATO members he felt were not putting enough resources into their defence budgets. He suggested at a campaign event in February 2024 that he would 'encourage' Russia to attack any country that did not meet its financial commitments within the alliance.[14] Trump also suggested on numerous occasions – more than fifty times, according to one calculation – that he could end the war in 'a day' or '24 hours'.[15] After he took office, it turned out not to be so.

NATO's future relations with Ukraine will inevitably be part of whatever kind of agreement ends the present phase of the Russo–Ukrainian conflict. The West – whatever moral imperatives will inform the role it plays in such an agreement – will have, though, to take Russia's views and likely responses into account in a way that was lacking in the alliance's enlargement of the 1990s and early 2000s.

The second point to consider is one major advantage that Putin has had over his Western counterparts during his time in office: continuity. The offices of the presidents of the US and France, the German chancellor and the British prime minister have all had multiple holders since Putin was first elected in 2000. In that same quarter-century, Russia has had two presidents, Putin and Medvedev: the latter only for four years, and only at Putin's pleasure. When he incurred Putin's displeasure – his decision not to veto Western military action in Libya being the most prominent cause – he was soon gone. Especially in the case of Putin, whose sense of Russian historical privilege and destiny is so strong, not having to face any serious domestic political opposition has been a huge advantage. He has been able to think years in advance, to set long-term goals, in the way that leaders subject to the changing fortunes of electoral politics simply cannot. The Russian foreign minister, Sergei Lavrov, has held his post since 2004. His long experience, and perfect command of English, gives him a clear advantage in dealing with Western counterparts with much less experience of international affairs, and of Russia in particular. His reported tricking of the then British foreign secretary, Liz Truss, into saying that the UK would never recognise Rostov and Voronezh (two regions of southern Russia, the sovereignty of which was not in dispute) as part of Russia is an example of how his sharp wittedness can be used to undermine his interlocutors.[16] Putin has had time to observe and understand Western political and media systems, and foreign policy, and find their vulnerabilities, in a way few of his counterparts can. This is not an argument for Western democracies retaining their leaders for decades on end. It is an argument for Western diplomats and policymakers understanding the advantages held by those they are dealing with when they deal with Russia. Fiona Hill's point that Putin is constantly thinking about Peter the Great and other great leaders in Russian history is worth recalling here: 'Putin thinks about this in all of these terms, and that's all embedded in his speeches. And our problem is we keep losing *his* plot. And he keeps seeing the same kind of plot ongoing in the U.S. and we never recognize how he's interpreting everything.'

Hill's point was even reportedly echoed by Lavrov himself, the *Financial Times* reporting in February 2023, a year after the escalation of the war, that the foreign minister had been caught 'completely by surprise' when the huge invasion force attacked Ukraine. The newspaper reported a conversation that an unnamed Russian oligarch had had with Lavrov about the invasion. Presumably embarrassed, or at least exasperated, by his ignorance of the plans, 'He has three advisers,' Lavrov reportedly replied. 'Ivan the Terrible. Peter the Great. And Catherine the Great.'[17]

Putin, with his references to the ancient chronicles of Kievan Rus', clearly likes to see himself as one of the heirs of Russia's great imperialist leaders. His eventual reputation will rest upon how the world comes to see his war on Ukraine. In the West, with the exception of the admirers he has acquired – generally on the far right or left of the European political spectrum – it is not likely to be at all favourable. Rather, he will be remembered as the Russian leader who attacked a neighbour simply because it sought to escape his country's influence. Arguably,

Putin has had opportunities to be remembered for other achievements. A genuine departure from power in 2008 might have earned him the reputation of the leader who helped to establish a Russian tradition of peaceful transitions of power though the ballot box (though it is hard to imagine that this is recognition he would have valued). Perhaps more to his taste might have been to stop at the annexation of Crimea. The West did very little in response, and he could have gone down in history as the Russian leader who reclaimed what he – and the vast majority of his compatriots – undoubtedly saw as 'historically Russian land'. It was not enough. Perhaps motivated to see himself as a peer of Ivan, Peter or Catherine, Putin wanted more. Future Russian historians may come to write of him in those terms. They may not have the option of writing of him in any other terms. For many in the West, Putin will not be a great man of history so much as a product of his cynical, grubby era – albeit an effective one. Internationally, his greatest achievement has perhaps been to inspire other strongman leaders, and forms of illiberal democracy, whereas the West's intention at the end of the Cold War was the opposite: to inspire liberal democracy in Russia. Domestically, he understood that the suffering experienced in the chaotic years immediately after the collapse of communism could be harnessed for political advantage, and how promising order in place of chaos would deliver him the Kremlin. While Yeltsin's time as Russian president is chiefly remembered in the West as a time when relations were better, it was also the time when the use of armed force (as in Moscow in 1993, and in Chechnya in the two wars later in the decade) was firmly established as a means of solving political disputes. It was a time when journalists were murdered because of their work.

Emerging into the political spotlight as the wild 1990s drew to a close, Putin's KGB past did him no harm. If, in other countries of the former Soviet bloc, former members of the secret police were vilified, the same was not true to the same extent in Russia. The Marxist-Leninist political system may have been loathed in Soviet satellite states, its demise greeted as liberation. In Russia, it was more readily associated with imperial (though never referred to in such terms) and international power. For many Russians, the fall of the USSR was not liberation so much as loss. Putin understood that, and exploited it – while also believing it himself. How then to judge the apparent contradiction between his early years, when he seemed to accept NATO enlargement, when he offered support to the US after 9/11, and his later rage at all the West had done since the late Soviet era? It may be, as suggested above, that he did not feel in a position to act against NATO expansion. It may be that he changed. Certainly, that is the assessment of Jonathan Powell, who was chief of staff to the British prime minister, Tony Blair, when Blair became the first Western leader to visit Putin. In our 2023 interview, Powell recalled:

> He struck us as a much lower key figure than Yeltsin, quite small, quite reserved, more like a clerk or bureaucrat, than a threat. Now people say we should have understood that he was a KGB man through and through. I'm not sure human beings are like that. Human beings change over time. What I perceived from Putin was he changed as a result of hubris, basically, the more he was surrounded by servants and luxury the more he changed his nature, rather than being a sort of evil person.

The year after we spoke, in London in the autumn of 2023, Powell was appointed national security adviser to the Labour government that took office after winning the July 2024 British general election. His reflections on past dealings with Russia are therefore likely to influence future British policy.

One of the questions for the longer term is to try to understand what went wrong between 1991 and 2022. I have argued above that by the end of the 1990s, and the beginning of the Putin era, Russia's mistrust and resentment of the West had already reached such an extent that renewed confrontation was inevitable – though the nature and scale of that confrontation was not inevitable. A case can be made that

Putin's speech at the 2007 Munich Security Conference was the point of fracture, if indeed there was a single incident that finally broke the relationship. For Powell, the relationship was already doomed by the time Putin spoke at Munich. 'I think it started earlier, but maybe that's a particularly British perspective, because Iraq was really what broke it for us with Putin.' He recalled the gist of Putin's phone calls with Blair at that time, barely three years after Putin, still then only acting president, had invited Blair to the opera in his home town of Saint Petersburg: 'You guys never listen to us. We offered to share intelligence. We offered to do stuff. You go ahead and do this stuff without even telling us. You know, you just go ahead and do it. I mean, what kind of relationship is that? That was his line.'

Hill's account of the Kremlin's belief that the CIA knew that Saddam Hussein did not have weapons of mass destruction at the time of the invasion, and that the US, bent on regime change, decided to invade anyway, lends weight to this conclusion. It is also interesting to wonder whether Putin's isolation during the pandemic – remember the internet memes spawned by images of the long table at which he insisted on receiving guests, so as to ensure they kept their distance – led him to complete his plan to secure his place in the kind of Russian history that was the content of his essays on the Second World War and Ukraine. In power then already for more than twenty years, Putin had probably come to believe firmly in his own vision of the world – for who would contradict him? If the *Financial Times* story about Lavrov's conversation with the oligarch is to be believed, not only was Lavrov apparently not asked his view on the 2022 invasion of Ukraine, he was not even told it was going to happen. In Lavrov's case, this was perhaps not even the first time. He was reportedly also excluded from the meeting at which the decision to annex Crimea was taken.[18]

All these factors make it even harder for Western policymakers not to lose Putin's plot, as Hill's memorable phrase has it. For if even senior Russian ministers do not know his thoughts, how can outsiders? In the aftermath of the Salisbury poisonings in March 2018, the then British defence secretary, Gavin Williamson, gave the impression that he had 'lost Putin's plot' during the diplomatic row that followed the attacks on Yulia and Sergei Skripal. Instead of raising the stakes in the round of expulsions of embassy staff, Williamson argued, 'Russia should go away and should shut up'.[19] It did not, of course. In the years that followed it loomed larger in Western Europe's security nightmares than at any time since the Cold War. Williamson's petulant frustration was much mocked in the UK and in Russia. While such an outburst, however undiplomatic, was understandable in the context of such a terrifying incident, it also suggested a wider unfulfilled, and unrealistic, desire for Russia to keep completely out of European affairs. It will not. Fear and ignorance have contributed to the causes of past confrontation, as historians of the Cold War have observed. Of the period after Stalin's death, Vladislav Zubok has written, 'This new Soviet leadership did not even realize how much fear they evoked in the US State Department and in American society.'[20] Odd Arne Westad argued: 'The Cold War ended because years of closer association between East and West had reduced the fear that the two sides had for each other.'[21]

Closer association will return one day – even if that association is not amicable but purely practical, transactional. So understanding Russia better is imperative in the coming years – even as gaining first-hand knowledge of the country becomes harder to do for researchers, journalists, diplomats and policymakers. One practical step Western countries might take would be to increase the provision of Russian language teaching. This has sadly declined since the end of the Cold War – along, in the UK at least, with a general decline in language learning. It is shortsighted. Technology may facilitate basic understanding of language. It cannot convey the culture and political context that shape the expressions used in another language. While many of the Western diplomats posted to Russia during the period covered by this book have mastered the language to some extent, very few politicians have even the most basic understanding – presumably a fact that prompted the polite advice offered by the British Foreign Office interpreter, Tony Bishop, on his retirement. Prime ministers, presidents and foreign ministers cannot all be expected to learn Russian – but they need to have people close to them who understand the country's language, politics, culture and history. This will be hard when it has become so difficult, and for some, even dangerous, to visit Russia – but it is not to be dismissed. Juho Kusti Passikivi, president of Finland from 1946 to 1956, during a time when his country survived the predations of the USSR at the end of the Stalin era, once reflected on what he saw as the weaknesses of leadership among his contemporaries in bigger countries. 'Baldwin, Chamberlain, Roosevelt, Atlee, Bevin – ignorant, naïve, easily cheated. Do they know history? No. Do they know geography? No. Do they know foreign languages? No.'[22] He would perhaps have been impressed by the ability of Condoleezza Rice and Angela Merkel to speak Russian. Not all Western politicians of this era of dealing with Russia would have earned his approval. Yet such expertise is indispensable for future dealings with Russia – a country few Westerners have visited, and which has become extremely difficult, and even risky, to visit.

For Russia is not going to go away. Putin himself will not be in charge forever, but while he remains there he sits at the top of a system that the Russia expert Mark Galeotti has described as functioning 'in a similar way to a royal court'.[23] When Putin does leave office there is little prospect of significant change in the short term. Even if Putin's administration were to fall, unlike at the time of Russia's major twentieth century crises, in 1917 and 1991, there is no alternative party or system waiting to take over. There is no serious opposition in Russia, and that which remains, silenced, in prison or in exile, is not in any position to take power – even if the population would welcome them. More probable is that Putin would be replaced by someone from within the system. A change of policy might follow to the extent that there would be new overtures to the West (and perhaps to the US in particular, given the enduring desire to be seen as Washington's equal). In a world where the UK's departure from the EU can go from fringe political campaign to government policy, however, where Donald Trump can win two terms as president of the US, where Volodymyr Zelensky can go from actor to wartime leader, Russia too could surprise. It is just neither likely, nor obvious how.

There is no returning to the world before the escalation of the war in Ukraine in February 2022. Any future Russian president, even one desiring an improvement of relations with the West, will be hard pressed to cede territory won from Ukraine at such great cost in blood and treasure. Russia and the West are not destined to be enemies as if it were some kind of natural state of affairs. They will need to learn from the mistakes they both made after 1991 if they are to rebuild their relationship on the successes of the period – trade and diplomatic cooperation – that are now buried in the past as the buried dead of a new era of European war haunt the future.

Acknowledgements

This book was many years in the making, in the sense that the question of when the Russian leadership once again came to see the West as an enemy had long preoccupied me. It was not until January 2022 that I began to formulate my thoughts into a book proposal. My first thanks must therefore go to Joanna Godfrey, with whom I had an initial discussion in the London office of Yale University Press late that month. Some four weeks later, Russia launched its massive assault on Ukraine. Joanna's patient advice and wise counsel were invaluable from the proposal stage, which coincided with a major diplomatic and military crisis that affected the subject of the book, right through the entire process. In more than thirty years as a journalist and more than a decade as an author, I have been privileged to work with some excellent editors. Joanna is among the best. Joanna's colleagues at Yale – assistant editor Frazer Martin, and managing editor and design manager Rachael Lonsdale – provided invaluable support, guidance and assistance. I am extremely grateful to the copy-editor, Rachel Bridgewater, for checking the text so carefully and thoughtfully.

I would like to thank those contributors whom I interviewed, all of whom have busy schedules that they did not allow to prevent their giving generously of their time. The extracts from our interviews such as they appear in this book cannot on their own give an adequate impression of just how important these meetings were in assisting me to shape my ideas.

My former BBC colleagues James Coomarasamy and Christopher Booth were very helpful, commenting on my arguments as they were formulated. Their opinion was especially valuable as, like me, they are members of a generation who hoped the world would develop differently after the end of the Cold War.

My thanks also to another generation, those whom I taught on the BA Journalism, Politics and History and the MA International Journalism at City St George's, University of London while I was researching and writing the book. My lectures on Russia and our discussions together helped me to focus the many thoughts the process prompted. That process would not have been possible in the way it was had I not been granted sabbatical leave in 2024. I am grateful for the university's support for my work.

I would like to thank the staff of the archives where I worked: the National Archives in Kew, West London; the Hoover Institution at Stanford University; and a special mention to David A. Langbart of the US National Archives at College Park, Maryland.

There are some people whom I would like to thank, but cannot name. They include the anonymous reviewers who commented on the complete first draft of the book. I thank them for their clear-eyed observations and suggestions. There are also a number of Russian citizens whom, times being as they are, I should probably not name but who were kind enough to assist me in the early stages.

My wife, Mette Jørgensen Rodgers, and I met when we were both working as journalists in Gaza in the early years of this century. We subsequently spent three years in Moscow together. Endless conversations about world affairs and many, many other subjects have been one of the most treasured things in my life. My thanks as always to her and to our daughters, Freya and Sophia – whose decision to study beyond the shores of the UK where they mostly grew up suggests they have inherited their parents' love of learning through travel.

Notes

PREFACE

1. Maureen Perrie, *The Cambridge History of Russia, Vol. 1* (Cambridge: Cambridge University Press, online edn, 2008), p. 3.

CHAPTER 1

1. Jeni Klugman and Sheila Marnie, 'Poverty', in Brigitte Granville and Peter Oppenheimer (eds), *Russia's Post-Communist Economy* (Oxford: Oxford University Press, 2001), pp. 452–3.
2. The National Archives of the UK (TNA), FCO 176/314 'Briefs Concerning Russia'.
3. Chrystia Freeland, *Sale of the Century: The Inside Story of the Second Russian Revolution* (London: Abacus, 2005), pp. 56–7.
4. Freeland, *Sale of the Century*, pp. 56–7 and 16.
5. Vladislav Zubok, *Collapse: The Fall of the Soviet Union* (New Haven and London: Yale University Press, 2021), p. 294.
6. Lilia Shevtsova, '1993: Russia's Small Civil War', Carnegie Moscow Center commentary, first posted 3 October 2013, accessed 8 December 2023. Available at https://carnegie.ru/commentary/53189.
7. Strobe Talbott, *The Russia Hand: A Memoir of Presidential Diplomacy* (New York: Random House, 2002), p. 91.
8. Bill Clinton, *My Life* (New York: Alfred A. Knopf, 2004), p. 549.
9. William J. Clinton Presidential Library declassification 2015-0782-M-1, published at https://nsarchive.gwu.edu/document/16847-document-05-memorandum-telephone-conversation. Accessed 29 November 2024.

10. US Department of State, Date/Case ID: 08 MAY 2000 200000982. Available at https://nsarchive.gwu.edu/document/16852-document-10-secretary-christopher-s-meeting. Accessed 29 November 2024.

11. Warren Christopher, *In the Stream of History: Shaping Foreign Policy for a New Era* (Stanford, CA: Stanford University Press, 1998), p. 94.

12. Sir Roderic Lyne, interview with the author, London, 8 November 2023.

13. https://www.usaid.gov/news-information/fact-sheets/usaid-russia. Accessed 5 January 2025.

14. Elizabeth Teague, 'Russia's Constitutional Reforms of 2020', *Russian Politics*, vol. 5 (2020), p. 320.

15. TNA DEFE13/270, Fall to Immediate FCO, 221525 October 1993.

16. Tom Parfitt, *High Caucasus: A Mountain Quest in Russia's Haunted Hinterland* (London: Headline, 2023), p. 247.

17. *Guardian*, 31 December 1994, p. 14.

18. Andrew Higgins, 'The War that Continues to Shape Russia, 25 years later', *New York Times*, 10 December 2019. Available at https://www.nytimes.com/2019/12/10/world/europe/photos-chechen-war-russia.html. Accessed 5 January 2024.

19. Carlotta Gall and Thomas de Waal, *Chechnya: A Small Victorious War* (London: Pan Macmillan, 2005), p. 16.

20. Gall and de Waal, *Chechnya*, p. 11.

21. Gall and de Waal, *Chechnya*, p. 12.

22. TNA FCO 179/729, Mackenzie to Guthrie, 23 July 1992.

23. TNA FCO 179/729, Mackenzie to Guthrie, 23 July 1992.

24. TNA FCO 179/729, 'Moscow Conference 1–4 June 1992 Military Reforms in a Democratic Society' Report by R. M. Davey.

25. Vladimir Shkolnikov, Martin McKee and David A Leon, 'Changes in Life Expectancy in Russia in the mid-1990s', *The Lancet*, vol. 357, no. 9260 (2001), p. 917.

26. Available at https://johnmajorarchive.org.uk/1995/05/09/mr-majors-speech-at-the-memorial-complex-at-poklonnaya-gora-9-may-1995/. Accessed 25 November 2024.

27. Steven Erlanger, 'V-E DAY PLUS 50: THE SCENE; Visiting Leaders Try to Honor a Past Victory and Protest a New War', *New York Times*, 10 May 1995. Available at https://www.nytimes.com/1995/05/10/world/v-e-day-plus-50-scene-visiting-leaders-try-honor-past-victory-protest-new-war.html. Accessed 10 January 2024.

28. William J. Clinton, 'Remarks to Students at Moscow State University', 10 May 1995. Available at https://www.govinfo.gov/content/pkg/PPP-1995-book1/pdf/PPP-1995-book1-doc-pg672.pdf. Accessed. 19 August 2025.

29. Associated Press despatch from Moscow, first published 4 March 1995. Available at https://www.nytimes.com/1995/03/04/world/thousands-in-moscow-mourn-slain-tv-journalist.html. Accessed 7 November 2024.

30. Malcolm Muggeridge, *Chronicles of Wasted Time* (London: Collins, 1972), p. 227.

31. Clemens Grafe and Kaspar Richter, 'Taxation and Public Expenditure', in Granville and Oppenheimer, *Russia's Post-Communist Economy*, p. 161.

32. Yuliy A. Nisnevich, 'Elections of Deputies of the State Duma of the Second Convocation (1995–1999): The Success of the Anti-reform Opposition, the

Failure of the "Party of Power" and the Defeat of the Democrats (to the 30th Anniversary of the Russian Federation)', *Post-Soviet Issues*, vol. 8, no. 3 (2021), pp. 379–96. DOI: 10.24975/2313-8920-2021-8-3-379-396.

33. Daniel Triesman, 'Why Yeltsin Won', *Foreign Affairs*, vol. 75, no. 5 (Sept–Oct 1996), p. 64.

34. 'Russia: Stabilization and Reform', Address by Michel Camdessus, managing director of the IMF, at the U.S.–Russia Business Council, Washington, DC, 1 April 1996. Available at https://www.imf.org/en/News/Articles/2015/09/28/04/53/spmds9604. Accessed 12 January 2024.

35. Michael Kramer, 'Rescuing Boris', *Time*, 15 July 1996. Available at https://content.time.com/time/subscriber/article/0,33009,984833-12,00.html. Accessed 12 January 2024.

36. Triesman, 'Why Yeltsin Won', p. 67.

37. 'Yeltsin: I had five heart attacks', BBC News, 20 January 2004. Available at http://news.bbc.co.uk/1/hi/world/europe/3415271.stm. Accessed 25 November 2024.

38. Talbott, *The Russia Hand*, p. 59.

39. Talbott, *The Russia Hand*, p. 106.

40. Christopher, *In the Stream of History*, p. 96

41. Andrei Kozyrev, *The Firebird: The Elusive Fate of Russian Democracy* (Philadelphia, PA: University of Pennsylvania Press, 2020), p. 192.

42. Kozyrev, *The Firebird*, p. 193.

43. Talbott, *The Russia Hand*, pp. 89–90.

44. Clinton, *My Life*, p. 550.

CHAPTER 2

1. 'NATO – Declassified: A short history of NATO'. Available at https://www.nato.int/cps/en/natohq/declassified_139339.htm. Accessed 12 January 2024.

2. Jamie Shea, interview with the author, London, 16 March 2023. All subsequent quotations attributed to Shea are taken from this interview unless otherwise stated.

3. TNA FCO 176/345, Boris Yeltsin to John Major, 15 September 1992 (translation in the archive with a copy of the original, in Russian).

4. Clinton, *My Life*, pp. 654–5.

5. Christopher, *In the Stream of History*, p. 129.

6. TNA FCO 176/345, John Major to Boris Yeltsin, 2 November 1993.

7. Madeleine Albright, *Madame Secretary: A Memoir* (New York: Harper Perennial, 2013), p. 169.

8. Albright, *Madame Secretary*, p. 167.

9. Chatham House, 'Transcript Q&A 20 Years On: Perspectives on the Fall of the Soviet Union' (2011).

10. Talbott, *The Russia Hand*, p. 93.

11. M.E. Sarotte, *Not One Inch: America, Russia, and the Making of Post-Cold War Stalemate* (New Haven and London: Yale University Press, 2021), p. 1.

12. John Lough, interview with the author, London, 2 September 2024.

13. TNA FCO 179/729, From Minister, Berlin, 27 January 1992, 'Discussion with the Russian Minister in Berlin'.

14. TNA FCO 179/729, R. Court UK Del NATO to I Bond, FCO. 071747Z Feb 1993.

15. Anders Aslund, *How Capitalism Was Built: The Transformation of Central and Eastern Europe, Russia, and Central Asia* (Cambridge: Cambridge University Press, online edn, 2012), p. 133.

16. *The Russian Economic Barometer*, 2000. Cited in Aslund, *How Capitalism Was Built*, p. 136.

17. Aslund, *How Capitalism Was Built*, p. 133.

18. Niko Gobbin and Bruno Merlevede, 'The Russian Crisis: A Debt Perspective', *Post Communist Economies*, vol. 12, no. 2 (2000), p. 148.

19. Illarionov, cited in Aslund, *How Capitalism Was Built*, p. 135.

20. 'Russian MP murdered', BBC News, 20 November 1998. Available at http://news.bbc.co.uk/1/hi/world/europe/218818.stm. Accessed 6 September 2025.

21. William J. Burns, *The Back Channel: American Diplomacy in a Disordered World* (London: Hurst, 2021), p. 89.

22. 'CONFLICT IN THE BALKANS: IN MOSCOW; 2 Gunmen Attack U.S. Site And Flee', *New York Times*, 29 March 1999. Available at https://www.nytimes.com/1999/03/29/world/conflict-in-the-balkans-in-moscow-2-gunmen-attack-us-site-and-flee.html. Accessed 19 April 2024.

23. 'Yeltsin's popularity in single digits', UPI, 5 April 1999. Available at https://www.upi.com/Archives/1999/04/05/Yeltsins-popularity-in-single-digits/8155923284800/. Accessed 19 April 2024.

24. Calder Walton, 'The New Spy Wars: How China and Russia Use Intelligence Agencies to Undermine America', *Foreign Affairs*, 19 July 2023. Available at https://www.foreignaffairs.com/china/russia-china-intelligence-new-spy-wars-undermine-america. Accessed 19 April 2024.

25. 'Confrontation over Pristina airport', BBC News, 9 March 2000. Available at http://news.bbc.co.uk/1/hi/world/europe/671495.stm. Accessed 30 April 2024.

26. The name given to the area of Pristina where NATO forces established their base. See https://jfcnaples.nato.int/kfor.

27. Shea, interview with the author, London, 16 March 2023.

28. 'Dagestan rebels call in Chechen warlord', BBC News, 11 August 1999. Available at http://news.bbc.co.uk/1/hi/world/monitoring/417696.stm. Accessed 3 May 2024.

29. 'Chechen Says He Leads Revolt in Nearby Area', *New York Times*, 12 August 1999. Available at https://www.nytimes.com/1999/08/12/world/chechen-says-he-leads-revolt-in-nearby-area.html. Accessed 3 May 2024.

30. 'Moscow blast suspects arrested', BBC News, 10 September 1999. Available at http://news.bbc.co.uk/1/hi/world/europe/444268.stm. Accessed 3 May 2024.

31. 'Rebels stage new invasion of Dagestan', *The Independent*, 6 September 1999. Available at https://www.independent.co.uk/news/world/rebels-stage-new-invasion-of-dagestan-1116858.html. Accessed 3 May 2024.

32. Boris Yeltsin, *Midnight Diaries* (London: Phoenix, 2000), p. 24.

33. Laure Mandeville, 'Alexandre Lebed: "Le pouvoir veut déstabiliser la Russie"', *Le Figaro*, no. 17147 (29 September 1999), p. 2.

34. Sophie Shihab, 'La Russie ne peut plus, ni moralement ni physiquement, diriger le nord du Caucase', *Le Monde*, 18 September 1999. Not having access to the transcript of the original interview, I have translated into English Lebed's words

as they appeared in French in the article. The same is true of the *Le Monde* interview with Maskhadov cited later. I am grateful to my former doctoral student, now colleague at City St George's, University of London, Dr Pauline Renaud, for finding the articles in the newspaper archive.

35. 'Russian tycoon Boris Berezovsky found dead at his UK home', BBC News, 23 March 2013. Available at https://www.bbc.co.uk/news/uk-21913356.

36. John B. Dunlop, *The Moscow Bombings of September 1999: Examinations of Russian Terrorist Attacks at the Onset of Vladimir Putin's Rule* (Stuttgart: Ibidem Verlag, 2012), p. 57.

37. Dunlop, *The Moscow Bombings of September 1999*, p. 58.

38. Dunlop, *The Moscow Bombings of September 1999*, p. 10.

39. Timothy J. Colton and Michael McFaul, *Popular Choice and Managed Democracy: The Russian Elections of 1999 and 2000* (Washington, DC: Brookings Institution Press, 2003), p. 173.

40. 'Yeltsin's resignation speech', BBC News, 31 December 1999. Available at http://news.bbc.co.uk/1/hi/world/monitoring/584845.stm Accessed 19 January 2024.

41. Paul D'Anieri, *Ukraine and Russia: From Civilized Divorce to Uncivil War* (Cambridge: Cambridge University Press, 2019), p. 63.

42. Records of the USIA (RG 306), National Archives. Available at https://www.archives.gov/research/foreign-policy/related-records/rg-306. Accessed 3 December 2024.

43. NARA RG 306 USIA Worldwide Survey Box 195092–195100.

44. NARA RG 306 USIA Worldwide Survey Box 193057 (cont.)–193061.

45. NARA RG 306 USIA Worldwide Survey Box 13065–13067.

46. NARA RG 306 USIA Worldwide Survey Box 194005–194018.

47. NARA RG 306 USIA Worldwide Survey Box 195100–196023.

48. NARA RG 306 USIA Worldwide Survey Box 197001–197017.

49. NARA RG 306 USIA Worldwide Survey Box 197037–197048.

50. TNA DEFE 13/300, Britmilrep to MODUK 201519Z Feb 95.

51. Philip Short, *Putin: His Life and Times* (London: Bodley Head, 2022), p. 119.

52. Vladimir Putin, *First Person: An Astonishingly Frank Self-Portrait by Russia's President Vladimir Putin* (London: Hutchinson, 2000), p. 85.

CHAPTER 3

1. For a fuller account of the restrictions placed on media coverage, please see my earlier book, *Assignment Moscow: Reporting on Russia from Lenin to Putin* (London: Bloomsbury, 2023), pp. 165–9.

2. James Hughes, *Chechnya: From Nationalism to Jihad* (Philadelphia, PA: University of Pennsylvania Press, 2007), p. 94.

3. Cited in Olga Oliker, *Russia's Chechen Wars, 1994–2000* (Santa Monica, CA: Rand Corporation, 2001), pp. 45–6.

4. 'Operating on the enemy in the two Chechen wars', BBC News, 8 October 2012. Available at https://www.bbc.co.uk/news/magazine-19811823. Accessed 24 May 2022.

5. 'Blair to press Putin on Chechnya', BBC News, 11 March 2000. Available at http://news.bbc.co.uk/1/hi/world/europe/673520.stm. Accessed 22 May 2024.

6. Jonathan Powell, interview with the author, London, 20 September 2023.
7. Tony Blair, *A Journey* (London: Hutchinson, 2010), p. 243.
8. Powell, interview with the author, London, 20 September 2023.
9. Sir Roderic Lyne, interview with the author, London, 8 November 2023.
10. Bettina Renz, *Russia's Military Revival* (Cambridge: Polity, 2018), p. 26.
11. United States National Security Archive, Cable from US Embassy Moscow to Secretary of State, 'Pollsters on Putin's Popularity, Election Popularity, Election', 200658 Mar 00.
12. United States National Security Archive, US Embassy Moscow to Secretary of State, 'Russian Presidential Elections – Reasonably Free and Fair', 281537 Mar 00.
13. Talbott, *The Russia Hand*, p. 7.
14. *Russian Economic Trends*, vol. 9, no. 4 (Nov 2000). DOI: 10.1111/1467-9426.00142.
15. 'Putin opens up for CNN's Larry King', CNN, 8 September 2000. Available at http://edition.cnn.com/2000/WORLD/europe/09/08/russia.putin.03. Accessed 4 June 2019.
16. Michael McFaul, *From Cold War to Hot Peace: The Inside Story of Russia and America* (London: Allen Lane, 2018), p. 64.
17. Condoleezza Rice, *No Higher Honour: A Memoir of my Years in Washington* (London: Simon & Schuster, 2011), p. 63.
18. 'Address to a Joint Session of Congress and the American People', 20 September 2001. Available at https://georgewbush-whitehouse.archives.gov/news/releases/2001/09/20010920-8.html. Accessed 3 June 2024.
19. Angela Stent, *The Limits of Partnership: U.S.–Russia Relations in the Twenty-First Century*, updated edn (New Jersey and Woodstock, Oxfordshire: Princeton University Press, 2014), p. 64.
20. Stent, *The Limits of Partnership*, p. 64.
21. Stent, *The Limits of Partnership*, p. 65.
22. George Robertson, telephone interview with the author, London, 14 February 2024.
23. The Rome Declaration, 28 May 2002, p. 6. Available at https://www.nato.int/docu/comm/2002/0205-rome/rome-eng.pdf. Accessed 4 June 2024.
24. All citations from this news conference are from a transcript provided by Lord (George) Robertson's office. A recording of the news conference is also available at nato.int/multi/audio/2002/s020528z.mp3. Accessed 16 May 2025.
25. TNA PREM 49/2552, David Manning to Simon MacDonald, 29 May 2002.
26. Interview with Russian TV channel RTR, BBC Monitoring, 14 December 2003.
27. Yevgeny Primakov, *A World Challenged: Fighting Terrorism in the Twenty-First Century* (Washington, DC: Brookings Institution Press, 2004), p. 90.
28. Erin E. Arvedlund, 'Russia Offers to Forgive 65% of Iraq's Debt', *New York Times*, 22 December 2003. Available at https://www.nytimes.com/2003/12/22/international/europe/russia-offers-to-forgive-65-of-iraqs-debt.html. Accessed 4 June 2024; and Peter Baker, 'In Reversal, Russia Agrees to Discuss Debt Relief for Iraq', *Washington Post*, 19 December 2003. Available at https://www.washington-post.com/archive/politics/2003/12/19/in-reversal-russia-agrees-to-discuss-debt-relief-for-iraq/ec204f1c-4b4a-4ed3-a4de-b36f03224be3. Accessed 4 June 2024.
29. OPEC monthly oil market report, published March 2003.

30. Sir David Manning, interview with the author, London, 6 December 2023.
31. Primakov, *A World Challenged*, p. 59.
32. Powell, interview with the author, London, 20 September 2023.
33. Fiona Hill and Clifford Gaddy, *Mr. Putin: Operative in the Kremlin (Geopolitics in the 21st Century)* (Washington, DC: Brookings Institution Press, 2015), p. 278.
34. George Robertson, telephone interview with the author, London, 14 February 2024.
35. 'Russia recalls envoy in London', UPI Archives, 18 December 1998. Available at https://www.upi.com/Archives/1998/12/18/Russia-recalls-envoy-in-London/9955913957200/. Accessed 19 August 2025.
36. Condoleezza Rice, 'Campaign 2000: Promoting the National Interest', *Foreign Affairs*, vol. 79, no. 1 (January/February 2000), p. 45.
37. William Perry, Speech at Marshall Ceremony, Garmisch, Germany, 28 April 1997. William Perry Papers, Box No 1 2019C102-B10.01701.A.
38. William Perry, Speech at United States Air Force Academy, 8 May 1997. William Perry Papers, Box No 1 2019C102-B10.01701.A.
39. 'Triple Threat', *Hoover Digest*, no. 3 (1998). William Perry Papers, Box No. 4.
40. Citations from this news conference from a transcript provided by Lord (George) Robertson's office. A recording of the news conference is also available at nato.int/multi/audio/2002/s020528z.mp3. Accessed 16 May 2025.

CHAPTER 4

1. Mark Franchetti, *Sunday Times*, 27 October 2002, p. 2.
2. Artem Krechetnikov, 'Moscow theatre siege: Questions remain unanswered', BBC News, 24 October 2012. Available at https://www.bbc.com/news/world-europe-20067384. Accessed 6 June 2024.
3. Franchetti, *Sunday Times*, p. 2.
4. Richard Sakwa, 'The 2003–2004 Russian Elections and Prospects for Democracy', *Europe-Asia Studies*, vol. 57, no. 3 (May 2005), p. 372.
5. Russian Central Electoral Commission figures, cited in Sakwa, 'The 2003–2004 Russian Elections', p. 372.
6. Sakwa, 'The 2003–2004 Russian Elections', p. 376.
7. Russian Central Electoral Commission figures, cited in Sakwa, 'The 2003–2004 Russian Elections', p. 388.
8. 'Russia's Alcohol Policy: A Continuing Success Story', *The Lancet*, vol. 394, no. 10205 (5–11 October 2019), p. 1205.
9. Life expectancy at birth, male (years) – Russian Federation', World Bank Group. Available at https://data.worldbank.org/indicator/SP.DYN.LE00.MA.IN?locations=RU. Accessed 6 June 2024.
10. Philip Hanson, 'The Russian Economic Puzzle: Going Forwards, Backwards or Sideways?', *International Affairs*, vol. 83, no. 5 (2007), p. 869.
11. Hanson, 'The Russian Economic Puzzle', p. 870.
12. 'Profile: Mikhail Khodorkovsky', BBC News, 22 December 2013. Available at https://www.bbc.com/news/world-europe-12082222. Accessed 7 June 2024.
13. 'Nine out of ten developing countries urgently need practical support to fight corruption, highlights new index', Transparency International, 7 October 2003.

Available at https://images.transparencycdn.org/images/2003_CPI_PressRelease_EN.pdf. Accessed 7 June 2024.

14. Susan B. Glasser and Peter Baker, 'Russian Tycoon And Putin Critic Arrested in Raid', *The Washington Post*, 25 October 2003. Available at https://www.washingtonpost.com/archive/politics/2003/10/26/russian-tycoon-and-putin-critic-arrested-in-raid/22e60f62-2db0-4dc3-b95c-cc90c0cbc1bf. Accessed 7 June 2024.

15. Andrew Jack, 'Russian Liberal Party warns raid may harm poll chances', *Financial Times*, 25/26 October 2003, p. 8.

16. 'Taming Russia's Ambitious Oligarchs', *Financial Times*, 28 October 2003, p. 22.

17. 'Foreign direct investment, net inflows (BoP, current US$) – Russian Federation', World Bank Group. Available at https://data.worldbank.org/indicator/BX.KLT.DINV.CD.WD?locations=RU. Accessed 7 June 2024.

18. C.j. Chivers Br and Erin Arvedlund, 'Russian Oil Tycoon Is Convicted and Sentenced to 9 Years in Jail', *New York Times*, 31 May 2005. Available at https://www.nytimes.com/2005/05/31/international/europe/russian-oil-tycoon-is-convicted-and-sentenced-to-9.html. Accessed 7 June 2024.

19. 'Factbox – Who is jailed tycoon Mikhail Khodorkvsky?', Reuters, 30 December 2010. Available at https://www.reuters.com/article/idUSTRE6BT23B. Accessed 7 June 2024.

20. Steve Lee Myers and Erin E. Arvedlund, 'Oil Tycoon's Arrest Scares Russian Financial Markets', *New York Times*, 28 October 2003. Available at https://www.nytimes.com/2003/10/28/world/oil-tycoon-s-arrest-scares-russian-financial-markets.html. Accessed 7 June 2024.

21. Ivan Zassoursky, *Media and Power in Post-Soviet Russia* (Armonk, NY: M.E. Sharpe, 2004), p. 4.

22. Elena Vartanova, 'The Russian Media Model in the Context of Post-Soviet Dynamics', in Daniel C. Hallin and Paolo Mancini (eds), *Comparing Media Systems Beyond the Western World* (Cambridge: Cambridge University Press, 2012), p. 136.

23. See 'Argumenty i Fakty Digital Archive', East View Information Services. Available at https://www.eastview.com/resources/gpa/argumenty-i-fakty; 'Which Soviet newspapers are available online?', UNC University Libraries. Available at https://guides.lib.unc.edu/sovietnewspapers. Both accessed 8 June 2024.

24. Genine Babakian, 'From the Archive: Thousands Mourn Murder of Russian Reporter Kholodov', *Moscow Times*, 21 October 1994. Republished 17 October 2014. Accessed 7 June 2024.

25. Rodgers, *Assignment Moscow*, p. 153.

26. Andrei Richter and Paul Janensch, 'Analyzing Russian Media: Study offers Praise, Criticism for Coverage of War in Chechnya', *Editor and Publisher*, vol. 128, no. 26 (July 1995).

27. For a fuller account of the different working conditions for journalists in the two Chechen wars, please see Chapter 8 of my book *Assignment Moscow*.

28. 'Putin versus the oligarchs?' *The Economist*, 17 June 2000, p. 47.

29. See https://www.rt.com/about-us. Accessed 8 June 2024.

30. Angus Roxburgh, *The Strongman: Vladimir Putin and the Struggle for Russia* (London: I.B. Tauris, 2013), p. 185.

31. 'Beslan school siege: Russia "failed" in 2004 massacre', BBC News. Available at https://www.bbc.com/news/world-europe-39586814. Accessed 10 June 2024.

32. 'President Vladimir Putin arrived at Beslan District Hospital', President of Russia, 4 September 2004. Available at http://en.kremlin.ru/events/president/news/31678. Accessed 19 August 2025.

33. 'President Vladimir Putin address to the Nation', President of Russia, 4 September 2004. Available at http://en.kremlin.ru/events/president/news/31682. Accessed 19 August 2025.

34. 'Address by President Vladimir Putin', President of Russia, 4 September 2004. Available at http://en.kremlin.ru/events/president/transcripts/22589. Accessed 19 August 2025.

35. 'Address by President Vladimir Putin', President of Russia, 4 September 2004. Available at http://en.kremlin.ru/events/president/transcripts/22589. Accessed 19 August 2025.

36. 'President Vladimir Putin spoke by phone with US President George W. Bush', President of Russia, 1 September 2004. Available at http://en.kremlin.ru/events/president/news/31670. Accessed 19 August 2025.

37. Anna Politkovskaya, 'Poisoned by Putin', *Guardian*, 9 September 2004. Available at https://www.theguardian.com/world/2004/sep/09/russia.media. Accessed 10 June 2024.

38. Politkovskaya, 'Poisoned by Putin'.

39. Zubok, *Collapse*, p. 383.

40. 'The two Victors', *The Economist*, 25 November 2004. Available at https://www.economist.com/europe/2004/11/25/the-two-victors. Accessed 10 June 2024.

41. 'President Vladimir Putin made a telephone call to Viktor Yanukovich to congratulate him on his victory in the Ukrainian presidential election', President of Russia, 22 November 2004. Available at http://en.kremlin.ru/events/president/news/32209. Accessed 21 August 2025.

42. 'The two Victors'.

43. Mikhail Zygar, *War and Punishment: The Story of Russian Oppression and Ukrainian Resistance* (London: Weidenfeld and Nicholson, 2023), p. 226.

44. Cited in Andrei Shleifer and Daniel Treisman, 'A Normal Country: Russia after Communism', *The Journal of Economic Perspectives*, vol. 19, no. 1 (Winter, 2005), p. 155.

45. 'Russia needs new roads to accommodate rise in car ownership', Interfax, 24 October 2000.

46. Sabra Ayres, 'Malls more than a capital idea in Russia', *New York Times*, 26 September 2006. Available at https://www.nytimes.com/2006/09/26/business/worldbusiness/26iht-remoscow.2942219.html. Accessed 11 June 2024.

47. 'Statement by Group of Eight Leaders', US Department of State, 16 July 2006. Available at https://2001-2009.state.gov/p/eur/rls/prsrl/69054.htm. Accessed 11 June 2024.

48. 'Bush, Putin Get Together Before G-8', CBS News, 14 July 2006. Available at https://www.cbsnews.com/news/bush-putin-get-together-before-g-8. Accessed 11 June 2024.

49. 'In pictures: Russian G8 summit', BBC News, 15 July 2006. Available at http://news.bbc.co.uk/2/hi/in_pictures/5183258.stm. Accessed 11 June 2024.

50. 'Documents of the G8 Summit in St Petersburg', President of Russia, 15 July 2006. Available at http://en.kremlin.ru/supplement/2781. Accessed 11 June 2024.

51. 'Documents of the G8 Summit in St Petersburg'.
52. FM AMEMBASSY MOSCOW (BURNS) TO SECSTATE WASHDC PRIORITY 7174 P 061133Z JUN 06, Department of State Virtual Reading Room. Accessed 11 June 2024.
53. 'Documents of the G8 Summit in St Petersburg'.
54. 'IFPI Hits Russian CD Plant With Counterfeiting Claims', *Billboard*, 23 December 2003. Available at https://www.billboard.com/music/music-news/ifpi-hits-russian-cd-plant-with-counterfeiting-claims-1473729. Accessed 11 June 2024.
55. Kozyrev, *The Firebird*, p. 9.
56. 'Foreign direct investment, net inflows (BoP, current US$)', World Bank Group. Available at https://data.worldbank.org/indicator/BX.KLT.DINV.CD.WD. Accessed 11 June 2024.
57. Anna Politkovskaya, A *Small Corner of Hell: Despatches from Chechnya*. (Chicago: Chicago University Press, 2003), p. 106.
58. Andrew Roth, 'Mastermind in Murder of Anna Politkovskaya Remains Unknown', *New York Times*, 9 June 2014. Available at https://www.nytimes.com/2014/06/10/world/europe/moscow-court-sentences-5-to-prison-for-contract-killing-of-anna-politkovskaya.html. Accessed 11 June 2024.
59. 'Russia behind Litvinenko murder, rules European rights court', BBC News, 21 September 2021. Available at https://www.bbc.com/news/world-58637572. Accessed 11 June 2024.
60. 'Annual Address to the Federal Assembly of the Russian Federation', President of Russia, 25 April 2005. Available at http://en.kremlin.ru/events/president/transcripts/22931. Accessed 19 August 2025.
61. 'Liberalism in Crisis: What Is to Be Done?', Khodorkovsky, 1 April 2004. Available at https://khodorkovsky.com/liberalism-in-crisis-what-is-to-be-done. Accessed 12 June 2024.

CHAPTER 5

1. Serhii Plokhy, *The Last Empire* (New York: Basic Books, 2014), p. 49.
2. Rice, *No Higher Honour*, p. 357.
3. D'Anieri, *Ukraine and Russia*, p. 112.
4. D'Anieri, *Ukraine and Russia*, p. 114.
5. D'Anieri, *Ukraine and Russia*, p. 156.
6. 'FT Briefing: Ukraine's gas dispute with Russia', *Financial Times*, 2 January 2006. Available at https://www.ft.com/content/6890fa5c-795f-11da-8d99-0000779e2340. Accessed 19 August 2025.
7. Thomas Catan and Tom Warner. 'Russia and Ukraine reach gas agreement', *Financial Times*. Available at https://www.ft.com/content/6ea768c4-7c8c-11da-936a-0000779e2340. Accessed 19 August 2025.
8. Rice, *No Higher Honour*, p. 412.
9. John Lough, *Germany's Russia Problem: The Struggle for Balance in Europe* (Manchester: Manchester University Press, 2022), pp. 138–9.
10. Lough, *Germany's Russia Problem*, p. 139.
11. Putin, *First Person*, p. 77.

12. Putin, *First Person*, p. 79.
13. Olga Kryshtanovskaya and Stephen White, 'Putin's Militocracy', *Post-Soviet Affairs*, vol. 19, no. 4 (October 2003), p. 289. DOI: 10.2747/1060-586X. 19.4.289.
14. Henry Foy. '"We need to talk about Igor": the rise of Russia's most powerful oligarch', *Financial Times*, 1 March 2018. Available at https://www.ft.com/ content/dc7d48f8-1c13-11e8-aaca-4574d7dabfb6. Accessed 19 August 2025.
15. See https://www.rosneft.com/governance/board/item/6078. Accessed 1 August 2024.
16. OPEC data cited in 'Oligarchs, power and profits: the history of BP in Russia', *Financial Times*, 24 March 2022. Available at https://www.ft.com/content/ e9238fa2-65a2-4753-a845-ce8129f93a0c. Accessed 4 September 2024.
17. 'Oligarchs, power and profits: the history of BP in Russia'.
18. 'TNK-BP chief is "forced out" of Russia', *Financial Times*, 24 July 2008. Available at https://www.ft.com/content/8f5c2610-59aa-11dd-90f8-000077b07658. Accessed 4 September 2024.
19. Vladimir Soldatkin, 'New blow for BP in Russia as office raided', Reuters, 31 August 2011. Available at https://www.reuters.com/article/business/environment/ new-blow-for-bp-in-russia-as-office-raided-idUSTRE77U1EP. Accessed 4 September 2024.
20. 'Oligarchs, power and profits: the history of BP in Russia'.
21. John Lough, interview with the author, London, 2 September 2024.
22. 'The making of a neo-KGB state', *The Economist,*, 23 August 2007. Available at https://www.economist.com/briefing/2007/08/23/the-making-of-a-neo-kgb-state. Accessed 1 August 2024.
23. Agence France Presse report first published in 'Russian Patriarch Kirill Spied in Switzerland for KGB in 70s', *Moscow Times*, 6 February 2023. Available at https:// www.themoscowtimes.com/2023/02/06/russian-patriarch-kirill-spied-in-switzerland-for-kgb-in-70s-media-a80151. Accessed 20 June 2025.
24. Martin Sixsmith and Daniel Sixsmith, *Putin and the Return of History: How the Kremlin Rekindled the Cold War* (London: Bloomsbury, 2024), p. 236.
25. Cited in Zoe Knox, 'The Symphonic Ideal: The Moscow Patriarchate's Post-Soviet Leadership', *Europe-Asia Studies*, vol. 55, no. 4 (June 2003), p. 583. DOI: 10.1080/096681303200008.
26. Knox, 'The Symphonic Ideal', p. 588.
27. 'Russians Return to Religion, But Not to Church', Pew Research Center, 10 February 2014. Available at https://www.pewresearch.org/religion/2014/02/10/ russians-return-to-religion-but-not-to-church.Accessed 20 August 2024.
28. 'Moscow Diary: A Christian revival', BBC News, 28 January 2009. Available at http://news.bbc.co.uk/1/hi/world/europe/7856161.stm. Accessed 20 August 2024.
29. Michael Schwirtz, 'Dignitaries Attend Yeltsin's Funeral', *New York Times*, 25 April 2007. Available at https://www.nytimes.com/2007/04/25/world/europe/25cnd-yeltsin.html. Accessed 20 August 2024.
30. 'Statement on Behalf of a Group of Member States of the Commonwealth of Independent States on the Situation Surrounding the Monument to the Liberator Soldier in Tallinn', The Ministry of Foreign Affairs of the Russian Federation,

26 April 2007. Available at https://archive.mid.ru/en/web/guest/foreign_policy/news/-/asset_publisher/cKNonkJE02Bw/content/id/375312. Accessed 20 August 2024.

31. 'How a cyber attack transformed Estonia', BBC News, 27 April 2017. Available at https://www.bbc.co.uk/news/39655415. Accessed 20 August 2024.

32. Steven Lee Myers, 'Estonia removes Soviet-era war memorial after a night of violence', *New York Times*, 27 April 2007. Available at https://www.nytimes.com/2007/04/27/world/europe/27iht-estonia.4.5477141.html. Accessed 20 August 2024.

33. Jamie Shea, interview with the author, London, 16 March 2023.

34. For the English translation of Putin's speech, please see 'Speech and the Following Discussion at the Munich Conference on Security Policy', President of Russia. Available at http://en.kremlin.ru/events/president/transcripts/24034. The Russian version, with video recording, is available at http://kremlin.ru/events/president/transcripts/24034. Both accessed 30 August 2024.

35. Terminology referring to NATO's new members since the end of the Cold War is a matter of controversy, specifically whether the alliance can be said to have 'expanded'. Supporters of the policy say this word is incorrect on the grounds that states apply to join NATO, which 'enlarges' when those applications are successful. Not surprisingly, Putin used the word 'расширение', normally translated into English as 'expansion'.

36. Rice, *No Higher Honour*, p. 670.

37. Rice, *No Higher Honour*, p. 671.

38. Rice, *No Higher Honour*, p. 672.

39. Rice, *No Higher Honour*, p. 673.

40. 'Bucharest Summit Declaration', NATO, 03 April 2008. Available at https://www.nato.int/cps/en/natohq/official_texts_8443.htm. Accessed 30 August 2024.

41. Rice, *No Higher Honour*, p. 675.

42. Lyne, interview with the author, London, 8 November 2023.

43. 'Nato right to heed Russian anger over Ukraine accession plan, Angela Merkel says in memoirs', *Financial Times*, 21 November 2024. Available at https://www.ft.com/content/053c369e-0903-4062-a910-20d5dd31827f. Accessed 24 January 2025.

44. 'Ukraine and NATO – Evidence from public opinion surveys', Stockholm School of Economics, 30 October 2023. Available at https://www.hhs.se/en/about-us/news/site-publications/2023/ukraine-and-nato--evidence-from-public-opinion-surveys. Accessed 24 January 2025.

45. 'Putin sees Medvedev as successor', BBC News, 10 December 2007. Available at http://news.bbc.co.uk/1/hi/world/europe/7136347.stm. Accessed 2 September 2024.

46. Cited in 'Sergei Ivanon Talks Tough on Chechnya', *The Jamestown Monitor*, vol. 7, no. 148 (2 August 2001). Available at https://jamestown.org/program/sergei-ivanov-talks-tough-on-chechnya. Accessed 3 September 2024.

47. Rice, *No Higher Honour*, p. 62.

48. Data from the Central Election Commission of the Russian Federation, cited in William A. Clark, 'The Presidential Transition in Russia, March 2008', *Electoral Studies*, vol. 28 (2009), p. 342. DOI: 10.1016/j.electstud.2008.10.002.

49. 'A military parade took place on Red Square in Moscow to mark the sixty-third anniversary of Victory in the Great Patriotic War', President of Russia, 9 May 2008. Available at http://en.kremlin.ru/events/president/news/32. Accessed 3 September 2024.

50. Catherine Ashton, interview with the author, London, 25 June 2024.

51. Rice, *No Higher Honour*, p. 577.

52. Putin, *First Person*, p. 18.

53. Interview with the author, Washington, DC, 19 July 2024

54. Vladimir Putin, Hilton Hotel, Brussels, 11 November 2002. Available at https://www.nato.int/docu/speech/2002/s021111a.htm. Accessed 6 September 2024.

CHAPTER 6

1. Thomas de Waal, *The Caucasus: An Introduction* (Oxford: Oxford University Press, 2010), p. 134.

2. 'Military expenditure (% of GDP) – Georgia', World Bank Group. Available at https://data.worldbank.org/indicator/MS.MIL.XPND.GD.ZS?locations=GE. Accessed 9 September 2024.

3. 'Russia-Georgia "spy" row deepens', BBC News, 28 September 2006. Available at http://news.bbc.co.uk/1/hi/world/europe/5386656.stm. Accessed 9 September 2024.

4. 'Georgia's Nato bid irks Russia', BBC News, 28 November 2006. Available at http://news.bbc.co.uk/1/hi/world/europe/6190858.stm. Accessed 9 September 2024.

5. 'Kokoity: "Caucasian Laws" Superior to Western Democracy', Civil.Ge, 31 October 2006. Available at https://old.civil.ge/eng/article.php?id=13992&search. Accessed 9 September 2024.

6. 'Russian MFA Information and Press Department Commentary Regarding Questions from RIA Novosti on the Holding of a Referendum and Presidential Election in South Ossetia on November 12, 2006', The Ministry of Foreign Affairs of the Russian Federation, 10 November 2006. Available at https://www.mid.ru/en/foreign_policy/news/1636725. Accessed 9 September 2024.

7. 'Russian MFA Information and Press Department Commentary Regarding a Question from ITAR-TASS News Agency About the Results of the Referendum and Presidential Elections in South Ossetia', The Ministry of Foreign Affairs of the Russian Federation, 13 November 2006. Available at https://www.mid.ru/en/foreign_policy/news/1637547. Accessed 9 September 2024.

8. 'Russia recognises Georgian rebels', BBC News, 26 August 2008. Available at http://news.bbc.co.uk/1/hi/7582181.stm. Accessed 9 September 2024.

9. 'Address by President of the Russian Federation', President of Russia, 18 March 2014. Available at http://en.kremlin.ru/events/president/news/20603. Accessed 9 September 2024.

10. Judy Dempsey, 'Poles and Czechs to talk with U.S. about missile defense system', *New York Times*, 23 January 2007. Available at https://www.nytimes.com/2007/01/23/world/europe/23iht-germany.4313216.html. Accessed 10 September 2024.

11. McFaul, *From Cold War to Hot Peace*, p. 179.

12. Dempsey, 'Poles and Czechs to talk with U.S. about missile defense system'.

13. Robert Burns, 'U.S. Might Negotiate on Missile Defense', *Washington Post*, 24 April 2007. Available at https://www.washingtonpost.com/wp-dyn/content/article/2007/04/24/AR2007042400871.html. Accessed 10 September 2024.

14. 'Discussing missile defence', NATO News, 19 April 2007. Available at https://www.nato.int/docu/update/2007/04-april/e0419a.html. Accessed 10 September 2025.

15. Rice, *No Higher Honour*, p. 580.

16. Rice, *No Higher Honour*, p. 676.

17. 'Fact Sheet: U.S.–Russia Strategic Framework Declaration', The White House, 6 April 2008. Available at https://georgewbush-whitehouse.archives.gov/news/releases/2008/04/20080406-5.html. Accessed 10 September 2024.

18. Rice, *No Higher Honour*, p. 677.

19. Steven Lee Myers, 'In last meeting, Putin and Bush agree to disagree', *New York Times*, 6 April 2008. Available at https://www.nytimes.com/2008/04/06/world/europe/06iht-bush.4.11709723.html. Accessed 10 September 2024.

20. 'Statement of the Russian Ministry of Foreign Affairs Concerning the Signing of the US-Czech Agreement on Deployment of Elements of the US Global Missile Defense System on the Territory of the Czech Republic', The Ministry of Foreign Affairs of the Russian Federation, 8 July 2008. Available at https://www.mid.ru/en/foreign_policy/news/1587969. Accessed 10 September 2024.

21. 'Statement by the Ministry of Foreign Affairs of the Russian Federation in Connection with Georgia's Provocative Actions in South Ossetia', The Ministry of Foreign Affairs of the Russian Federation, 4 July 2008. Available at https://www.mid.ru/en/foreign_policy/news/1734571. Accessed 10 September 2024.

22. 'Statement of the Russian Ministry of Foreign Affairs Concerning the Exacerbation of the Situation in the Georgian-Abkhaz and Georgian-Ossetian Zones of Conflict', The Ministry of Foreign Affairs of the Russian Federation, 9 July 2008. Available at https://www.mid.ru/en/foreign_policy/news/1588015. Accessed 10 September 2024.

23. 'Minister of Foreign Affairs Sergey Lavrov Meets with South Ossetian President Eduard Kokoity', The Ministry of Foreign Affairs of the Russian Federation, 14 July 2008. Available at https://www.mid.ru/en/foreign_policy/news/1589412. Accessed 10 September 2024.

24. J. Rodgers and A. Lanoszka, 'Russia's Rising Military and Communication Power: From Chechnya to Crimea', *Media, War & Conflict*, vol. 16, no. 2 (2003), p. 142. DOI: 10.1177/17506352211027084.

25. 'FACTBOX: Facts about the 2008 war in Georgia', Reuters, 4 August 2009. Available at https://www.reuters.com/article/world/factbox-facts-about-the-2008-war-in-georgia-idUSTRE5732TH. Accessed 11 September 2024.

26. 'Vladimir Putin "wanted to hang Georgian President Saakashvili by the balls"', *The Times* 14 November 2008. Available at https://www.thetimes.com/article/vladimir-putin-wanted-to-hang-georgian-president-saakashvili-by-the-balls-mbz2p0mjjlz?msockid=36bf362024bb65ec111e399c258364a4. Accessed 11 September 2024.

27. 'Independent International Fact-Finding Mission on the Conflict in Georgia' (also known as the Tagliavini report), 20 September 2009. Accessed via 'Russian jets attack Georgian town', BBC News, 9 August 2008. Available at http://news.bbc.co.uk/1/hi/world/europe/7550804.stm. Accessed 11 September 2024.

28. Tagliavini report, p. 19.
29. Tagliavini report, p. 24.
30. Tagliavini report, p. 26.
31. Timothy Heritage, 'Georgia started war with Russia: EU-backed report', Reuters, 30 September 2008. Available at https://www.reuters.com/article/world/georgia-started-war-with-russia-eu-backed-report-idUSTRE58T4MO. Accessed 11 September 2024.
32. For a fuller account of the 2008 media war between Russia and Georgia, please see Chapter 4 of my 2012 book, *Reporting Conflict* (Basingstoke: Palgrave Macmillan).
33. Sergei Lavrov, interviewed for the BBC by James Rodgers, Moscow, 9 August 2008. Quote is from an extract from the interview held in the author's personal archive.
34. Rick Fawn and Robert Nalbandov, 'The Difficulties of Knowing the Start of War in the Information Age: Russia, Georgia and the War over South Ossetia, August 2008', *European Security*, vol. 21, no. 1 (2012), p. 57. DOI: 10.1080/09662839.2012.656601.
35. Andrei Illarionov, 'The Russian Leadership's Preparation for War', in Svante E. Cornell and S. Frederick Starr (eds), *The Guns of August 2008: Russia's War in Georgia* (Armonk and London: M. E. Sharpe, 2009), p. 50.
36. Rodgers and Lanoszka, 'Russia's rising military and communication power', p. 142.
37. Vasilii Kashin, 'Defense Innovation in Russia in the 2010s', *Journal of Strategic Studies*, vol. 44, no. 6 (2021), p. 907. DOI: 10.1080/01402390.2021.1974172.
38. Kashin, 'Defense innovation in Russia in the 2010s', p. 901.
39. Rodgers and Lanoszka, 'Russia's rising military and communication power', p. 142.
40. Alec Luhn, 'Ex-Soviet countries on front line of Russia's media war with the west', *Guardian*, 6 January 2015. Available at https://www.theguardian.com/world/2015/jan/06/-sp-ex-soviet-countries-front-line-russia-media-propaganda-war-west. Accessed 12 September 2024.
41. Steven Lee Myers, 'White House Unveils $1 Billion Georgia Aid Plan', *New York Times*, 3 September 2008. Available at https://www.nytimes.com/2008/09/04/world/europe/04cheney.html. Accessed 13 September 2024.
42. 'We must make Moscow pay for this blow against democracy', *The Times*, 17 August 2008. Available at https://www.thetimes.com/article/0d345281-bd55-4ebb-9c00-594ba394162b. Accessed 13 September 2024.
43. Fiona Hill, interview with the author, Washington, DC, 19 July 2024.
44. Sir Roderic Lyne, interview with the author, London, 24 June 2024
45. Laurie Bristow, interview with the author, Cambridge, 12 September 2023. All quotations subsequently attributed to Bristow come from this interview unless otherwise indicated.
46. Rice, *No Higher Honour*, p. 686.
47. 'Alexei Kudrin: A guarantor of fiscal discipline', *Financial Times*, 17 April 2008. Available at https://www.ft.com/content/86ea34f4-0b6c-11dd-8ccf-0000779fd2ac. Accessed 16 September 2024.
48. McFaul, *From Cold War to Hot Peace*, p. 79
49. McFaul, *From Cold War to Hot Peace*, p. 82.

50. McFaul, *From Cold War to Hot Peace*, pp. 74–5.
51. McFaul, *From Cold War to Hot Peace*, p. 75.
52. McFaul, *From Cold War to Hot Peace*, p. 98.
53. 'Clinton gift of "reset" button lost in translation', The Associated Press YouTube channel, 7 March 2009. Available at https://www.youtube.com/watch?v=Ee4P fhogtdQ. Accessed 16 September 2024.
54. McFaul, *From Cold War to Hot Peace*, p. 98.
55. Tony Brenton, interview with the author, Cambridge, England, 23 April 2023.
56. McFaul, *From Cold War to Hot Peace*, p. 79.
57. McFaul, *From Cold War to Hot Peace*, p. 88.
58. McFaul, *From Cold War to Hot Peace*, p. 94.
59. McFaul, *From Cold War to Hot Peace*, p. 106.
60. 'U.S.-Russia Relations: "Reset" Fact Sheet', White House, 24 June 2010. Available athttps://obamawhitehouse.archives.gov/the-press-office/us-russia-relations-reset-fact-sheet. Accessed 16 September 2024.
61. McFaul, *From Cold War to Hot Peace*, p. 168 (italics in original).
62. Catherine Ashton, *And Then What?: Despatches from the Heart of 21st-Century Diplomacy from Kosovo to Kyiv* (London: Elliott and Thompson, 2023), p. 182.

CHAPTER 7

1. Putin, *First Person*, p. 69.
2. McFaul, *From Cold War to Hot Peace*, pp. 168–9.
3. Charles Clover, *Black Wind, White Snow: Russia's New Nationalism* (New Haven and London: Yale University Press, 2022), p. 18.
4. Vladimir Putin. Article in *Nezavisimaya Gazeta*, 23 January 2012. Quoted in Clover, *Black Wind, White Snow*, p. 15.
5. 'White House Fact Sheet on The Strategic Arms Reduction Treaty (START)', The American Presidency Project, 31 July 1991. Available at https://www.presidency.ucsb.edu/documents/white-house-fact-sheet-the-strategic-arms-reduction-treaty-start. Accessed 24 September 2024.
6. 'START I at a Glance', Arms Control Association, last updated July 2022. Available at https://www.armscontrol.org/factsheets/start-i-glance. Accessed 24 September 2024.
7. 'White House Fact Sheet on The Strategic Arms Reduction Treaty (START)'.
8. 'The Strategic Offensive Reductions Treaty (SORT) At a Glance', Arms Control Association.Availableathttps://www.armscontrol.org/factsheets/strategic-offensive-reductions-treaty-sort-glance.
9. 'US-Russian Strategic Offensive Reductions Treaty (As Delivered)', US Department of State, 9 July 2002. Available at https://2001-2009.state.gov/secretary/former/powell/remarks/2002/11743.htm. Accessed 24 September 2024.
10. 'New START Treaty', United States Department of State. Available at https://www.state.gov/new-start. Accessed 24 September 2024.
11. 'Russian-US Treaty on Reduction and Limitation of Strategic Offensive Arms has been signed', President of Russia, 8 April 2010. Available at http://en.kremlin.ru/events/president/news/7396. Accessed 24 September 2024.
12. 'New START Treaty'.

13. 'Presidential Address to Federal Assembly', President of Russia, 21 February 2023. Available at http://en.kremlin.ru/events/president/news/70565. Accessed 24 September 2024.
14. Ulrich Kühn, 'The End of Conventional Arms Control and the Role of US Congress', *Journal for Peace and Nuclear Disarmament*, vol. 2, no. 1 (2019), p. 256. DOI: 10.1080/25751654.2019.1607993.
15. 'Foreign Ministry statement on the completion of the procedure for the Russian Federation's withdrawal from the Treaty on Conventional Armed Forces in Europe (CFE Treaty)', The Ministry of Foreign Affairs of the Russian Federation, 7 November 2023. Available at https://www.mid.ru/en/foreign_policy/news/1913546. Accessed 24 September 2024.
16. Terence Neilan, 'Bush Pulls Out of ABM Treaty; Putin Calls Move a Mistake', *New York Times*, 13 December 2001. Available at https://www.nytimes.com/2001/12/13/international/bush-pulls-out-of-abm-treaty-putin-calls-move-a-mistake.html. Accessed 24 September 2024.
17. 'A Statement Regarding the Decision of the Administration of the United States to Withdraw from the Antiballistic Missile Treaty of 1972', President of Russia, 13 December 2001. Available at http://en.kremlin.ru/events/president/transcripts/21444. Accessed 24 September 2024.
18. 'Intermediate-Range Nuclear Forces Treaty (INF Treaty)', US Department of State. Available at https://2009-2017.state.gov/t/avc/trty/102360.htm. Accessed 24 September 2024.
19. 'Donald Trump's decision to pull out of Russia nuclear treaty: why now?', CNN Politics, 22 October 2018. Available at https://edition.cnn.com/2018/10/21/politics/trump-russia-inf-treaty-decision/index.html. Accessed 24 September 2024.
20. 'U.S. Withdrawal from the INF Treaty on August 2, 2019', United States Department of State, 2 August 2019. Available at https://2017-2021.state.gov/u-s-withdrawal-from-the-inf-treaty-on-august-2-2019. Accessed 24 September 2024.
21. 'Foreign Ministry statement on the withdrawal of the United States from the INF Treaty and its termination', The Ministry of Foreign Affairs of the Russian Federation, 2 August 2019. Available at https://www.mid.ru/en/foreign_policy/news/1467241. Accessed 24 September 2024.
22. Sarah Bidgood, 'US–Russia Relations and the Future of Arms Control: How the Comprehensive Nuclear-Test-Ban Treaty could Restore Engagement on Nuclear Issues', *The Nonproliferation Review*, vol. 25, nos 3–4 (2018), p. 308. DOI: 10.1080/10736700.2018.1512203.
23. ITAR-TASS news agency, Moscow, in Russian, 1322 14 Jul 05/BBCMonitoring/(c) BBC. Accessed 24 September 2024.
24. Steven Lee Myers, 'U.S. Suspects Russia Set Off Nuclear Test', *New York Times*, 29 August 1997. Available at https://www.nytimes.com/1997/08/29/world/us-suspects-russia-set-off-nuclear-test.html. Accessed 26 September 2024.
25. 'Results of Special Panel Meeting on Novaya Zemlya Test Site', CIA, 28 October 1997. Approved for release November 2004. Available at https://www.cia.gov/readingroom/docs/DOC_0001150395.pdf. Accessed 26 September 2024.
26. The Associated Press, 'U.S. Says Russian Tremor Was Not Nuclear', *New York Times*, 5 November 1997. Available at https://www.nytimes.com/1997/11/05/world/us-says-russian-tremor-was-not-nuclear.html. Accessed 26 September 2024.

27. 'The Comprehensive Nuclear-Test-Ban Treaty', CTBTO. Available at https://www.ctbto.org/our-mission/the-treaty. Accessed 26 September 2024.
28. 'The Russian Federation's support for the Comprehensive Nuclear-Test-Ban Treaty', CTBTO. Available at https://www.ctbto.org/news-and-events/news/russian-federations-support-comprehensive-nuclear-test-ban-treaty. Accessed 26 September 2024.
29. 'Moscow voices serious concern over North Korea nuclear test', TASS, 9 September 2016. Available at https://tass.com/politics/898815. Accessed 26 September 2024.
30. Filipp Lebedev and Mark Trevelyan, 'Russia passes law pulling ratification of nuclear test ban treaty', Reuters, 26 October 2023. Available at https://www.reuters.com/world/europe/russian-upper-house-approves-de-ratification-nuclear-test-ban-treaty-2023-10-25. Accessed 17 October 2025.
31. 'Law revoking the ratification of the Comprehensive Nuclear-Test-Ban Treaty', President of Russia, 2 November 2023. Available at http://en.kremlin.ru/acts/news/72635. Accessed 26 September 2024.
32. 'Memorandum on security assurances in connection with Ukraine's accession to the Treaty on the Non-Proliferation of Nuclear Weapons', Budapest, 5 December 1994. Available at https://treaties.un.org/doc/Publication/UNTS/Volume%203007/Part/volume-3007-I-52241.pdf. Accessed 26 September 2024.
33. Alison Pargeter, *Libya: The Rise and Fall of Qaddafi* (New Haven and London: Yale University Press, 2012), p. 216.
34. Ashton, *And Then What?*, p. 106.
35. 'Resolution 1973 (2011) Adopted by the Security Council at its 6498th meeting, on 17 March 2011', UN Security Council. Available at https://documents.un.org/doc/undoc/gen/n11/268/39/pdf/n1126839.pdf. Accessed 17 October 2025.
36. 'Readout of President Obama's call with Russian President Medvedev', White House. Available at https://obamawhitehouse.archives.gov/the-press-office/2011/03/24/readout-president-obama-s-call-russian-president-medvedev. Accessed 17 October 2025.
37. Ashton, *And Then What?*, p. 114.
38. Monterey Initiative in Russian Studies, 'The Ambassadorial Series: Deans of U.S.-Russia Diplomacy Transcript of the Ambassador Michael McFaul Interview', 16 June 2021. Interview conducted 10 May 2021. Available at https://nsarchive.gwu.edu/document/23523-transcript-ambassador-michael-mcfaul-interview. Accessed 7 October 2024.
39. Hillary Clinton, then US secretary of state.
40. https://www.reuters.com/article/world/putin-likens-un-libya-resolution-to-crusades-idUSTRE72K3JR/. March 21, 2011. Accessed 26 September 2025.
41. Zygar, *War and Punishment*, p. 272.
42. 'Putin likens U.N. Libya resolution to crusades', Reuters, 21 March 2011. Available at https://www.reuters.com/article/world/putin-likens-un-libya-resolution-to-crusades-idUSTRE72K3JR. Accessed 27 September 2024.
43. McFaul, *From Cold War to Hot Peace*, p. 189.
44. McFaul, *From Cold War to Hot Peace*, p. 192.
45. 'Dmitry Medvedev signed the laws on amendments to the Russian Constitution regarding the Government's responsibility to deputies and the raising of the terms of office for the head of state and members of parliament', President of Russia, 30 December 2008. Available at http://en.kremlin.ru/events/president/news/2684. Accessed 28 September 2024.

46. 'United Russia party congress', President of Russia, 24 September 2011. Available at http://en.kremlin.ru/events/president/news/12802. Accessed 28 September 2024.

47. Population by per capita money income. From 'Living Standards', Federal State Statistics Service, 11 August 2018. Available at https://eng.rosstat.gov.ru/living. Accessed 28 September 2024.

48. 'Putin "booed" at Moscow martial arts event', YouTube. Available at https://www.youtube.com/watch?v=nS48UuVXbjQ&t=2s.

49. Russian Federation Elections to the State Duma, 4 December 2011, OSCE/ODIHR Election Observation Mission Final Report. Available at https://www.osce.org/files/f/documents/f/5/86959.pdf. Accessed 6 October 2024.

50. Levada data quoted in Stephen White and Ian McAllister, 'Did Russia (Nearly) have a Facebook Revolution in 2011?: Social Media's Challenge to Authoritarianism', *Politics*, vol. 34, no. 1 (February 2014), p. 82. DOI: 10.1111/1467-9256.12037.

51. 'Партия жуликов и воров' in Russian.

52. 'За честные выборы' in Russian. The phrase could also be translated as 'for honest elections'.

53. 'Russian election: Biggest protests since fall of USSR', BBC News, 10 December 2011. Available at https://www.bbc.com/news/world-europe-16122524. Accessed 6 October 2024.

54. 'Russian election: Biggest protests since fall of USSR'.

55. 'A Russian awakening', *The Economist*, 11 December 2011. Available at https://www.economist.com/eastern-approaches/2011/12/11/a-russian-awakening. Accessed 19 August 2025.

56. David M. Herszenhorn and Ellen Barry, 'After Russian Vote, Putin Claims Clinton Incited Unrest', *New York Times*, 8 December 2011. Available at https://www.nytimes.com/2011/12/09/world/europe/putin-accuses-clinton-of-instigating-russian-protests.html. Accessed 7 October 2024.

57. Телевизор никого не впечатляет, ОМОН особо никого не пугает.

58. Alexei Navalny, 'Навальный', LiveJournal, 21 December 2011. Available at https://navalny.livejournal.com/2011/12/21. Accessed 7 October 2024.

59. Jan Matti Dollbaum, Morvan Lallouet and Ben Noble, *Navalny: Putin's Nemesis, Russia's Future?* (Oxford, Oxford University Press: 2021; online edn, Oxford Academic, 20 January 2022), p. 78.

60. Dollbaum, Lallouet and Noble, *Navalny*, p. 110.

61. 'Putin tells stadium rally "battle" is on for Russia', BBC News, 23 February 2012. Available at https://www.bbc.com/news/world-europe-17136644. Accessed 7 October 2024.

62. Russian Central Election Committee figures cited in 'OSCE/ODIHR Election Observation Mission Final Report, Russian Federation Presidential Election 4 March 2012', 11 May 2012, p. 25. Available at https://www.osce.org/files/f/documents/2/c/90461.pdf. Accessed 7 October 2024.

63. 'Prokhorov Says He's No "Kremlin Stooge," Lays Out Campaign Platform', RFE/RL, 20 January 2012. Available at https://www.rferl.org/a/prokhorov_lays_out_presidential_election_platform/24458038.html. Accessed 7 October 2024.

64. Russian Central Election Committee figures cited in 'OSCE/ODIHR Election Observation Mission Final Report', p. 2.

65. 'Presidential Elections in Russia', US Department of State, 5 March 2012. Available at https://2009-2017.state.gov/r/pa/prs/ps/2012/03/185210.htm. Accessed 7 October 2024.

66. Paul Chaisty and Stephen Whitefield, 'Forward to Democracy or Back to Authoritarianism?: The Attitudinal Bases of Mass Support for the Russian Election Protests of 2011–2012', *Post-Soviet Affairs*, vol. 29, no. 5 (2013), p. 388. DOI: 10.1080/1060586X.2013.807605.

67. D.B. Oreshkin, 'Presidential Elections in the Russian Federation on March 4, 2012: Evolution of Regional Support', *Regional Research of Russia*, vol. 2, no. 3 (2012), pp. 268–9.

68. Zygar, *War and Punishment*, p. 273.

CHAPTER 8

1. This figure is imprecise, and contested. Media reports, for example, Mary Catherine Wellons, 'Sochi by the numbers', CNBC, 10 February 2024, available at https://www.cnbc.com/2014/02/10/sochi-by-the-numbers.html, use it. But others, for example, Paul Farhi, 'Did the Winter Olympics in Sochi really cost $50 billion? A closer look at that figure', *Washington Post*, 10 February 2024, available at https://www.washingtonpost.com/lifestyle/style/did-the-winter-olympics-in-sochi-really-cost-50-billion-a-closer-look-at-that-figure/2014/02/10/a29e37b4-9260-11e3-b46a-5a3d0d2130da_story.html, question it. In his 2015 paper, 'After Sochi 2014: Costs and Impacts of Russia's Olympic Games', the geographer Martin Müller gave the figure $55bn. *Eurasian Geography and Economics*, vol. 55, no. 6 (2014), p. 628. DOI: 10.1080/15387216.2015.1040432.

2. 'Sochi 2014 Olympic Medal Table – Gold, Silver & Bronze', Olympics.com. Available at https://olympics.com/en/olympic-games/sochi-2014/medals. Accessed 8 October 2024.

3. 'Winter Olympics: Putin cautions gay visitors to Sochi', BBC News, 17 January 2014. Available at https://www.bbc.com/news/world-europe-25785161. Accessed 8 October 2024.

4. 'Russia: Sochi Games Highlight Homophobic Violence', Human Rights Watch, 3 February 2014. Available at https://www.hrw.org/news/2014/02/03/russia-sochi-games-highlight-homophobic-violence. Accessed 8 October 2024.

5. 'Association Agreement between the European Union and its Member States, of the one part, and Ukraine, of the other part', *Official Journal of the European Union* (29 May 2014). Available at https://publications.europa.eu/resource/cellar/4589a50c-e6e3-11e3-8cd4-01aa75ed71a1.0006.03/DOC_1. Accessed 8 October 2024.

6. Timothy Snyder, *Bloodlands: Europe Between Hitler and Stalin* (London: Vintage, 2015)

7. Elizabeth Piper, 'Special Report: Why Ukraine spurned the EU and embraced Russia', Reuters, 19 December 2013. Accessed 8 October 2024.

8. Office of the UN High Commissioner for Human Rights, 'Accountability for killings in Ukraine from January 2014 to May 2016', p. 9. Available at https://www.ohchr.org/sites/default/files/Documents/Countries/UA/OHCHRThematicReportUkraineJan2014-May2016_EN.pdf. Accessed 8 October 2024.

9. 'Putin: Russia helped Yanukovych to flee Ukraine', BBC News, 24 October 2014. Available at https://www.bbc.com/news/world-europe-29761799. Updated 11 November 2014. Accessed 8 October 2024.

10. Doina Chiacu and Arshad Mohammed, 'Leaked audio reveals embarrassing U.S. exchange on Ukraine, EU', Reuters, 7 February 2014. Available at https://www.reuters.com/article/world/leaked-audio-reveals-embarrassing-us-exchange-on-ukraine-eu-idUSBREA1601K. Accessed 9 October 2024.

11. Andrew Wilson, *Ukraine Crisis: What it Means for the West* (New Haven and London: Yale University Press, 2014), p. 108.

12. Wilson, *Ukraine Crisis*, p. 110.

13. Andrei Vasiliev, 'The Crimean "Army"', openDemocracy, 14 March 2014. Available at https://www.opendemocracy.net/en/odr/crimean-army. Accessed 9 October 2024.

14. Wilson, *Ukraine Crisis*, p. 112.

15. 'Direct Line with Vladimir Putin', President of Russia, 17 April 2014. Available at http://en.kremlin.ru/events/president/news/20796. Accessed 9 October 2024.

16. Carol Morello, Pamela Constable and Anthony Faiola, 'Crimeans vote to break away from Ukraine, join Russia', *Washington Post*, 16 March 2014. Available at https://www.washingtonpost.com/world/2014/03/16/ccec2132-acd4-11e3-a06a-e3230a43d6cb_story.html. Accessed 9 October 2024.

17. 'Statement by the Press Secretary on Ukraine', White House, 16 March 2014. Available at https://obamawhitehouse.archives.gov/the-press-office/2014/03/16/statement-press-secretary-ukraine. Accessed 9 October 2024.

18. 'Executive Order on recognising Republic of Crimea', President of Russia, 17 March 2014. Available at http://en.kremlin.ru/events/president/news/20596. Accessed 9 October 2024.

19. 'Address by President of the Russian Federation', President of Russia, 18 March 2014. Available at http://en.kremlin.ru/events/president/news/20603. Accessed 9 October 2024.

20. 'The Ukraine Crisis and the Resumption of Great-Power Rivalry', Russia in Global Affairs, 14 July 2014. Available at https://eng.globalaffairs.ru/articles/the-ukraine-crisis-and-the-resumption-of-great-power-rivalry. Accessed 9 October 2024.

21. Richard Sakwa, *Frontline Ukraine: Crisis in the Borderlands* (London: I.B. Tauris, 2015), p. 9.

22. Clover, *Black Wind, White Snow*, p. 330.

23. 'Address by President of the Russian Federation'.

24. Putin's approval rating. Levada Center website. Available at https://www.levada.ru/en/ratings. Accessed 9 October 2024.

25. Samuel Greene and Graeme Robertson, *Putin v. the People: The Perilous Politics of a Divided Russia* (New Haven and London: Yale University Press, 2019), p. 107.

26. John Kerry, Secretary of State, Chief of Mission Residence, Paris, France, 30 March 2014. 'Press Availability – Paris, France', US Department of State. Available at https://2009-2017.state.gov/secretary/remarks/2014/03/224158.htm. Accessed 10 October 2024.

27. 'Comment by the Russian Foreign Minister, Sergey Lavrov, and his answers to questions from the mass media summarising his negotiations with the US secretary of state, John Kerry, Moscow, 30 March 2014', The Ministry of Foreign

Affairs of the Russian Federation, 31 March 2014. Available at https://www.mid.ru/en/foreign_policy/news/1709708. Accessed 10 October 2024.

28. See https://russkiymir.ru/en/fund. Accessed 10 October 2024.
29. Policy statement by Federal Chancellor Angela Merkel on the situation in Ukraine, Thursday 13 March 2014 in German Bundestag. Available at https://www.bundesregierung.de/breg-en/service/archive/archive/policy-statement-by-federal-chancellor-angela-merkel-on-the-situation-in-ukraine-443796. Accessed 10 October 2024.
30. 'Ukraine crisis: Kerry and Lavrov in push for solution', BBC News, 29 March 2014. Available at https://www.bbc.com/news/world-europe-26803688. Accessed 10 October 2024.
31. Wilson, *Ukraine Crisis*, p. 124.
32. Wilson, *Ukraine Crisis*, p. 131.
33. Wilson, *Ukraine Crisis*, p. 133.
34. 'Ukraine crisis: Forgotten death of Russian soldier', BBC News, 18 September 2014. Available at https://www.bbc.co.uk/news/world-europe-29249643. Accessed 15 October 2024.
35. '"Persistent and grave" human rights violations in eastern Ukraine – UN report', UN News, 1 June 2015. Available at https://news.un.org/en/story/2015/06/500292. Accessed 15 October 2024.
36. 'MH17 – The Open Source Evidence', Bellingcat, 8 October 2015. Available at https://www.bellingcat.com/news/uk-and-europe/2015/10/08/mh17-the-open-source-evidence. Accessed 15 October 2024.
37. 'Summary of the day in court: 17 November 2022 – Judgment', District Court of The Hague, 17 November 2022. Available at https://www.courtmh17.com/en/summaries-and-news/news/summary-of-the-day-in-court-17-november-2022-judgment.htm. Accessed 15 October 2024.
38. Steve Rosenberg, 'Igor Girkin shot down a passenger jet, then insulted Putin. Which one put him in jail?', BBC News, 25 January 2024. Available at https://www.bbc.co.uk/news/world-europe-68091877. Accessed 21 August 2025.
39. Karoun Demirjian, 'Russians have many theories about the MH17 crash. One involves fake dead people', *Washington Post*, 22 July 2014. Available at https://www.washingtonpost.com/world/russians-have-many-theories-about-the-mh17-crash-one-involves-fake-dead-people/2014/07/22/9a1c5ec9-11b6-4384-b585-53fff62e5779_story.html. Accessed 15 October 2024.
40. 'Катастрофа «Боинга» под Донецком', Levada Center, 30 July 2014. Available at https://www.levada.ru/2014/07/30/katastrofa-boinga-pod-donetskom. Accessed 15 October 2024. The Russian word 'ополченцы' that I have translated as 'volunteers' is sometimes translated as 'home guard'. It comes from a verb meaning 'to take up arms'.
41. 'MH17 – The Open Source Evidence'.
42. 'Briefing by the Russian Foreign Minister, Sergey Lavrov, for representatives of foreign and Russian mass media Moscow, 28 July 2014', The Ministry of Foreign Affairs of the Russian Federation, 28 July 2014. Available at https://www.mid.ru/en/foreign_policy/news/1628290. Accessed 16 October 2024.
43. 'MH17 crash: Obama warns Russia of isolation', *Financial Times*, 21 July 2014. Available at https://www.ft.com/content/6012c9a2-109e-11e4-b116-00144feabdc0. Accessed 16 October 2024.

44. 'Kremlin says Russia has no plans to get back to G8', TASS, 13 January 2017. Available at https://tass.com/politics/924897. Accessed 16 October 2024.
45. Zygar, *War and Punishment*, p. 301.
46. 'Briefing by the Russian Foreign Minister, Sergey Lavrov, for representatives of foreign and Russian mass media Moscow, 28 July 2014'.
47. 'The Russian Embargo: Impact on the Economic and Employment Situation in the EU', European Parliament. Available at https://www.europarl.europa.eu/RegData/etudes/BRIE/2014/536291/IPOL_BRI(2014)536291_EN.pdf. Accessed 16 October 2024.
48. 'Text of the Geneva Statement on Ukraine released by the US, EU, Ukraine and Russia', U.S. Mission to International Organizations in Geneva, 17 April 2014. Available at https://geneva.usmission.gov/2014/04/18/text-of-the-geneva-statement-on-ukraine-released-by-the-us-eu-ukraine-and-russia. Accessed 16 October 2024.
49. D'Anieri, *Ukraine and Russia*, p. 238.
50. D'Anieri, *Ukraine and Russia*, p. 247.
51. Duncan Allen, 'The Minsk Conundrum: Western Policy and Russia's War in Eastern Ukraine', Chatham House, 22 May 2020. Updated 17 December 2020. Available at https://www.chathamhouse.org/2020/05/minsk-conundrum-western-policy-and-russias-war-eastern-ukraine-0/minsk-2-agreement. Accessed 21 June 2025.
52. 'Doorstep statement by the NATO Secretary General before the meetings of the North Atlantic Council and the NATO-Ukraine Commission', NATO, 2 March 2014. Available at https://www.nato.int/cps/en/natohq/opinions_107663.htm. Accessed 16 October 2024.
53. 'Remarks by the NATO Secretary General, Anders Fogh Rasmussen at the Press Conference held following the meeting of the NATO-Russia Council at NATO HQ, Brussels', NATO, 5 March 2014. Available at https://www.nato.int/cps/en/natolive/opinions_107743.htm. Accessed 16 October 2024.
54. Jens Stoltenberg, interview with the author, NATO headquarters, Brussels, 8 September 2023.
55. 'Former Nato chief Jens Stoltenberg: "So far, we have called Putin's bluff"', *Financial Times*, 4 October 2024. Available at https://www.ft.com/content/5b63bdc1-9e74-4464-92df-a5aa83c5b221. Accessed 4 October 2024.

CHAPTER 9

1. Steven Erlanger, 'Russian Nationalist Wants To Rebuild Czars' Empire', *New York Times*, 13 December 1993. Available at https://www.nytimes.com/1993/12/13/world/russian-nationalist-wants-to-rebuild-czars-empire.html. Accessed 19 October 2024.
2. McFaul, *From Cold War to Hot Peace*, p. 331.
3. McFaul, *From Cold War to Hot Peace*, p. 332.
4. 'David Cameron: Syria empowering new al-Qaeda generation', BBC News, 17 December 2012. Available at https://www.bbc.co.uk/news/uk-politics-20762098. Accessed 19 October 2024.

5. 'Remarks by the President to the White House Press Corps', White House, 20 August 2012. Available at https://obamawhitehouse.archives.gov/the-press-office/2012/08/20/remarks-president-white-house-press-corps. Accessed 19 October 2024.

6. 'United Nations Mission to Investigate Allegations of the use of Chemical Weapons in the Syrian Arab Republic: Report on the Investigation of Alleged Use of Chemical Weapons in the Ghouta Area Of Damascus'. Available at https://front.un-arm.org/wp-content/uploads/2013/09/FS_SG_CW_Bilingue.pdf. Accessed 19 October 2024.

7. 'FULL TRANSCRIPT: Secretary of State John Kerry's remarks on Syria on Aug. 30', *Washington Post*, 30 August 2013. Available at https://www.washingtonpost.com/world/national-security/running-transcript-secretary-of-state-john-kerrys-remarks-on-syria-on-aug-30/2013/08/30/f3a63a1a-1193-11e3-85b6-d27422650fd5_story.html. Accessed 17 October 2025.

8. McFaul, *From Cold War to Hot Peace*, p. 352; 'Syria crisis: Cameron loses Commons vote on Syria action', BBC News, 30 August 2013. Available at https://www.bbc.co.uk/news/uk-politics-23892783. Accessed 19 October 2024.

9. 'Remarks by the NATO Secretary General, Anders Fogh Rasmussen at the Press Conference held following the meeting of the NATO-Russia Council at NATO HQ, Brussels', NATO, 5 March 2014. Available at https://www.nato.int/cps/en/natolive/opinions_107743.htm. Accessed 22 October 2024.

10. Alan Rappeport, 'Syria's Chemical Arsenal Fully Destroyed, U.S. Says', *New York Times*, 18 August 2014. Available at https://www.nytimes.com/2014/08/19/world/middleeast/syrias-chemical-arsenal-fully-destroyed-us-says.html.

11. McFaul, *From Cold War to Hot Peace*, p. 356.

12. Dmitry Trenin, 'The Ukraine Crisis and the Resumption of Great-Power Rivalry', Russia in Global Affairs, 14 July 2014. Available at https://eng.globalaffairs.ru/articles/the-ukraine-crisis-and-the-resumption-of-great-power-rivalry. Accessed 22 October 2024.

13. Sergei Radchenko, *To Run the World: The Kremlin's Cold War Bid for Global Power* (Cambridge: Cambridge University Press, 2024), p. 375.

14. Roy Allison, 'Russia and Syria: Explaining Alignment with a Regime in Crisis', *International Affairs*, vol. 89, no. 4 (July 2013), p. 796.

15. 'Foreign Policy of the Russian Federation', approved 12 February 2013. Available at https://beijing.mid.ru/en/countries/rossiya/kontseptsiya_vneshney_politiki_rossii. Accessed 22 October 2024.

16. '70th session of the UN General Assembly', President of Russia, 28 September 2015. Available at http://en.kremlin.ru/events/president/news/50385. Accessed 22 October 2024.

17. 'Russian aviation performed high-accuracy strikes against international terrorist organization ISIS', The Ministry of Defence of the Russian Federation, 30 September 2015. Available at https://eng.mil.ru/en/news_page/country/more.htm?id=12059172@egNews. Accessed 22 October 2024.

18. 'Воздушные удары по объектам террористической группировки ИГИЛ', YouTube, 30 September 2015. Available at https://www.youtube.com/watch?v=hiA0JUdWR6M&t=46s. Accessed 22 October 2024.

19. Thomas Gibbons-Neff, 'How a 4-Hour Battle Between Russian Mercenaries and U.S. Commandos Unfolded in Syria', *New York Times*, 24 May 2018. Available at

https://www.nytimes.com/2018/05/24/world/middleeast/american-commandos-russian-mercenaries-syria.html. Accessed 25 January 2025.

20. Jade McGlynn, *Memory Makers: The Politics of the Past in Putin's Russia* (London: Bloomsbury Academic, 2023), p. 90.

21. Report of the Independent International Commission of Inquiry on the Syrian Arab Republic. First published 21 January 2021. Available at https://documents.un.org/doc/undoc/gen/g21/014/36/pdf/g2101436.pdf. Accessed 22 October 2024.

22. 'Obama: Russia Is "A Regional Power," Not Top Geopolitical Foe', NBC News, 25 March 2014. Available at https://www.nbcnews.com/storyline/ukraine-crisis/obama-russia-regional-power-not-top-geopolitical-foe-n61601. Accessed 22 October 2024.

23. OPEC Monthly Oil Market Report, 16 January 2014. Available at https://www.opec.org/opec_web/static_files_project/media/downloads/publications/MOMR_January_2014.pdf. Accessed 23 October 2024

24. OPEC Monthly Oil Market Report.

25. D.B. Kuvalin and A.K. Moiseev, 'Russian Enterprises at the End of 2014: Adjustment to Crisis Developments in the National Economy and Views on the Consequences of Economic Sanctions', *Studies on Russian Economic Development*, vol. 26, no. 3 (2015), p. 295.

26. 'GDP growth (annual %) – Russian Federation', World Bank Group. Available at https://data.worldbank.org/indicator/NY.GDP.MKTP.KD.ZG?locations=RU. Accessed 23 October 2024.

27. 'Russian economy hit by oil price slide', BBC News, 25 January 2016. Available at https://www.bbc.co.uk/news/business-35398423. Accessed 23 October 2024.

28. 'Putin Says Russian Officials "Can't Afford" 10-Day Holiday', *Moscow Times*, 26 December 2014. Available at https://www.themoscowtimes.com/2014/12/26/putin-says-russian-officials-cant-afford-10-day-holiday-a42593. Accessed 23 October 2024.

29. 'Sochi Olympics a "monstrous scam" – Russian opposition', BBC News, 30 May 2013. Available at https://www.bbc.co.uk/news/world-europe-22720228. Accessed 24 October 2024.

30. Boris Nemtsov and Leonid Martynyuk, trans. Kerkko Paananen, 'Winter Olympics in the Subtropics', Путин. Итоги, 2013. Available at https://www.putin-itogi.ru/winter-olympics-in-the-subtropics. Accessed 24 October 2024.

31. 'Russia opposition politician Boris Nemtsov shot dead', BBC News, 28 February 2015. Available at https://www.bbc.co.uk/news/world-europe-31669061. Accessed 24 October 2024.

32. 'Condolences to Dina Eidman', President of Russia, 28 February 2015. Available at http://en.kremlin.ru/events/president/news/47763. Accessed 24 October 2024.

33. 'Boris Nemtsov: Murdered Putin rival "tailed" by agent linked to FSB hit squad', BBC News, 28 March 2022. Available at https://www.bbc.co.uk/news/world-europe-60878663. Accessed 24 October 2024.

34. This interview was given to the Russian news website Sobesednik on 10 February and subsequently quoted extensively in Western media, for example in Joshua Yaffa, 'Assassination in Moscow', *New Yorker*, 27 February 2015. Available at https://www.newyorker.com/news/news-desk/assassination-in-moscow. Accessed 24 October 2024.

35. 'Nemtsov's final report says 220 Russian troops have died in Ukraine', *Financial Times*, 12 May 2015. Available at https://www.ft.com/content/dae1ee18-f8b7-11e4-8e16-00144feab7de. Accessed 24 October 2024.

36. Mark Fitzpatrick, 'Assessing the JCPOA', *Adelphi Series*, vol. 57, nos 466–7 (2017), p. 19. DOI: 10.1080/19445571.2017.1555914.

37. Ashton, *And Then What?*, p. 178.

38. Fitzpatrick, 'Assessing the JCPOA', pp. 20–1.

39. Ashton, interview with the author, London, 26 June 2024.

40. 'UK spied on Russians with fake rock', BBC News, 19 January 2012. Available at https://www.bbc.co.uk/news/world-europe-16614209. Accessed 25 October 2024.

41. Powell, interview with the author, London, 20 September 2023.

42. 'Groups condemn Russian NGOs law', BBC News, 18 January 2006. Available at http://news.bbc.co.uk/1/hi/world/europe/4624064.stm. Accessed 25 October 2024.

43. Carroll Bogert, 'Russia and NGOs: A photo-op for Putin', *New York Times*, 7 July 2006. Available at https://www.nytimes.com/2006/07/07/opinion/07iht-edbogert.2142310.html. Accessed 25 October 2024.

44. 'Ten Alleged Secret Agents Arrested in the United States', US Department of Justice, 28 June 2010. Available at https://www.justice.gov/opa/pr/ten-alleged-secret-agents-arrested-united-states. Accessed 25 October 2024.

45. 'Laptop from Operation Ghost Stories', FBI. Available at https://www.fbi.gov/history/artifacts/laptop-from-operation-ghost-stories. Accessed 25 October 2024.

46. 'How the FBI Busted Anna Chapman and the Russian Spy Ring', ABC News, 1 November 2011. Available at https://abcnews.go.com/blogs/politics/2011/11/how-the-fbi-busted-anna-chapman-and-the-russian-spy-ring. Accessed 25 October 2024.

47. 'How the FBI Busted Anna Chapman and the Russian Spy Ring'.

48. 'The secrets of Anna Chapman', BBC News, 28 March 2011. Available at https://www.bbc.co.uk/news/world-europe-12876927. Accessed 25 October 2024.

49. 'Spies swapped by US and Russia at Vienna airport', BBC News, 9 July 2010. Available at https://www.bbc.co.uk/news/10564994. Accessed 25 October 2024.

50. 'Sergei Skripal: Who is the former Russian intelligence officer?', BBC News, 29 March 2018. Available at https://www.bbc.co.uk/news/world-europe-43291394. Accessed 25 October 2024.

51. Glenn Greenwald, 'NSA collecting phone records of millions of Verizon customers daily', *Guardian*, 6 June 2013. Available at https://www.theguardian.com/world/2013/jun/06/nsa-phone-records-verizon-court-order. Accessed 25 October 2024.

52. 'Edward Snowden granted Russian citizenship', BBC News, 26 September 2022. Available at https://www.bbc.co.uk/news/world-europe-63036991. Accessed 25 October 2024.

53. 'The Putin Interviews – Vladimir Putin on Edward Snowden – Official Clip w/ Oliver Stone, SHOWTIME', YouTube. Available at https://www.youtube.com/watch?v=UD4eIM-8Vrc. Accessed 25 October 2024.

54. Fiona Hill, *There is Nothing for You Here: Finding Opportunity in the 21st Century* (New York: Mariner Books, 2023), p. 183.

55. Hill, *There is Nothing for You Here*, p. 182.

56. '18 revelations from Wikileaks' hacked Clinton emails', BBC News, 27 October 2016. Available at https://www.bbc.co.uk/news/world-us-canada-37639370. Accessed 30 October 2024.
57. Robert S. Mueller, 'Report On The Investigation Into Russian Interference In The 2016 Presidential Election', US Department of Justice, March 2019, p. 3. Available at https://www.justice.gov/storage/report_volume2.pdf. Accessed 30 October 2024.
58. Hill, *There is Nothing for You Here*, p. 183.
59. Mueller, 'Report On The Investigation Into Russian Interference', p. 3.
60. Hill, *There is Nothing for You Here*, p. 184.
61. Ciaran Martin, speaking at 'Disinformation and Smearing in British Politics: 100 years since the Zinoviev Letter', Queen Mary, University of London, 29 October 2024.
62. Intelligence and Security Committee of Parliament, 'Russia', 21 July 2020, p. 1. Available at https://isc.independent.gov.uk/wp-content/uploads/2021/03/CCS207_CCS0221966010-001_Russia-Report-v02-Web_Accessible.pdf. Accessed 25 January 2025.
63. Intelligence and Security Committee of Parliament, 'Russia', p. 16.
64. Catherine Belton, *Putin's People: How the KGB Took Back Russia and then Took on the West* (London: William Collins, 2020), p. 352.
65. Hill, *There is Nothing for You Here*, p. 221.
66. Hill, *There is Nothing for You Here*, p. 231.
67. 'Salisbury Attack – Suspects Identified', Counter Terrorism Policing, 5 September 2018. Updated 22 November 2018. Available at https://www.counterterrorism.police.uk/suspectsidentified. Accessed 31 October 2024.
68. 'The GRU Globetrotters: Mission London', Bellingcat, 28 June 2019. Available at https://www.bellingcat.com/news/uk-and-europe/2019/06/28/the-gru-globetrotters-mission-london. Accessed 31 October 2024.
69. 'Men claiming to be Salisbury novichok attack suspects speak to Russian state TV', Guardian News, YouTube, 13 September 2018. Available at https://www.youtube.com/watch?v=iNEWMrdSNfc. Accessed 31 October 2024.
70. In Russian, 'Это мог быть кто угодно' ('It could have been anyone') 'Дело Скрипалей' ('The Skripal Affair'), Levada Center, 25 October 2018. Available at https://www.levada.ru/2018/10/25/delo-skripalej. Accessed 31 October 2024.
71. Duncan Allen, 'The UK's response to the March 2018 Salisbury attack: "this appalling act against our country"', Chatham House, 30 October 2018. Updated 14 December 2018. Available at https://www.chathamhouse.org/2018/10/managed-confrontation-uk-policy-towards-russia-after-salisbury-attack-0/uks-response-march. Accessed 31 October 2024.
72. 'Russia election: Trump congratulates Putin over victory', BBC News, 21 March 2018. Available at https://www.bbc.co.uk/news/world-europe-43476895. Accessed 31 October 2024.
73. 'Russia election: Vladimir Putin wins by big margin', BBC News, 19 March 2024. Available at https://www.bbc.co.uk/news/world-europe-43452449. Accessed 31 October 2024.
74. Carol D. Leonnig, David Nakamura and Josh Dawsey, 'Trump's national security advisers warned him not to congratulate Putin. He did it anyway', *Washington*

Post, 20 March 2018. Available at https://www.washingtonpost.com/politics/trumps-national-security-advisers-warned-him-not-to-congratulate-putin-he-did-it-anyway/2018/03/20/22738ebc-2c68-11e8-8ad6-fbc50284fce8_story.html. Accessed 31 October 2024.

75. Hill, *There is Nothing for You Here*, p. 227.
76. Catherine Lucey and Josh Lederman, 'Trump declares US leaving "horrible" Iran nuclear accord', AP News, 8 May 2018. Available at https://apnews.com/article/north-america-donald-trump-ap-top-news-politics-iran-cead755353a1455b-bef08ef289448994. Accessed 31 October 2024.
77. Hill, *There is Nothing for You Here*, p. 226.
78. Hill, *There is Nothing for You Here*, p. 231.
79. Hill, interview with the author, Washington, DC, 19 July 2024.
80. 'News conference following talks between the presidents of Russia and the United States', President of Russia, 16 July 2018. Available at http://en.kremlin.ru/events/president/news/58017. Accessed 31 October 2024.
81. Margarita Simonyan on X, 9 November 2016: 'Людей достала война. Людей достали СМИ. Людей достал агрессивный либерализм. Людей достали иммигранты. Хорошо или плохо, но это факт.' Available at https://x.com/M_Simonyan/status/796234496911798272. Accessed 31 October 2024.
82. Lionel Barber, Henry Foy and Alex Barber, 'Vladimir Putin says liberalism has "become obsolete"', *Financial Times*, 28 June 2019. Available at https://www.ft.com/content/670039ec-98f3-11e9-9573-ee5cbb98ed36. Accessed 31 October 2024.
83. Roula Khalaf, 'Alex Younger: The Russians did not create the things that divide us – we did that', *Financial Times*, 30 September 2020. Available at https://www.ft.com/content/c544d058-6dad-4549-8319-470975281d0a. Accessed 31 October 2024.

CHAPTER 10

1. 'Putin gives Trump a World Cup soccer ball, tells him "now the ball is in your court"', Fox News, 16 July 2018. Available at https://www.foxnews.com/politics/putin-gives-trump-a-world-cup-soccer-ball-tells-him-now-the-ball-is-in-your-court?msockid=36bf362024bb65ec111e399c258364a4. Accessed 1 November 2024.
2. 'Russia's new faith . . . in itself', BBC News, 28 June 2008. Available at http://news.bbc.co.uk/1/hi/programmes/from_our_own_correspondent/7477352.stm. Accessed 1 November 2024.
3. 'Sepp Blatter: Russia will host 2018 World Cup despite Crimea', BBC Sport, 21 March 2014. Available at https://www.bbc.co.uk/sport/football/26691561. Accessed 1 November 2024.
4. James Riach, 'FBI investigating Fifa's awarding of 2018 and 2022 World Cups – report', *Guardian*, 3 June 2015. Available at https://www.theguardian.com/football/2015/jun/03/fbi-investigating-fifa-2018-2022-world-cup. Accessed 1 November 2024.
5. 'Непредвиденные расходы: как менялась смета ЧМ-2018', РБК, 8 June 2014. Available at https://www.rbc.ru/society/08/06/2018/5b02f8039a7947289e44a869.

Accessed 2 November 2024; Holly Ellyatt, 'Russia World Cup will give economy a boost', CNBC, 14 June 2014. Available at https://www.cnbc.com/2018/06/14/russia-world-cup-will-give-economy-a-boost.html. Accessed 2 November 2024.

6. I referred to this in some of my own journalism from the time: 'World Cup 2018: Wins For Russia On And Off The Field', Forbes, 2 July 2018. Available at https://www.forbes.com/sites/jamesrodgerseurope/2018/07/02/world-cup-2018-wins-for-russia-on-and-off-the-field. Accessed 2 November 2024. In the autumn of 2024, the tweet itself was no longer available.

7. 'Moscow official says West is trying to deny Russia World Cup', BBC News, 1 April 2018. Available at https://www.bbc.co.uk/news/world-europe-43609505. Accessed 2 November 2024.

8. Samuel Osborne, 'Theresa May's Russia statement in full as she expels 23 spies over nerve agent attack', *The Independent*, 14 March 2018. Available at https://www.independent.co.uk/news/uk/politics/theresa-may-russia-statement-in-full-spies-expel-nerve-agent-salisbury-poisoning-a8255661.html. Accessed 2 November 2024.

9. 'Briefing by Foreign Ministry Spokesperson Maria Zakharova, Moscow, March 29, 2018', The Ministry of Foreign Affairs of the Russian Federation, 29 March 2018. Available at https://www.mid.ru/en/foreign_policy/news/1567230. Accessed 2 November 2024.

10. 'Russia to raise its pension age for the first time in modern history', Meduza, 14 June 2018. Available at https://meduza.io/en/news/2018/06/14/russia-to-raise-its-pension-age-for-the-first-time-in-modern-history. Accessed 2 November 2024.

11. 'Russia will raise pension ages that date back to Stalin', *The Economist*, 30 June 2018. Available at https://www.economist.com/europe/2018/06/30/russia-will-raise-pension-ages-that-date-back-to-stalin. Accessed 2 November 2024.

12. 'Alcohol-related deaths drop in Russian Federation due to strict alcohol control measures, new report says', World Health Organization, 1 October 2019. Available at https://www.who.int/europe/news/item/01-10-2019-alcohol-related-deaths-drop-in-russian-federation-due-to-strict-alcohol-control-measures-new-report-says. Accessed 11 November 2024.

13. 'Life expectancy at birth, male (years) – Russian Federation', World Bank Group. Available at https://data.worldbank.org/indicator/SP.DYN.LE00.MA.IN?locations=RU. Accessed 2 November 2024.

14. 'Survival to age 65, male (% of cohort) – Russian Federation', World Bank Group. Available at https://data.worldbank.org/indicator/SP.DYN.TO65.MA.ZS?locations=RU. Accessed 2 November 2024.

15. 'Survival to age 65, female (% of cohort) – Russian Federation', World Bank Group. Available at https://data.worldbank.org/indicator/SP.DYN.TO65.FE.ZS?locations=RU. Accessed 2 November 2024.

16. 'Russia's Putin softens pension reforms after outcry', BBC News, 29 August 2018. Available at https://www.bbc.co.uk/news/world-europe-45342721. Accessed 2 November 2024.

17. 'Если вы останетесь дома, это значит, что с вашего молчаливого согласия власть продолжит грабить нашу страну', Navalny.com, 9 September 2018. Available at https://navalny.com/2018/09/08. Accessed 4 November 2024.

18. 'Алексей Навальный', Navalny.com, 9 September 2018. Available at https://navalny.com/2018/09/09. Accessed 4 November 2024.

19. 'не дайте себя запугать', Navalny.com, 10 September 2018. Available at https://navalny.com/2018/09/10. Accessed 4 November 2024.

20. Elisabeth Schimpfossl and Ilya Yablokov, 'Coercion or Conformism? Censorship and Self-censorship among Russian Media Personalities and Reporters in the 2010s', *Demokratizatsiya*, vol. 22, no. 2 (Spring 2014), p. 295.

21. Maria Makutina, 'Почему социологические службы не смогли спрогно зировать результаты выборов московского мэра', Газета.Ru, 9 September 2013. Available at https://www.gazeta.ru/politics/2013/09/09_a_5645357.shtml. Accessed 4 November 2024.

22. 'Laying down the law: Medvedev vows war on Russia's "legal nihilism"', *Financial Times*, 24 December 2008. Available at https://www.ft.com/content/e46ea1d8-c6c8-11dd-97a5-000077b07658. Accessed 4 November 2024.

23. 'People and Corruption: Europe and Central Asia', Transparency International, 2016. Available at https://www.transparency.org/en/gcb/europe-and-central-asia/europe-central-asia-2016, p. 33. Accessed 6 November 2024.

24. 'Medvedev Not Offended by Being Called "Dimon"', *Moscow Times*, 21 May 2013. Available at https://www.themoscowtimes.com/2013/05/21/medvedev-not-offended-by-being-called-dimon-a24231. Accessed 6 November 2024. Timakova's words in Russian, 'Он вам не Димон', literally mean 'He's not Dimon to you'.

25. 'Navalny Video Accusing Medvedev Of Corruption Posted On Government Websites Radio Free Europe/ Radio Liberty', 11 June 2017. Available at https://www.rferl.org/a/navalny-video-medvedev-corruption-posted-goverment-websites/28541102.html. Accessed 21 August 2025.

26. 'Don't call him "Dimon"', YouTube, 2 March 2017. Available at https://www.youtube.com/watch?v=qrwlk7_GF9g&t=313s. Accessed 6 November 2024.

27. 'Russian billionaire Arkady Rotenberg says "Putin Palace" is his', BBC News, 30 January 2021. Available at https://www.bbc.co.uk/news/world-europe-55872249. Accessed 21 June 2025.

28. Alexei Navalny, 'Putin's palace. History of world's largest bribe', YouTube, 19 January 2021. Available at https://www.youtube.com/watch?v=ipAnwilMncI&t=638s. Accessed 6 November 2024.

29. 'Amnesty strips Alexei Navalny of "prisoner of conscience" status', BBC News, 24 February 2021. Available at https://www.bbc.co.uk/news/world-europe-56181084. Accessed 6 November 2024.

30. 'Chess star squares up to Putin', BBC News, 13 April 2007. Available at http://news.bbc.co.uk/1/hi/world/europe/6551725.stm. Accessed 6 November 2024.

31. 'Garry Kasparov not returning to Russia out of fear of prosecution', *Financial Times*, 6 June 2013. Available at https://www.ft.com/content/0fc438d4-ce8f-11e2-ae25-00144feab7de. Accessed 6 November 2024.

32. 'Russia's State Duma adopts Stable Runet law', TASS, 16 April 2021. Available at https://tass.com/politics/1053917. Accessed 7 November 2024.

33. 'Russia ready for global internet shutdown, can sustain its own web – MPs', RT, 16 April 2019. Available at https://www.rt.com/russia/456717-russia-internet-law-signed. Accessed 7 November 2024.

34. National Cyber Strategy of the United States of America, September 2018. Available at https://trumpwhitehouse.archives.gov/wp-content/uploads/2018/09/National-Cyber-Strategy.pdf. Accessed 7 November 2024.
35. 'No great firewall: Russian PM says Moscow doesn't want to "regulate" web, only protect its interests', RT, 29 March 2019. Available at https://www.rt.com/russia/455072-medvedev-russia-internet-law. Accessed 7 November 2024.
36. 'Thousands of Russians protest against internet restrictions', Reuters, 10 March 2019. Available at https://www.reuters.com/article/world/thousands-of-russians-protest-against-internet-restrictions-idUSKBN1QR0IU. Accessed 7 November 2024.
37. 'Kremlin takes on sweeping internet connection powers', *Financial Times*, 1 November 2019. Available at https://www.ft.com/content/644198da-fc9f-11e9-a354-36acbbb0d9b6. Accessed 7 November 2024.
38. Jane Wakefield, 'Russia "successfully tests" its unplugged internet', BBC News, 24 December 2019. Available at https://www.bbc.co.uk/news/technology-50902496. Accessed 7 November 2024.
39. Schimpfossl and Yablokov, 'Coercion or Conformism?', p. 308.
40. Arkady Ostrovsky, *The Invention of Russia: The Journey from Gorbachev's Freedom to Putin's War* (London: Atlantic Books, 2015), p. 317.
41. 'The Concept of the Foreign Policy of the Russian Federation', The Ministry of Foreign Affairs of the Russian Federation, 31 March 2023. Available at https://www.mid.ru/en/foreign_policy/fundamental_documents/1860586. Accessed 8 November 2024.
42. 'Russia's Putin signs NGO "foreign agents" law', Reuters, 21 July 2012. Available at https://www.reuters.com/article/world/russias-putin-signs-ngo-foreign-agents-law-idUSBRE86K05M. Accessed 8 November 2024.
43. McFaul, *From Cold War to Hot Peace*, p. 359.
44. McFaul, *From Cold War to Hot Peace*, p. 362.
45. 'Russia: Four years of Putin's "Foreign Agents" law to shackle and silence NGOs', Amnesty International, 18 November 2018. Available at https://www.amnesty.org/en/latest/news/2016/11/russia-four-years-of-putins-foreign-agents-law-to-shackle-and-silence-ngos-2. Accessed 8 November 2024.
46. Sheila Fitzpatrick, *On Stalin's Team: The Years of Living Dangerously in Soviet Politics* (Princeton and Oxford: Princeton University Press, 2015), p. 98.
47. For a fuller account of Harrison's story, please see my earlier book *Assignment Moscow*, pp. 59–63.
48. 'Foreign Agents Registration Act, US Department of Justice. Available at https://www.justice.gov/nsd-fara. Accessed 8 November 2024.
49. Andrew E. Kramer, 'Russia May Make All Outside News Media Register as "Foreign Agents"', *New York Times*, 15 November 2017. Available at https://www.nytimes.com/2017/11/15/world/europe/russia-news-media-foreign-agents.html. Accessed 8 November 2024.
50. 'Russia labels reporters foreign agents after Nobel award', BBC News, 8 October 2021. Available at https://www.bbc.co.uk/news/world-europe-58840084. Accessed 8 November 2024.
51. Daren Butler and Bulent Usta, 'Ecumenical Patriarch signs decree granting Ukraine church independence', Reuters, 5 January 2019. Available at https://

www.reuters.com/article/world/ecumenical-patriarch-signs-decree-granting-ukraine-church-independence-idUSKCN1OZ0AP. Accessed 8 November 2024.

52. '"Inappropriate" for Pompeo to discuss Ukrainian church affairs with Kiev – Putin', RT, 20 December 2018. Available at https://www.rt.com/news/447030-putin-pompeo-ukraine-orthodoxy. Accessed 8 November 2024.

53. 'Concert to mark the fifth anniversary of Crimea's reunification with Russia', President of Russia, 18 March 2019. Available at http://en.kremlin.ru/events/president/news/60096. Accessed 11 November 2024.

54. 'Meeting with members of the public from the French Republic', President of Russia, 18 March 2019. Available at http://en.kremlin.ru/events/president/news/60094. Accessed 11 November 2024.

55. 'Marine Le Pen says sanctions on Russia are not working'. *The Economist*, 3 November 2022. Available at https://www.economist.com/europe/2022/11/03/marine-le-pen-says-sanctions-on-russia-are-not-working. Accessed 21 August 2025.

56. 'Crimean bridge: Who – or what – caused the explosion?', BBC News, 9 October 2022. Available at https://www.bbc.co.uk/news/world-europe-63192757. Accessed 11 November 2024; 'Ukraine claims responsibility for new attack on key Crimea bridge', CNN, 17 July 2023. Available at https://edition.cnn.com/2023/07/16/europe/russia-crimea-bridge-intl-hnk/index.html. Accessed 11 November 2024; 'Crimea bridge reopens after Ukraine says it carried out underwater explosion', BBC News, 3 June 2025. Available at https://www.bbc.co.uk/news/live/cr58e9yr2ezt. Accessed 21 June 2025.

57. 'Comment by the Information and Press Department on the 70th anniversary of the North Atlantic Treaty Organization', The Ministry of Foreign Affairs of the Russian Federation, 4 April 2019. Available at https://archive.mid.ru/foreign_policy/news/-/asset_publisher/cKNonkJE02Bw/content/id/3601456. Accessed 12 November 2024.

58. 'NATO: good for Europe and good for America: Address to the United States Congress by NATO Secretary General Jens Stoltenberg', NATO, 3 April 2019. Available at https://www.nato.int/cps/en/natohq/opinions_165210.htm. Accessed 12 November 2024.

59. MFA Russia on X: '#Zakharova: On @NATO's 70th birthday, we would like to wish the alliance inner peace and less nervousness. We hope it avoids focusing on obsessions and phobias #NATO70', 4 April 2019. Available at https://t.co/vzS9ILZKoy. Accessed 12 November 2024.

60. 'Press point by NATO Secretary General Jens Stoltenberg and US President Donald Trump', NATO, 3 December 2019. Available at https://www.nato.int/cps/en/natohq/opinions_171542.htm. Accessed 11 November 2024.

61. 'The untold story of the most chaotic Nato summit ever', *Financial Times*, 4 July 2024. Available at https://www.ft.com/content/8985b970-0015-479f-9585-7a9b234715a4. Accessed 11 November 2024.

62. 'Brexit timeline: events leading to the UK's exit from the European Union', House of Commons Library, 6 January 2021. Available at https://commonslibrary.parliament.uk/research-briefings/cbp-7960. Accessed 17 October 2025.

63. 'Lavrov on Brexit: Russia will cooperate with UK and EU, whatever the outcome', TASS, 16 January 2019. Available at https://tass.com/politics/1040290. Accessed 24 November 2024.

CHAPTER 11

1. Government of Russia on X, 1 January 2020. Available at https://t.co/3BUBBiIDlX. Accessed 12 November 2024.

2. 'Twenty foreign armies invited to take part in Russia's Victory Day Parade', TASS, 10 February 2020. Available at https://tass.com/defense/1118425. Accessed 12 November 2024.

3. James Rodgers, 'Tanks For The Memory: The Soviet T-34 Is Now A Movie Star', Forbes, 18 January 2018. Available at https://www.forbes.com/sites/jamesrodgerseurope/2019/01/18/tanks-for-the-memory-the-soviet-t-34-is-now-a-movie-star. Accessed 21 June 2025.

4. 'Иностранные делегации на юбилеях Победы в Москве', TASS, 7 May 2015. Available at https://tass.ru/obschestvo/1953908/amp. Accessed 12 November 2024.

5. 'Texts adopted – Importance of European remembrance for the future of Europe', European Parliament, 19 September 2019. Available at https://www.europarl.europa.eu/doceo/document/TA-9-2019-0021_EN.html. Accessed 12 November 2024.

6. 'Russia-Poland row over start of WW2 escalates', BBC News, 31 December 2019. Available at https://www.bbc.co.uk/news/world-europe-50955273. Accessed 12 November 2024.

7. Ambasador Mark Brzezinski on X, 30 December 2019. Available at https://x.com/USAmbPoland/status/1211588565475430400. Accessed 12 November 2024.

8. 'Putin Calls Former Polish Ambassador "Anti-Semitic Pig"', Moscow Times, 25 December 2019. Available at https://www.themoscowtimes.com/2019/12/25/putin-calls-former-polish-ambassador-anti-semitic-pig-a68739. Accessed 12 November 2024.

9. '20 questions with Vladimir Putin', TASS. Available at https://putin.tass.ru/en. Accessed 12 November 2024.

10. Julian Borger, 'Landmark second world war ceremony in Moscow poses dilemma for UK and US', Guardian, 20 February 2020. Available at https://www.theguardian.com/world/2020/feb/25/russia-world-war-ii-75th-anniversary-uk-us. Accessed 12 November 2024.

11. 'Kremlin says Putin does not need a coronavirus test as he has no symptoms', Reuters, 20 March 2020. Available at https://www.reuters.com/article/world/kremlin-says-putin-does-not-need-a-coronavirus-test-as-he-has-no-symptoms-idUSKBN2171BQ. Accessed 14 November 2024.

12. 'Russia's coronavirus cases top 1,200', TASS, 28 March 2020. Available at https://tass.com/society/1136939. Accessed 14 November 2024.

13. Anton Zverev and Olga Popova, 'Coronavirus lockdown drives jump in vodka and whisky sales in Russia', Reuters, 9 April 2020. Available at https://www.reuters.com/article/business/coronavirus-lockdown-drives-jump-in-vodka-and-whisky-sales-in-russia-idUSKCN21R16S. Accessed 14 November 2024.

14. 'Economists Forecast 6th Year of Falling Incomes for Russians', Moscow Times, 29 May 2019. Available at https://www.themoscowtimes.com/2019/05/29/economists-forecast-6th-year-of-falling-incomes-for-russians-a65791. Accessed 12 November 2024.

15. 'Russia's economy shrank 3% last year – revised data', Reuters, 1 April 2021. Available at https://www.reuters.com/article/markets/russias-economy-shrank-3-last-year-revised-data-idUSR4N2LK05S. Accessed 14 November 2024.

16. 'Constitutional amendments', Levada Center, 19 March 2020. Available at https://www.levada.ru/en/2020/03/19/constitutional-amendments. Accessed 14 November 2024.

17. Henry Foy and John Burn-Murdoch, 'Russia's Covid death toll could be 70 per cent higher than official figure', *Financial Times*, 11 May 2020. Available at https://www.ft.com/content/77cd2cba-b0e2-4022-a265-e0a9a7930bda. Accessed 14 November 2024.

18. Ivan Nechepurenko, 'A Coronavirus Mystery Explained: Moscow Has 1,700 Extra Deaths', *New York Times*, 11 May 2020. Available at https://www.nytimes.com/2020/05/11/world/europe/coronavirus-deaths-moscow.html. Accessed 14 November 2024.

19. Daria Litvinova, 'Russia slams New York Times, Financial Times on virus deaths', AP News, 14 May 2020. Available at https://apnews.com/article/12c8f559a4ec43f72035e6d1ca58271a. Accessed 14 November 2024.

20. Chris Baraniuk, 'Covid-19: What Do We Know About Sputnik V and Other Russian Vaccines?', *BMJ*, vol. 372, no. 743 (19 March 2021). Available at https://www.bmj.com/content/372/bmj.n743. Accessed 14 November 2024. DOI: 10.1136/bmj.n743.

21. 'Coronavirus: Russia's Putin gets vaccine but without cameras', BBC News, 23 March 2021. Available at https://www.bbc.co.uk/news/world-europe-56498847. Accessed 14 November 2024.

22. 'Russians spread fake news over Oxford coronavirus vaccine', *The Times*, 16 October 2020. Available at https://www.thetimes.com/uk/politics/article/russians-spread-fake-news-over-oxford-coronavirus-vaccine-2nzpk8vrq?t=1731602074504. Accessed 14 November 2024.

23. 'Coronavirus: Dominic Raab "absolutely confident" Russia behind vaccine hack attempt', Sky News, 19 July 2020. Available at https://news.sky.com/story/coronavirus-dominic-raab-absolutely-confident-russia-behind-vaccine-hack-attempt-12031779. Accessed 14 November 2024.

24. The White House 45 Archived on X: 'On May 8, 1945, America and Great Britain had victory over the Nazis! "America's spirit will always win. In the end, that's what happens"'. 8 May 2020. Available at https://t.co/umCOwRXWlB. Accessed 15 November 2024.

25. 'Forgetting someone? WH attributes victory over Nazis to "America & UK" in bizarre VE-Day message, gets schooled on Twitter', RT World News, 9 May 2020. Available at https://www.rt.com/news/488217-victory-day-us-nazis-russia. Accessed 15 November 2020.

26. '75th Anniversary of the Great Victory: Shared Responsibility to History and our Future', President of Russia, 19 June 2020. Available at http://en.kremlin.ru/events/president/news/63527. Accessed 15 November 2024.

27. Churchill to Stalin, sent 27 September 1944, received 27 September 1944. In David Reynolds and Vladimir Pechatnov, *The Kremlin Letters: Stalin's Wartime Correspondence with Churchill and Roosevelt* (New Haven and London: Yale University Press, 2018), p. 470.

28. James Rodgers, 'Russia's Victory Parade: A Reminder Of WWII Glory, Putin's New Challenges', Forbes, First 24 June 2020. Available at https://www.forbes.com/sites/jamesrodgerseurope/2020/06/24/russias-victory-parade-a-reminder-of-wwii-glory-and-new-challenges. Accessed 15 November 2024.

29. 'Russia's constitutional amendments enter into force July 4', TASS, 4 July 2020. Available at https://tass.com/politics/1174507. Accessed 15 November 2024.

30. 'Putin urges Russians to cast ballots on Constitution, says every vote counts', TASS, 30 June 2020. Available at https://tass.com/politics/1173213. Accessed 15 November 2024.

31. Gabrielle Tétrault-Farber and Alexander Marrow, 'Kremlin calls vote allowing Putin to rule until 2036 a triumph as Russians ponder his next move', Reuters, 2 July 2020. Available at https://www.reuters.com/article/us-russia-putin-vote/kremlin-calls-vote-allowing-putin-to-rule-until-2036-a-triumph-as-russians-ponder-his-next-move-idUSKBN2431TM. Accessed 15 November 2024.

32. Martin Crutsinger, 'IMF downgrades outlook for global economy in face of virus', AP News, 24 June 2020. Available at https://apnews.com/article/virus-outbreak-the-great-depression-financial-markets-us-news-ap-top-news-2be55cbdf80ca8049655570c6f756027. Accessed 15 November 2024.

33. 'Парад для одного зрителя. Сколько это стоит?' (A parade for one spectator. How much does it cost?), Navalny.com, First 22 June 2020. Available at https://navalny.com/2020/06/22. Accessed 18 November 2024.

34. 'Alexei Navalny: "Poisoned" Russian opposition leader in a coma', BBC News, 20 August 2020. Available at https://www.bbc.co.uk/news/world-europe-53844958. Accessed 18 November 2024.

35. 'Alexei Navalny poisoned with nerve agent novichok, says Germany', *Financial Times*, 2 September 2020. Available at https://www.ft.com/content/5d9aeac2-3ff4-4e91-ba2f-ec43fde2a794. Accessed 21 November 2024.

36. 'Alexei Navalny: Russia opposition leader poisoned with Novichok – Germany', BBC News, 2 September 2020. Available at https://www.bbc.co.uk/news/world-europe-54002880. Accessed 18 November 2024.

37. Tim Lister, Clarissa Ward and Sebastian Shukla, 'Alexey Navalny dupes Russian spy into revealing how he was poisoned', CNN, 21 December 2020. Available at https://edition.cnn.com/2020/12/21/europe/russia-navalny-poisoning-underpants-ward/index.html. Accessed 18 November 2024.

38. Mary Ilyushina, Laura Smith-Spark and Jennifer Hansler, 'Vladmir Putin says if Russia wanted to kill opposition leader Navalny, it would have "finished" the job', CNN, 17 December 2020. Available at https://edition.cnn.com/2020/12/17/europe/putin-annual-press-conference-intl/index.html. Accessed 18 November 2024.

39. 'Алексей Навальный: отношение и отравление', Levada Center, 2 October 2020. Available at https://www.levada.ru/2020/10/02/aleksej-navalnyj-otnoshenie-i-otravlenie. Accessed 18 November 2024.

40. Thomas Escritt, 'Who is Vadim Krasikov, Russian hitman freed from German jail in prisoner swap?', Reuters, 1 August 2024. Available at https://www.reuters.com/world/europe/vadim-krasikov-russian-hitman-sprung-german-jail-prisoner-swap-2024-08-01. Accessed 18 November 2024.

41. 'Alexey Navalny: The 2020 60 Minutes Interview', 60 Minutes, YouTube, posted 4 August 2023 (recorded 2020). Available at https://www.youtube.com/watch?v=iyvpZuwKwZE. Accessed 18 November 2024.

42. 'Alexei Navalny: "More than 3,000 detained" in protests across Russia', BBC News, 23 January 2021. Available at https://www.bbc.co.uk/news/world-europe-55778334. Accessed 17 October 2025.

43. Andrew Osborn and Polina Nikolskaya, 'Rivals allege mass fraud as Russian pro-Putin party wins big majority', Reuters, 20 September 2021. Available at https://www.reuters.com/world/europe/pro-putin-party-heads-russian-election-win-after-navalny-clampdown-2021-09-19. Accessed 19 November 2024.

44. 'Итоговая явка на выборах в РФ составила 51,72%', Interfax, 24 September 2021. Available at https://www.interfax.ru/russia/793344. Accessed 19 November 2024.

45. Zygar, *War and Punishment*, p. 326.

46. 'Протокол центральної виборчої комісії', Ukrainian central election commission. Available at https://www.cvk.gov.ua/wp-content/uploads/2019/11/vpu_2019_protokol_cvk_30042019.pdf. Accessed 19 November 2024.

47. 'Conflict-related civilian casualties in Ukraine', United Nations Human Rights Monitoring Mission in Ukraine, 27 January 2022. Available at https://ukraine.un.org/sites/default/files/2022-02/Conflict-related%20civilian%20casualties%20as%20of%2031%20December%202021%20%28rev%2027%20January%202022%29%20corr%20EN_0.pdf. Accessed 19 November 2024.

48. 'Volodymyr Zelenskyy's Inaugural Address', Official website of the President of Ukraine, 20 May 2019. Available at https://www.president.gov.ua/en/news/inavguracijna-promova-prezidenta-ukrayini-volodimira-zelensk-55489. Accessed 19 November 2024.

49. Zygar, *War and Punishment*, p. 346.

50. 'Foreign Threats to the 2020 US Federal Elections', National Intelligence Council, 15 March 2021. Available at https://www.dni.gov/files/ODNI/documents/assessments/ICA-declass-16MAR21.pdf. Accessed 19 November 2024.

51. Patrick Reevell, 'Putin challenges Biden to debate after president calls him a "killer"', ABC News, 18 March 2021. Available at https://abcnews.go.com/International/putin-challenges-biden-president-calls-killer/story?id=76539031. Accessed 19 November 2024.

52. 'Moscow Takes Measures in Response to "Threatening" NATO Actions', *Moscow Times*, 13 April 2021. Available at https://www.themoscowtimes.com/2021/04/13/moscow-takes-measures-in-response-to-threatening-nato-actions-a73581. Accessed 19 November 2024.

53. 'OFFICIAL Russian military build-up near Ukraine numbers more than 100,000 troops, EU says', Reuters, 19 April 2021. Available at https://www.reuters.com/world/europe/russian-military-build-up-near-ukraine-numbers-more-than-150000-troops-eus-2021-04-19. Accessed 19 November 2023.

54. 'Russia to pull troops back from near Ukraine', BBC News, 22 April 2021. Available at https://www.bbc.co.uk/news/world-europe-56842763. Accessed 19 November 2024.

55. 'Article by Vladimir Putin "On the Historical Unity of Russians and Ukrainians"', President of Russia, 12 July 2021. Available at http://en.kremlin.ru/events/president/news/66181. Accessed 19 November 2024.

56. Serge A. Zenkovsky, *Medieval Russia's Epics, Chronicles, and Tales* (New York: E.P. Dutton and Co., 1963), p. 11.

57. Sarah Rainsford, 'Sarah Rainsford: My last despatch before Russian expulsion', BBC News, 31 August 2021. Available at https://www.bbc.co.uk/news/world-europe-58395121. Accessed 19 November 2024.
58. 'Press release on Russian draft documents on legal security guarantees from the United States and NATO', The Ministry of Foreign Affairs of the Russian Federation, 17 December 2021. Available at https://www.mid.ru/en/foreign_policy/news/1790809. Accessed 19 November 2024.
59. 'Treaty between The United States of America and the Russian Federation on security guarantees', The Ministry of Foreign Affairs of the Russian Federation, 17 December 2021. Available at https://mid.ru/ru/foreign_policy/rso/nato/1790818/?lang=en. Accessed 19 November 2024.

CHAPTER 12

1. Caroline Wheeler, 'Liz Truss accuses Putin of Ukraine "puppet" plan', *Sunday Times*, 23 January 2022. Available at https://www.thetimes.com/article/liz-truss-accuses-putin-of-ukraine-puppet-plan-s9xd7dmqc. Accessed 6 January 2025.
2. Michael D. Shear, 'Biden says the U.S. believes Putin has decided to invade Ukraine', *New York Times*, 18 February 2022. Available at https://www.nytimes.com/2022/02/18/world/europe/biden-holds-urgent-talks-with-nato-leaders-amid-growing-signs-that-war-is-imminent-in-ukraine.html?action=click&pgtype=Article&module=&state=default&region=footer&context=breakout_link_back_to_briefing. Accessed 6 January 2025.
3. Alexander Marrow and Aleksandar Vasovic, 'West warns military build-up near Ukraine growing, not shrinking', Reuters, 17 February 2022. Available at https://www.reuters.com/world/europe/russian-pullout-meets-uk-scepticism-ukraine-defence-website-still-hacked-2022-02-16. Accessed 7 January 2025.
4. Stephen Hutchings, Vera Tolz, Precious Chatterje-Doody, Rhys Crilley and Marie Gillespie, 'Media Communication Strategies in Putin's Russia', in *Russia, Disinformation, and the Liberal Order: RT as Populist Pariah* (Ithaca, NY: Cornell University Press, 2024), pp. 27–49. Available at http://www.jstor.org/stable/10.7591/jj.11981213.6.
5. Kozyrev, *The Firebird*, p. 197.
6. 'STATE OF THE UNION; Transcript of President Bush's Address on the State of the Union', *New York Times*, 29 January 1992. Available at https://www.nytimes.com/1992/01/29/us/state-union-transcript-president-bush-s-address-state-union.html. Accessed 21 June 2025.
7. Gregory Carleton, *Russia: The Story of War* (Cambridge, MA and London: The Belknap Press of Harvard University Press, 2017), p. 37.
8. TNA PREM 49/160, K.A. Bishop to Mr Thomas Eastern Dept, 18 November 1997.
9. Zygar, *War and Punishment*, p. 273.
10. Dmitry V. Trenin, 'The Ukraine Crisis and the Resumption of Great-Power Rivalry', Russia in Global Affairs, 14 July 2014. Available at https://eng.globalaffairs.ru/articles/the-ukraine-crisis-and-the-resumption-of-great-power-rivalry. Accessed 15 January 2025.

11. John J. Mearsheimer, 'Why the Ukraine Crisis is the West's Fault: The Liberal Delusions That Provoked Putin', *Foreign Affairs*, vol. 93, no. 5 (September/October 2014). Published on 18 August 2014. Available at https://www.foreignaffairs.com/ issues/2014/93/5. Accessed 17 October 2025.

12. Michael McFaul, Stephen Sestanovich and John J. Mearsheimer, 'Faulty Powers: Who Started the Ukraine Crisis?', *Foreign Affairs*, 17 October 2014. Available at https://www.foreignaffairs.com/articles/eastern-europe-caucasus/2014-10-17/ faulty-powers. Accessed 15 January 2025.

13. Sarotte, *Not One Inch*, p. 350.

14. 'Trump says he would "encourage" Russia to attack Nato allies who do not pay their bills', BBC News, 11 February 2024. Available at https://www.bbc.co.uk/ news/world-us-canada-68266447. Accessed 21 June 2025.

15. 'Fact check: It wasn't "in jest." Here are 53 times Trump said he'd end Ukraine war within 24 hours or before taking office', CNN, 25 April 2025. Available at https://edition.cnn.com/2025/04/25/politics/fact-check-trump-ukraine-war/ index.html. Accessed 21 June 2025.

16. 'Truss error is proof West doesn't understand Ukraine conflict: Kremlin', Reuters, 11 February 2022. Available at https://www.reuters.com/world/europe/kremlin-cites-truss-error-evidence-west-doesnt-understand-ukraine-conflict-2022-02-11. Accessed 16 January 2025.

17. Max Seddon, Christopher Miller and Felicia Schwartz, 'How Putin blundered into Ukraine – then doubled down', *Financial Times*, 23 February 2023. Available at https://www.ft.com/content/80002564-33e8-48fb-b734-44810afb7a49. Accessed 16 January 2025.

18. Mark Galeotti, *We Need to Talk about Putin: How the West Gets Him Wrong* (London: Penguin, 2019), p. 18.

19. Greg Heffer, 'Salisbury attack: Defence Secretary tells Russia to "go away and shut up"', Sky News, 15 March 2018. Available at https://news.sky.com/story/salisbury-attack-defence-secretary-tells-russia-to-go-away-and-shut-up-11290722. Accessed 24 January 2025.

20. Vladislav Zubok, *The World of the Cold War: 1945–1991* (London: Pelican, 2025), pp. 133–4.

21. Odd Arne Westad, *The Cold War: A World History* (London: Penguin, 2017), p. 579.

22. Kimmo Rentola, *How Finland Survived Stalin: From Winter War to Cold War, 1939–1950*, translated by Richard Robinson (New Haven and London: Yale University Press, 2024), p. 221.

23. Galeotti, *We Need to Talk about Putin*, p. 17.

Bibliography

ARCHIVES

The Hoover Institution, Stanford University, Stanford, California
    William Perry papers
    Michael McFaul papers
The National Archives of the United Kingdom
The National Archives at College Park, Maryland
The National Security Archive (United States of America) (online)

BOOKS

Albright, Madeleine. *Madame Secretary: A Memoir*, New York, Harper Perennial, 2013.

Ashton, Catherine. *And Then What?: Despatches from the Heart of 21st-century Diplomacy from Kosovo to Kyiv*, London, Elliott and Thompson, 2023.

Aslund, Anders. *How Capitalism Was Built: The Transformation of Central and Eastern Europe, Russia, and Central Asia*, Cambridge, Cambridge University Press, 2012.

Belton, Catherine. *Putin's People: How the KGB Took Back Russia and then Took on the West*, London, William Collins, 2020.

Blair, Tony. *A Journey*, London, Hutchinson, 2010.

Burns, William J. *The Back Channel: American Diplomacy in a Disordered World*, London, Hurst, 2021.

Carleton, Gregory. *Russia: The Story of War*, Cambridge, MA and London, The Belknap Press of Harvard University Press, 2017.

Christopher, Warren. *In the Stream of History: Shaping Foreign Policy for a New Era*, Stanford, CA, Stanford University Press, 1998.

Clinton, Bill. *My Life*, New York, Alfred A. Knopf, 2004.

Clover, Charles. *Black Wind, White Snow: Russia's New Nationalism*, New Haven and London, Yale University Press, 2021.

Colton, Timothy J., and Michael McFaul. *Popular Choice and Managed Democracy: The Russian Elections of 1999 and 2000*, Washington, DC, Brookings Institution Press, 2003.

Cornell, Svante E. and S. Frederick Starr (eds). *The Guns of August 2008: Russia's War in Georgia*, Armonk and London, M.E. Sharpe, 2009.

D'Anieri, Paul. *Ukraine and Russia: From Civilized Divorce to Uncivil War*, Cambridge, Cambridge University Press, 2019.

de Waal, Thomas. *The Caucasus: An Introduction*, Oxford: Oxford University Press, 2010.

Dollbaum, Jan Matti, Morvan Lallouet and Ben Noble. *Navalny: Putin's Nemesis, Russia's Future?*, Oxford, Oxford University Press, 2021; online edn, Oxford Academic, 20 January 2022.

Dunlop, John B. *The Moscow Bombings of September 1999: Examinations of Russian Terrorist Attacks at the Onset of Vladimir Putin's Rule*, Stuttgart, Ibidem Verlag, 2012.

Fitzpatrick, Sheila. *On Stalin's Team: The Years of Living Dangerously in Soviet Politics*, Princeton and Oxford, Princeton University Press, 2015.

Freeland, Chrystia. *Sale of the Century: The Inside Story of the Second Russian Revolution*, 2nd edn, London, Abacus, 2005.

Galeotti, Mark. *We Need to Talk about Putin: How the West Gets Him Wrong*, London, Penguin, 2019.

Gall, Carlotta and Thomas de Waal. *Chechnya: A Small Victorious War*, London, Pan Macmillan, 2005.

Granville, Brigitte and Peter Oppenheimer (eds). *Russia's Post-Communist Economy*, Oxford, Oxford University Press, 2001.

Greene, Samuel A. and Graeme B. Robertson. *Putin v. the People: The Perilous Politics of a Divided Russia*, New Haven and London, Yale University Press, 2019.

Hill, Fiona. *There is Nothing for You Here: Finding Opportunity in the 21st Century*, New York, Mariner Books, 2023.

Hill, Fiona and Clifford Gaddy. *Mr. Putin: Operative in the Kremlin (Geopolitics in the 21st Century)*, Washington, DC, Brookings Institution Press, 2015.

Hughes, James. *Chechnya: From Nationalism to Jihad*, Philadelphia, PA, University of Pennsylvania Press, 2007.

Hutchings, Stephen, Vera Tolz, Precious Chatterje-Doody, Rhys Crilley and Marie Gillespie. *Russia, Disinformation, and the Liberal Order: RT as Populist Pariah*, Ithaca, NY, Cornell University Press, 2024.

Kozyrev, Andrei. *The Firebird: The Elusive Fate of Russian Democracy*, Philadelphia, PA, University of Pennsylvania Press, 2020.

Litvinenko, Alexander (with Yuri Felshtinsky). *Blowing Up Russia*, translated by Geoffrey Andrews, London, Gibson Square, 2007.

Lough, John. *Germany's Russia Problem: The Struggle for Balance in Europe*, paperback edn, Manchester, Manchester University Press, 2022.

McFaul, Michael. *From Cold War to Hot Peace: The Inside Story of Russia and America*, London, Allen Lane, 2018.

McGlynn, Jade. *Memory Makers: The Politics of the Past in Putin's Russia*, London, Bloomsbury Academic, 2023.

Muggeridge, Malcolm. *Chronicles of Wasted Time, Volume 1: The Green Stick*, London, Collins, 1972.

Oliker, Olga. *Russia's Chechen Wars, 1994–2000*, Santa Monica, CA, Rand Corporation, 2001.

Ostrovksy, Arkady. *The Invention of Russia: The Journey from Gorbachev's Freedom to Putin's War*, London, Atlantic Books, 2015.

Parfitt, Tom. *High Caucasus: A Mountain Quest in Russia's Haunted Hinterland*, London, Headline, 2023.

Pargeter, Alison. *Libya: The Rise and Fall of Qaddafi*, New Haven and London, Yale University Press, 2012.

Perrie, Maureen (ed.). *The Cambridge History of Russia, Volume 1*, Cambridge, Cambridge University Press, online edn, 2008, https://doi.org/10.1017/CHOL 9780521812276.

Plokhy, Serhii. *The Last Empire: The Final Days of the Soviet Union*, New York, Basic Books, 2014.

Politkovskaya, Anna. *A Small Corner of Hell: Despatches from Chechnya*, Chicago, Chicago University Press, 2003.

Primakov, Yevgeny. *A World Challenged: Fighting Terrorism in the Twenty-First Century*, Washington, DC, Brookings Institution Press, 2004.

Putin, Vladimir (with Natalya Gevorkyan, Natalya Timakova and Andrei Kolesnikov). *First Person: An Astonishingly Frank Self-Portrait by Russia's President Vladimir Putin*, translated by Catherine A. Fitzpatrick, London, Hutchinson, 2000.

Radchenko, Sergei. *To Run the World: The Kremlin's Cold War Bid for Global Power*, Cambridge, Cambridge University Press, 2024.

Rentola, Kimmo. *How Finland Survived Stalin: From Winter War to Cold War, 1939–1950*, translated by Richard Robinson, New Haven and London, Yale University Press, 2024.

Renz, Bettina. *Russia's Military Revival*, Cambridge, Polity, 2018.

Reynolds, David and Vladimir Pechatnov. *The Kremlin Letters: Stalin's Wartime Correspondence with Churchill and Roosevelt*, New Haven and London, Yale University Press, 2018.

Rice, Condoleezza. *No Higher Honour: A Memoir of My Years in Washington*, London, Simon & Schuster, 2011.

Rodgers, James. *Reporting Conflict*, Basingstoke, Palgrave Macmillan, 2012.

Rodgers, James. *Assignment Moscow: Reporting on Russia from Lenin to Putin*, 2nd edn, London, Bloomsbury, 2023.

Roxburgh, Angus. *The Strongman: Vladimir Putin and the Struggle for Russia*, London, I.B. Tauris, 2013.

Sakwa, Richard. *Frontline Ukraine: Crisis in the Borderlands*, London, I.B. Tauris, 2015.

Sarotte, M.E. *Not One Inch: America, Russia, and the Making of Post-Cold War Stalemate*, New Haven and London, Yale University Press, 2021.

Short, Philip. *Putin: His Life and Times*, London, Bodley Head, 2022.

Sixsmith, Martin and Daniel Sixsmith. *Putin and the Return of History: How the Kremlin Rekindled the Cold War*, London, Bloomsbury, 2024.

Snyder, Timothy. *Bloodlands: Europe Between Hitler and Stalin*, London, Vintage, 2015.

Stent, Angela. *The Limits of Partnership: U.S.–Russia Relations in the Twenty-First Century*, updated edn, New Jersey and Woodstock, Oxfordshire, Princeton University Press, 2014.

Talbott, Strobe. *The Russia Hand: A Memoir of Presidential Diplomacy*, New York, Random House, 2002.

Vartanova, Elena. 'The Russian Media Model in the Context of Post-Soviet Dynamics', in Daniel C. Hallin and Paolo Mancini (eds), *Comparing Media Systems Beyond the Western World*, pp. 119–42, Cambridge, Cambridge University Press, 2012.

Wilson, Andrew. *Ukraine Crisis: What it Means for the West*, New Haven and London, Yale University Press, 2014.

Westad, Odd Arne. *The Cold War: A World History*, London, Penguin, 2017.

Yeltsin, Boris. *Midnight Diaries*, London, Phoenix, 2000.

Zassoursky, Ivan. *Media and Power in Post-Soviet Russia*, Armonk, NY, M.E. Sharpe, 2004.

Zenkovsky, Serge A. (ed.). *Medieval Russia's Epics, Chronicles, and Tales*, New York, E. P. Dutton and Co., 1963.

Zubok, Vladislav. *Collapse: The Fall of the Soviet Union*, New Haven and London, Yale University Press, 2021.

Zubok, Vladislav. *The World of the Cold War: 1945–1991*, London, Pelican, 2025.

Zygar, Mikhail. *War and Punishment: The Story of Russian Oppression and Ukrainian Resistance*, London, Weidenfeld and Nicholson, 2023.

Index

Page numbers in **bold** refer to maps; plate numbers are indicated by *p*.